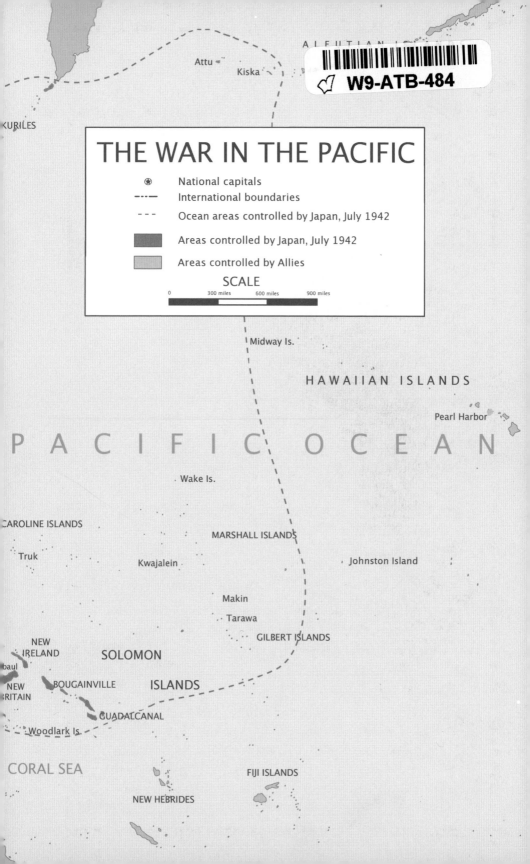

ALEUTIAN ISLANDS

Attu

Kiska

KURILES

W9-ATB-484

# THE WAR IN THE PACIFIC

⊛     National capitals

-----     International boundaries

- - -     Ocean areas controlled by Japan, July 1942

    Areas controlled by Japan, July 1942

    Areas controlled by Allies

## SCALE

| 0 | 300 miles | 600 miles | 900 miles |

Midway Is.

HAWAIIAN ISLANDS

Pearl Harbor

P A C I F I C   O C E A N

Wake Is.

CAROLINE ISLANDS

MARSHALL ISLANDS

Truk

Kwajalein

Johnston Island

Makin

Tarawa

NEW
IRELAND

SOLOMON

GILBERT ISLANDS

Rabaul

NEW
BRITAIN

BOUGAINVILLE

ISLANDS

GUADALCANAL

Woodlark Is.

CORAL SEA

FIJI ISLANDS

NEW HEBRIDES

# A TALE OF
# TWO SUBS

# A TALE OF TWO SUBS

## AN UNTOLD STORY OF WORLD WAR II, TWO SISTER SHIPS, AND EXTRAORDINARY HEROISM

## JONATHAN J. McCULLOUGH

GRAND
CENTRAL
PUBLISHING

New York   Boston

Grand Central Publishing
Hachette Book Group USA
237 Park Avenue
New York, NY 10017

Visit our Web site at www.HachetteBookGroupUSA.com.

Printed in the United States of America

First Edition: May 2008
10 9 8 7 6 5 4 3 2 1

Grand Central Publishing is a division of Hachette Book Group USA, Inc.
The Grand Central Publishing name and logo is a trademark of
Hachette Book Group USA, Inc.

Library of Congress Cataloging-in-Publication Data
McCullough, Jonathan J.
A tale of two subs : an untold story of World War II, two sister ships, and
extraordinary heroism / Jonathan J. McCullough.—1st ed.
p. cm.
Includes index.
Summary: "There was no way for the commander of the USS Sailfish
to know that the Japanese aircraft carrier he just torpedoed actually had
on board several crew members of the USS Sculpin, the sister sub to the
Sailfish, which had been sunk just days earlier by enemy fire. This is the
extraordinary story of the events that led to this amazing twist of fate and
what happened to the Sculpin survivors."—Provided by the publisher
ISBN-13: 978-0-446-17839-6
ISBN-10: 0-446-17839-X
1. Sculpin (Submarine)   2. Sailfish (Submarine)   3. World War, 1939–
1945—Naval operations—Submarine.   4. World War, 1939–1945—Naval
operations, American.   5. World War, 1939–1945—Naval operations,
Japanese.   6. World War, 1939–1945—Campaigns—Pacific Ocean.
7. World War, 1939–1945—Prisoners and prisons, Japanese.   I. Title.
D774.S37M33 2008
940.54'510973—dc22
2007039789

For Kathryn, James, and Sadie

# Author's Note

The remarkable story of the two sister submarines USS *Sculpin* (SS-191) and USS *Sailfish* (SS-192) began at the Portsmouth Navy Yard. The builders constructed the boats side by side from the keels up, and as the new ships came off the ways and became fully operational submarines, their crews became intimately familiar with each other. From the time the ships officially joined the Navy's Silent Service until the beginning of World War II and beyond, the officers and crew had gone to the Naval Academy or the sub school together, played baseball games and poker together, traded parts and went on leave together.

This is the story of how their fates curiously intertwined in a combination of events that no one could have foreseen. It is drawn from research that included interviews with survivors; archival records from the submarine base library and museum in Groton, the National Archives in Maryland, the Naval Historical Center in Washington, and the Wenger (Cryptologic) Naval Security Group Command Display in Pensacola; as well as innumerable books, articles, and interview transcripts. Although the dialogue and conversations are not verbatim transcripts from recordings within the submarines, they are reconstructed from direct quotes contained in written eyewitness accounts, patrol reports, eyewitness recollections from interviews, and standard submarine command language from that era.

This is also the story of how the Allies in the Pacific used the powerful knowledge gained by secret radio decryption activities to win the war, and the ultimate sacrifice of Captain John Philip Cromwell to ensure its secrecy from the Japanese. Although his devotion to duty won him a Medal of Honor for saving thousands of American lives, it caused unavoidable grief to his family and curiously sealed the fate of many men from the uss *Sculpin* during their terrible ordeal for survival. In the many accounts of the terrifying war beneath the sea during World War II, none parallel the unusual events surrounding the loss of the *Sculpin*, Cromwell's decision to sacrifice himself, and the part the sister ship would play in the *Sculpin* sailors' incredible reversals of fortune.

# A TALE OF
# TWO SUBS

# 1

## Darkness Visible

One of the lookouts was the first to see it, twenty minutes before midnight. They were standing on the bridge in the moist heat, their hands and faces buffeted by gusts of warm pinprick rain as they scanned the sea, the horizon, and the sky. The water rushed and lapped along the submarine's hull, the diesels thrummed hypnotically along the deck with a reassuring buzz that the watch standers felt in the soles of their feet.

*There, there it is again...* Panning across the horizon with his binoculars, the lookout's view passed through something subtly darker than the utter black around it, or perhaps it was a hole in the random haze of surface squalls that was somehow too consistent. His eyes lingered along its periphery so as to make out its boundaries.

"Mr. Mendenhall..." he called out uncertainly to the officer of the deck. The gauzy veil of rain lifted and the phantom coalesced. His heart quickened in a flash of recognition.

"Mr. Mendenhall! Ship dead ahead!"

The lieutenant swung his binoculars around, overcompensating a bit as the unmistakable silhouette of a large man-of-war came into view. The other lookouts tensed immediately but kept their binoculars up and scanned their sectors furiously, as though by extra effort their eyes might draw steel out from the shadows.

"Sound general quarters! Make ready tubes one through four!" Mendenhall shouted as he got the binoculars ready to send accurate readings to the men below.

Roused by the insistent *dong dong dong* of the klaxon, the skipper, Lucius Chappell, came clambering up the ladder to the bridge, where he got his first glimpse of the ship. It was huge, long, and low with three stacks. So far into enemy waters, it was doubtless Japanese. The skipper racked his brain to determine what kind of ship he was observing. For years, he had pored over the images of silhouettes and haphazard photographs in ship identification booklets for just this occasion. It looked to him like a *Tenryu*-class cruiser, and it had drawn out of the dark night so quickly that if he didn't attack it or submerge, the lookouts on the other ship might draw a bead on his sub, the USS *Sculpin*, and blow her out of the water. Chappell had only seconds to decide.

Down the hatch in the conning tower below, the fire control party anxiously waited his orders. Chappell called out the information to them as he tracked the ship with the binoculars: "Set depth five feet…Bearing, mark!…Range…Angle on the bow…Speed, ten knots."

Agonizing moments went by as the target crawled farther along. They needed two points to draw an accurate line along the ship's path to calculate where the torpedoes would intersect, if the cruiser didn't get them first.

While they were waiting, the portside lookout called, "Two ships on the port bow!" Far out in the gloom, in column with the cruiser, the skipper spotted a ship he couldn't quite make out, and then saw one of Japan's most important capital ships: an aircraft carrier.

It was every sub skipper's dream prize, the number one target for the entire U.S. Navy. Perhaps most important, it represented a chance at revenge for the attack on Pearl Harbor just over two months ago. But just as quickly as his hopes were raised, he realized that the flattop was going too fast, and that it was too far away. It was too late to shift targets; they'd never be able to get into a firing position. He would try to get the cruiser instead, and he told the crew so.

"Final bearing and shoot. Range, one-five double-oh yards. Bearing, mark!"

Moments passed as they waited for the ship to come into the crosshairs.

"Set!" came a voice from below the conning tower.

"Fire one!" the skipper ordered.

The ship shuddered momentarily as the massive *shusshh* of hundreds of pounds of compressed air ejected the torpedo from the tube.

"One's away, sir."

"Fire two!"

They watched as the second so-called fish left the tubes, and even though the torpedoes were several feet below the surface, their noisy steam engines made a gruesome sewing machine–like noise that was audible from the bridge. The phosphorescent wakes churned up by the torpedoes' racing propellers receded ahead of the ship.

"Both fish running hot and normal," the soundman called out. Using hydrophones akin to underwater microphones, he listened to the course of the torpedoes as they sped away to determine if they were making a circular path back to the boat. Sometimes a malfunctioning torpedo would circle back and return to sink a submarine. Under the right conditions, the soundman, or sonar operator, could also hear the sound and bearing—or direction— of other ships' propellers out to a fair distance. This information could be crucial when a submarine was too deep to use its periscope, or the conditions on the surface were too dangerous to come up.

Anticipating a counterattack, the skipper decided to pull the plug. "Lookouts below!" he called. The men quickly darted down the hatch as he pulled the chain on the diving horn twice: *oo-OO-gah! oo-OO-gah!*

"Dive! Dive!" he yelled into the intercom on the bridge.

A spume of air shot up through the deck as *Sculpin* gradually nosed downward. To submerge, the ship took on thousands of gallons of water into its tanks. The enormous burbling noise made it impossible for the sonar operator to hear what happened next. Lieutenant Mendenhall took one last look over his shoulder before going down the hatch. A massive explosion shook the water, but it was short of the target—the torpedo had exploded prematurely. The wake of the second torpedo seemed to be on course as he turned to go down the hatch, but four seconds later, it, too, exploded. By the time they submerged, precisely four minutes had passed since the lookout first spotted the cruiser.

As the ship dove, the skipper raised the periscope to take a look at the flattop. The waves lapped around the periscope as Chappell strained to see it there in the distance, then the water rushed in from all sides and everything turned black as the dark sea covered them up. He ordered a change of course to put some distance between them and the cruiser. Any convoy with a carrier and a cruiser was bound to have destroyers—submarine killers—as escorts.

Mendenhall reported the premature torpedo. If the skipper had any thoughts about the torpedoes, he kept them to himself. There was something wrong with those torpedoes...there had to be.

Lieutenant Jack Turner had relieved Lieutenant Mendenhall as officer of the deck. Now that the *Sculpin* was submerged, he also served as the diving officer. As the boat sank he gave orders to the crewmen in the control room below the conning tower to control the ship's depth, speed, and course.

Unlike surface craft, submarines move not in two dimensions but three. If a sub took on too much water in its ballast tanks, it would be heavier than the sea around it and sink like a stone. Not enough water would make it buoyant, and it would pop up to the surface. "Compensation" is the thin line of equilibrium between the two, and once the ship submerged and attained a buoyancy roughly the same as the water around it, the crew could easily change the depth by steering the sub up and down like an airplane with rudders in the fore and aft parts of the ship—known as the bow and stern planes. If the ship lost propulsion, the water wouldn't move over the planes, making it difficult to control depth. The planesmen stood at their stations next to each other in the control room with large stainless steel steering wheels. Each had a shallow depth gauge with fine gradations so that they could make crucial depth control adjustments at periscope depth, close to the surface. If the ship went down too far, the periscope might dunk under the surface and render the skipper blind. If the ship bobbed up to the surface, or broached, a target ship might spot them and try to ram, drop depth charges, or fire on the hapless sub. At deeper levels, the diving officer and planesmen watched a deep depth gauge as well as the trim, or angle of the ship, on an indicator that resembled an arc-shaped carpenter's level that showed in degrees whether the ship was pointed upward or downward.

The diving officer might also adjust the up angle or down angle of the ship by shifting water to special trim tanks fore and aft with the trim pump, but since the trim pump was noisy as a jackhammer, they would do this only as a last resort. The enemy also had his ears—or sonar—in the water. If a sub used the noisy trim pumps, an alert soundman on a destroyer could zero in, lay in a course, and depth-charge the sub to oblivion.

The diving officer also gave orders to the helmsman, who stood at a large stainless steel steering wheel about chest high that controlled the ship's rudder. On orders from the diving officer the helmsman kept an eye on a compass and steered the boat port or starboard; when the ship came to the specified course, he straightened out to "rudder amidships." He also transmitted orders of a change in speed by ringing them up on the annunciators—the circular indicators with two sets of arrows pointing to "STOP—⅓—⅔—FULL," in either direction, forward or backward. Whenever he rang up a change in speed, the men in the maneuvering room who were responsible for adjusting the motors to come to the required speed would acknowledge the order by moving the arrows to the new speed on their corresponding annunciators.

In turn, the men in the maneuvering room stood their station far aft in the ship between the two engine rooms at a huge electrical panel bristling with meters and switches that befit a scene from Dr. Frankenstein's laboratory. Using giant levers standing about hip-high, they directed the electricity from the batteries to the electric motors that propelled the ship. Forward of the panel stood the control cubicle, a cage containing a rat's nest of cloth-wrapped wires as thick as a man's thigh, bus bars, fuses, and switches. Admittance to the caged-off room was strictly forbidden under nearly all circumstances, because at peak capacity a horrifying five million watts ran through the various wires— enough not only to electrocute a man but also immolate him to cinders and a cloud of oily smoke within seconds.

While the ship came to the ordered depth, the soundman in the conning tower swept the hydrophones 360 degrees around the ship. Listening intently on the old-style headphones, he could make out several ships' propellers, or screws as they were called. But just as the squalls had hidden the ships from observation on the surface, the sheets of rain pounding on the surface of the sea sounded like a confusing static haze that obscured the sounds the enemy ships made.

The crew in the control room waited for the counterattack and listened to the soundman's reports—several heavy screws shifted in and out. They hoped that the second torpedo had hit the cruiser. Was Mendenhall right? Had that first torpedo prematurely exploded? If so, the cruiser may have changed course and avoided the second torpedo. But it had been a perfect shot—maybe the cruiser was dead in the water and all they needed to do was finish it off. The skipper ordered that the torpedo tubes be reloaded, and after nearly an hour with no counterattack, he decided to risk a look and the sub came to sixty-five feet—the depth at which it could safely skim under the surface and make periscope observations. Seeing nothing, the captain surfaced the submarine and scrambled up the ladder to the bridge at half past midnight.

The night was pitch black, overcast, and rainy. Neither the captain nor the bridge crew was able to see the three ships they'd spotted before. As the storm intensified, the black clouds spit and rumbled with lightning. The lookouts watched when the strobelike flashes illuminated the far reaches of the sea, where they were just able to make out the silhouettes of two ships pulling away—one at about 5,000 yards and the other at 7,000 yards. The enemy ships were built for speed, not evasion like a submarine, and once alerted would easily outpace the *Sculpin*. As the submarine plied the waves on a course back to the site of their first attack, the lookouts couldn't see any smaller destroyers that would ordinarily accompany these large ships as escorts.

Chappell broke radio silence to broadcast an urgent contact report back to base to report the ships they'd seen, and received acknowledgment from headquarters. If the *Sculpin* couldn't sink the carrier, another submarine might do so. Barring that, the information about the carrier might give command a better picture of the Japanese fleet's disposition and intentions. Although few knew it at the time, intelligence would decide the outcome of the war.

The weather and visibility were still poor, shifting from a pitch black lucid to a deceptive rainy haze. It was a quarter past two when the lookouts saw the next ship, this time tentatively identified as a destroyer. Once again, the officer of the deck sounded general quarters—an order for the men to drop everything and man their battle stations—and the skipper came to the bridge. They began tracking the ship for a surface attack when, a couple of minutes later, the other lookouts began calling out sightings of two, three... five other destroyers. The bridge crew watched two of the ships turn toward the *Sculpin*. They were now surrounded by overwhelming odds and had lost the all-important advantage of surprise. They couldn't outrun the destroyers. The sub's only option was to dive, try to evade, and wait out the depth charges. Chappell gave the order to dive.

The British Admiralty developed the depth charge during the First World War to counter the German navy's U-boat fleet. They were roughly the size and shape of an oil barrel and contained approximately 500 pounds of high explosives. After determining the general location of a submerged submarine, the crew of a destroyer or smaller surface craft could set the depth at which the "ash cans" would explode, then roll them off special racks. The explosions were so powerful that the surface ship using them had to be underway, otherwise the shock waves and upheaval of hot gases might break the ship's keel in two. To their horror, the crews on many destroyers discovered that the concussions of the depth charges could seize hold of survivors bobbing in the water and instantaneously crush them till their bellies burst.

For the men on a submarine, a depth charge attack is essentially a crew of men separated from a series of 500-pound bomb explosions by ¾ inch of steel and some water. Depth is the submarine's ally, because the water's increased pressure there tends to contain the effects of a depth charge's concussion. But if the depth charge is particularly close when the submarine is at a great depth—a place where the sheer pressure of the water is already testing the sub's many valves and openings—the water's relative density actually reflects the shock waves of a close explosion with devastating results. At certain distances and depths, a depth charge may have no effect beyond a loud sound. If it is closer, the shock effect can shake a boat so much that pipes rupture, electrical relays break, and two-ton diesel engines lift off their chassis. Under certain conditions, a single well-placed charge can rupture a submarine's hull. In that case, the water doesn't just flood in; an instantaneous thunderclap compresses the air in a submarine compartment so quickly that any air actually ignites—whether it is in the compartment, in lungs, or in sinus cavities. It comes with such brutal speed, such force, and such pressure that a human body turns to jelly and splintered bones.

During the *Sculpin*'s rigorous prewar training, the crew had received depth charges from friendly destroyers, and since the commencement of the war they'd heard enemy depth charges from afar. But none of these experiences could prepare them for what was about to happen.

"Rig for depth charge," the skipper said through the 1MC, the shipwide intercom system. The crewmen swung the heavy, round-edged watertight doors between the compartments until they shut and dogged the massive clamps tight, sealing the men inside their tomblike pressure chambers. They then secured everything that might come loose and watched the depth and pressure gauges, hoping they would be able to put as much water between them and those destroyers as possible before the first depth charge. The needle on the deep depth gauge crossed 200…210…220…225…

The concussion hit so hard they thought the ship had split in half.

Lightbulbs along the overhead shattered in sparks and showers of broken glass in some of the compartments. The crewmen were left to wonder what had happened as they listened with ringing ears to the enormous, seething froth of bubbles run up eerily from below their feet, up the steel walls around them, and on up to the surface for what seemed like an eternity.

A damage report came from the conning tower: A clutch that retained the retractable radio antenna had slipped. The force of the blast drove the antenna straight into the boat. They were absorbing this information when thirty seconds after the first explosion, an even closer depth charge explosion shook the boat. The bulkheads zinged to the touch like a live electrical wire. Their guts shook inside their bellies. Even the skin on their faces, arms, and bodies heaved with the shaking ship. Caught unawares, some men's mandibles rattled back and forth involuntarily, their teeth chattering in what was called the dreaded "tooth rattler."

The emergency lighting came on, illuminating the compartments that had been left in the dark. Another damage report from the conning tower: The last blast had blown off a wrench-tightened nut holding in an electrical cable. A stream of water poured in through the packing around the cable. The men in the conning tower worked to control the leak but water was getting everywhere. It pooled up and started to snake insidiously down an electrical cable to the control room below, where, unknown to the crew, it collected in the high-voltage interior communications (IC) switchboard—a disaster waiting to happen.

About thirty seconds after the last depth charge came another. Everything not tied down simply shook loose or hummed itself quiet. Each explosion seemed closer than the last, affecting the men in ways they'd never experienced before.

A close depth-charging could play upon men's imaginations about the worst things that could happen on a submarine. For some, the explosions led to a quiet, debilitating mental paralysis.

The mere anticipation of the next depth charge could move a man to the limit of his endurance, and with one step further he entered a sort of dissociative state that left him unable to get out of his bunk. For others, it caused a sort of jittery, convulsive hysteria that gave them an uncontrollable compulsion to open the nearest hatch, no matter how deep they might be. On one submarine, a crewman became so unglued that his crewmates confined him belowdecks in what was for all purposes the ship's vegetable crisper. The spectacle of friends losing their wits was bad enough, but the sense of panic could spread like wildfire throughout a boat. One skipper would even relieve himself of command. Knowing full well that he set the tone for the entire boat, Lucius Chappell calmly endured, knowing that all eyes were on him and that any hesitation or flinch could amplify into sheer terror.

*BANG!*

The *Sculpin* rang all along its length as it shook from stem to stern like a saw blade. When they reached test depth of 250 feet, Turner, the diving officer, gave the order to level the boat into trim by planing up. The planesmen tried to move the wheels, but they stuck fast, steering the sub deeper like a runaway automobile with a frozen steering wheel. The furious rushing sound of the depth charge gases racing to the surface receded and was replaced with the unsettling twangs and cricks of the hull. They were now approaching 300 feet—fifty feet below the boat's test depth.

*BANG!*

Because the planes wouldn't budge, Turner had to use the noisy trim pump to shift water from the forward tanks to the stern tanks, so that the ship would point upward and climb.

The planesmen were still fighting against their wheels, which moved with great difficulty. The boat slowed its descent, and after making so much noise with the trim pump, Turner ordered a reduction of speed from ⅔ to a quieter ⅓ to elude the destroyers above. The crewmen in the maneuvering room acknowledged the order on the annunciator, then nothing. They waited tense moments for the motors to slow, but now in addition to the seized planes came word that the electrical switches wouldn't respond. Turner asked permission to go to the maneuvering room to get a report and see if he could fix the problem.

There was a lull in the depth charges. The soundman put his headphones on again and scanned around the boat, listening to the sounds of the destroyers above. The screws made a rhythmic sound between a click and a swish as they turned through the water; the rushing sound of the water churned up by the screws and the water racing over their hulls made a sound like a surging waterfall. The soundman heard no fewer than six to eight ships above; he couldn't be sure because they were so close that they might be masking one another as they crossed paths.

*BANG!*

Now came a report from the aft engine room: A hatch had unseated and they were taking on water in that compartment.

In the control room, there was a separate explosion. The room went dark as huge clouds of noxious black smoke billowed out from the IC box. The high-voltage device now crackled with sparks as flames licked up the walls of the control room, burning wire insulation and cork. The men choked on the thick clouds of asphyxiating, eye-burning smoke that ate up the oxygen in the compartment.

At 345 feet, the boat was working toward crush depth—at

which even the tightest openings would not hold fast, the depth where the ship would slowly fill the crew's compartments and fall even faster. If the sea was merciful, one pressure compartment after another would simply collapse in a thunderclap of seawater like a string of firecrackers, killing them all instantly. If a depth charge landed close enough, it could be the last thing they would ever hear. Then it came.

Pigboats. Iron coffins. Death traps. The unflattering sobriquets that regular Navymen—even submariners among them—used to describe submarines came from long observation and hard experience. The first subs introduced to the Navy early in the twentieth century were short, squat vessels that tended to bob up and down when underway like a sea porpoise, also known at that time as a sea pig. But the habitability and hygiene conditions on those cramped, moist, early subs lent a fitting double entendre to the term "pigboat," and the nickname stuck. One submariner—in the U.S. Navy pronounced subma-*reen*-er—coined a little doggerel verse about the early service that proved popular until well after the Bureau of Ships saw fit to provide toilets in their subs:

> *Submarines have no latrines,*
> *The men wear leatheren britches.*
> *They hang their tails out o'er the rails,*
> *And yell like sons-o-bitches.*

The other unfortunate nicknames came when the nation—and its Navy—was shocked as sub after sub went down in the decades that followed. The story nearly always came with the same tragic ending: All hands lost. When a sub went down, it simply disappeared. Alternatively, and even more maddening, were the occasions when the sub was just out of reach below the surface, the crew desperately trying to find a way out, their would-be rescuers powerless to help them, until the final moments when hope was not enough. There were practically never any survivors to tell what had happened, and if the ship was salvaged, there were only clues. The ships were extremely complex, and anything might have gone wrong.

On the day that the *Sculpin*'s sponsor, Mrs. Joseph R. Defrees, launched her at the Portsmouth Navy Yard on July 27, 1938, the *Sculpin* was to be the most technologically sophisticated—and complex—ship in the world. Inside the sleek hull were seven pressure chambers, with the conning tower comprising an eighth. The chambers sat inside the hull like sausage links, separated by bulkheads with watertight doors. The compartments were packed with a thicket of electrical cables, high-pressure air tubes, hydraulic lines, fuel lines, and tubes for pumping water.

In the forward torpedo room were four torpedo tubes, racks for reload torpedoes, and bunks for some of the crew. It was also where the soundman and his hydrophones were located. The next compartment was called officer's country, containing berths for the officers and petty officers, the captain's quarters, and the wardroom where the officers took their meals. This area was also called the forward battery because underneath the officers' quarters was a watertight compartment containing a massive bank of batteries to propel and operate the ship while submerged. Aft of these compartments and directly underneath the conning tower was the control room. Almost every imaginable tube or wire used to control the boat flowed into this room. Its walls were covered with electrical panels, hydraulic tubes, and manifolds for directing water and high-pressure air. In the *Sculpin*, the cramped control room contained the TDC, or Torpedo Data Computer, a highly sophisticated analog computer to plot a target's course. The control room also contained a little radio shack for transmitting, receiving, and decoding radio transmissions. Above it was the conning tower, where the attack party convened to observe a primitive form of radar, and fire the torpedoes. The skipper also made periscope observations from the conning tower. When he was through, the handles of the periscope would fold up and it would retract down through the floor, past the floor of the control room, and stay in the periscope well in the pump room below the control room.

The crew's quarters was the next compartment. There were not enough bunks for each man to have one of his own, so the crewmen "hotbunked." When one man woke up for that day's duties, another man would take his place in the bunk and get some sleep. Next came a tiny galley, where a chef's mate would cook for up to seventy crewmembers. Adjacent to this was the crew's mess where the enlisted men took their meals and spent time when not on duty. Under the galley, mess, and crew's quarters was the after battery.

The forward engine room followed, which had two massive Fairbanks-Morse diesels and a water distiller to desalinate water for the batteries and bathing, if there was enough left over. Behind this compartment was the control cubicle and maneuvering room to manage the engines and motors. And behind this was the after engine room with two more diesels, then the after torpedo room with four more torpedo tubes.

The various ballast, fuel, and other tanks used to sink and trim the boat accounted for the outer bulge around the middle of the ship below the waterline. The deck, from the jaunty bull nose on the bow to the rudder, was actually a superstructure built on the hull and lined with holes along the sides so that air could escape when diving. The deck was lined with teak slats, with a 3-inch deck gun aft of the conning tower. The boat's first crew would be known as "plankowners."

The many peculiarities of submarine service attracted a different kind of sailor; in many ways it was—and remains—an elite service. It was an all-volunteer force, and the crewmen got extra pay for the dangers involved. Although the lack of space and fresh water wasn't conducive to the spit-polish and saluting punctilio of the "bluewater navy" culture aboard surface craft, the crews fully observed the chain of command.

Like the enlisted men, the officers were likewise a bit different from their counterparts aboard surface craft. It was a good billet for recent graduates of the Naval Academy because they had a reasonable expectation to rise to the command of a vessel sooner than their classmates. And since the service was a relatively small part of the Navy, submarine officers and their families were part of a tight-knit community where nearly everyone knew one another or could rely on introductions. They drank, played cards, had potlatches, traded recipes, and commiserated with one another; everyone had the same experiences of dealing with Navy brass, or of finding an affordable place for their families to stay in New London, Connecticut, where the Navy built boats at the Electric Boat yard and conducted its famous sub school.

While at the sub school, officers and enlisted men alike learned to be extremely conscientious about performing their duties. Due to the complexity of submarines and the dangers inherent in operating them, the sub crews were arguably the most highly trained in the Navy. Any mistake, even a minor one, could sink a boat and kill all aboard. The staff drilled the men over and over again in the procedures for their respective duties, as well as cross training for other duties. The men received rigorous physical exams, and due to the close quarters aboard a submarine, they also received psychological exams to determine suitability for service in submarines.

The Navy also built submarines at the Portsmouth Navy Yard, where it built the *Sculpin* and her sister ship, the *Squalus*. The boat's sponsor, Mrs. Defrees, was married to an admiral, Joseph Rollie Defrees, and their son, Joe, followed the family tradition by going into the Navy. Although her mother's intuition could probably have surmised that her son might want to serve in submarines, as she broke the bottle on the stern and watched the ship slip away from her she could never have known that less than five years later, the nation would be at war, or that her son would be on the ship's final war patrol.

With the fire on the *Sculpin* raging out of control and the boat plummeting ever deeper, the men's sub school training took over like a rote survival instinct. Firemen rushed to the control room with carbon dioxide extinguishers and put out the flames. Jack Turner came back from the maneuvering room with the chief electrician's mate, John Pepersack, to ask the skipper for permission to enter the high-voltage control cubicle. Pepersack gave his assurance that he thought he could find the problem and fix it safely. Chappell gave his permission. The executive officer and second-in-command, Charles Henderson, relieved Turner as diving officer and slowly worked the boat upward while Turner went back with Pepersack.

The control cubicle was contained in the cage with high-voltage warning signs all around it. Turner held a lantern while Pepersack gingerly worked his way around massive wires, hot from the hundreds of amps of current surging through them. The depth charges had loosened a single tiny nut, which had lodged itself in the control levers, making it impossible to shift them to a slower speed. Pepersack dislodged it and made his way out to present it to the skipper with aw-shucks humility. The maneuvering room was able to shift the levers to the quieter ⅓ speed.

As the boat slowly inched up back to test depth, the planesmen were able to move their wheels. The skipper speculated that the sheer pressure of the water outside the boat at that depth had pressed against the shafts so hard that they seized.

# 2

---

# The Morning News

Although Wilfred J. Holmes may not have chosen it at first, by 1941, he was enjoying his retirement from the Navy. Holmes, who went by his initials, W.J., or his nickname, "Jasper," grew up on the banks of the Hudson River in New York. As the son of a Swedish immigrant, he had his own Ellis Island story; the original family name was Bessemark but his father had made a clean break with the Old World and enthusiastically embraced everything American. They were not particularly well off, and young Holmes knew that just about the only chance of getting into college was to get a coveted appointment to the U.S. Naval Academy. As luck would have it he was able to get in, and he continued his education with a graduate degree in electrical engineering from Columbia University in New York.

His thirteen-year career in the Navy had culminated in the command of his own submarine, the *S-30*, in what was sarcastically referred to at the time by envious sailors as the "pineapple" Navy based in Pearl Harbor. But over the years, he developed a nagging backache that in time became excruciating. He'd hoped it would get better and concealed it from his crew and superiors, but eventually the pain became unbearable. The diagnosis was arthritis of the spine, and though it was treatable at the time in a limited way, the Navy cashiered him as physically unfit for duty. It was 1936—the middle of the Depression—when he found himself out of work. Fortunately, his engineering degree helped him get a position at the University of Hawaii, and he taught there during the regular school year. During the summer months he wrote submarine stories for one of the nation's top magazines, *The Saturday Evening Post*, under the pen name "Alec Hudson," the surname derived from his old stomping grounds in New York state. His wife, Isabelle (or "Izzy," as he called her), was a shrewd and inquisitive woman every bit his equal, who acted as the local air raid warden in their Black Point neighborhood about a dozen miles from Pearl Harbor. They had a son, Eric, who was a student at the prestigious and exclusive Punahou School.

The Holmeses knew mostly Navy people, and of them, mostly submariners and their families like John DeTar, who was skipper of the uss *Tuna*, and Captain Dykeman, whose daughter Eric particularly admired. More than most, they socialized with the family of John Cromwell, who was the engineering officer on the staff of the Commander Submarines, Pacific (ComSubPac). Holmes and Cromwell had attended the Naval Academy at the same time, both had engineering degrees, and like Holmes, Cromwell had a health issue—high blood pressure.

In those years, Honolulu was a small town. The road leading to the naval station at Pearl Harbor was just a two-lane dirt road. There was only one beauty parlor worth noting, because it had exclusive European products, and because the young woman who ran it, Susie "Ruth" Kühn, charged very reasonable rates. Everybody seemed to know the wealthy, amiable, and somewhat odd Kühn family, who had immigrated from Germany in August

1935. Ruth's father, Bernard, was a physician, but he didn't run a practice, and when it came to speculation about the source of their prosperity, he gave vague explanations about coming into an inheritance, or profitable investment instruments. If so, they weren't local because he wasn't doing business in the islands and he wasn't trading stocks with the local brokers. But no matter, business was booming at the salon, so much so that Kühn's wife, Friedel, often helped Ruth when there was a rush. Ruth was a pretty and gregarious young woman who dated mostly sailors, and would eventually become engaged to a sailor. Her salon catered to the wives of high-ranking naval officers. "They talked so much that it was a relief when they left the place," she said.

Her mother, Friedel, also accompanied Dr. Kühn to the hills surrounding Honolulu or on his little sailboat around the harbor to conduct research for a history of the islands. Whether in the boat or on the hills, they examined the geography, took pictures, and made extensive mental notes. Dr. Kühn would also take his inquisitive young son, Hans, to the docks for a look at the Navy ships. Hans dressed in a Cracker Jack suit with a little Navy hat and charmed the sailors all along the waterfront. Though the good doctor couldn't go on the men-of-war for security reasons, the sailors often took Hans on a tour of the boat where he could admire all the neat-looking gadgets and ask all manner of questions.

But as the 1930s drew to a close, the docks became more restricted. Europe teetered closer to war when Hitler conducted a hostile annexation of the Sudetenland in Czechoslovakia and flouted the Treaty of Versailles by remilitarizing the Rhineland along the border with France. In the Pacific, the British, American, Dutch, and Australian governments reacted to Japan's

Greater East Asia Co-Prosperity Sphere and war atrocities in Manchuria with tighter trade restrictions. Unfortunately, their Pacific fleets couldn't enforce those policies if hostilities began as a result of the restrictions. In anticipation of a possible war with Germany and Japan, the U.S. Navy started calling reservists into active duty and started courting retired officers like Jasper Holmes.

Holmes demurred. His premature retirement from the Navy had caused not a small amount of anxiety, and he didn't want to risk his new career at the University of Hawaii. In any event, war wasn't a foregone conclusion for the United States in 1940, which was also a presidential election year. Even as France fell to the Nazis in June 1940, the country was opposed to fighting a war in Europe or anywhere else for that matter, and President Franklin Delano Roosevelt campaigned with a pledge not to send our boys to Europe. Late in 1940, however, the nation started the first peacetime draft, and shortly after he won the election, FDR announced the Lend-Lease program with Britain and the Soviet Union, whereby FDR could get around existing law to provide ships and war matériel to those important allies.

By mid-1941, the devastating war in Europe had been in full swing for nearly two years. Hitler's U-boats were choking off Britain's vital lifelines to war matériel, and now that Hitler had conquered continental Europe, he redirected his armies to the Eastern Front, where the Soviet Union staggered under the assault. While FDR's administration was otherwise occupied with the situation in Europe, diplomatic tensions with Japan waxed and waned down a path that led closer to war. In June 1941, commandant Admiral Claude C. Bloch called on Jasper Holmes to consider taking on a position as a combat intelligence officer for the Fourteenth Naval District, which was based in Hawaii. Holmes accepted, though neither man had an understanding of intelligence as it pertained to naval operations, let alone what a combat intelligence officer would do. Both took the arrangement to be a situation where the arthritic Holmes would do bureaucratic scut work, but as it turned out it would be a privileged vantage point to observe and participate in the secret, behind-the-scenes decision making at the highest levels that would win or lose the war.

Earlier that year in March, a twenty-nine-year-old diplomat named Tadashi Morimura came to the islands to act as chancellor at the Japanese consulate. He took up residence at a cottage on the grounds there and set about the task he'd been sent to accomplish, though not by Japan's Foreign Ministry. Morimura had studied English for several years and kept up on naval developments and the shipping news with the *Honolulu Star-Bulletin* and the *Honolulu Advertiser.*

He began to familiarize himself with Honolulu and the surrounding area, and although he'd previously had health issues that had very nearly destroyed his career, he spent time at a Japanese teahouse drinking heavily and chasing skirts with the U.S. Navy sailors. He particularly enjoyed talking to the geishas, who told him about their customers. The second floor had a telescope to take in the sights of Pearl Harbor, where the U.S. fleet lay anchored. At that time, this included the uss *Sculpin* and her sister ship, the *Sailfish.* In retrospect, Morimura and his superiors might have paid more attention to the submarine fleet, which for now was just an afterthought. Instead he gave the battleships and cruisers particular scrutiny, noting their comings and goings. For instance, they arrived to stay at harbor for the weekend and went back out to sea on Monday, though he had yet to discover where they went.

Morimura was not given to frequenting one place for too long, however. Constantly in motion, he might take some girlfriends for a ride around Oahu in a tourist boat, or go on long drives in a taxi or chauffeured consular car. Alternatively, having taken aeronautics training several years ago, he would rent a plane at John Rodgers Airport and fly around the area. He would also sometimes take a bus, dressed as a workman. He never took photographs, and saved his note taking for later. His evenings were spent writing reports and encoding them. Consul General Nagao Kita and Vice Consul Otojiro Okuda were likely the only ones in the Hawaiian Islands to receive his reports, and perhaps not even them. Couriers at the consulate took the encoded versions to the RCA offices in Honolulu so that they could be transmitted back to Japan as radiograms. "The Americans were very foolish," Morimura would say, years later.

Jasper Holmes also found himself busy, but unlike Morimura, he seemed to be spinning his wheels. District Intelligence (as distinct from the Fleet Intelligence) concerned itself mainly with counterintelligence—the detection of foreign intelligence operations. The main office was in downtown Honolulu, but they had a satellite office at the Navy Yard, where Holmes reported. His immediate superior there seemed to have no need of him to the extent that there was literally no place to put him. At a loss, he asked Bloch for direction and was told that he could "write my own ticket." At the time, the Navy didn't have a comprehensive program to plot the location and progress of merchantmen to and from the various ports across the Pacific. Sensing that this information would be valuable at the outbreak of war, Holmes busied himself by reading the shipping news and picking up gossip about the comings and goings of the various vessels at the shipping offices.

Holmes realized that many ships at sea transmitted a daily weather report that included temperature, wind speed, and barometric pressure. These reports were forwarded to the weather service to make forecasts for the West Coast of the United States, but more important to him, the radio transmissions included the longitude and latitude of the ships. Deciding to leave no stone unturned, he went down to the same local RCA office that the Japanese consulate used, to inquire whether he could get a daily rundown of these reports. The representative there said that he might help Holmes if there were some sort of emergency, but that the transmissions were technically a private matter, and that they couldn't provide what he needed as a matter of routine. Holmes was disappointed, and thinking that the matter was over, he consoled himself that at least he might have a good source of information should the need arise.

But it wasn't over. The next day he received a call from the office of Captain Irving Mayfield, who was the Fourteenth Naval District's intelligence officer. They'd learned that Holmes had been illegally seeking unauthorized information that was protected by a law passed in 1934, and whose penalties included serious jail time and thousands of dollars in fines. Holmes hadn't intended to stir up a hornet's nest and didn't pursue it further; he'd only wanted accurate information for his plot. A close reading of the act would have led him to the conclusion that he could be authorized by the carrier, in this case RCA, and that Captain Mayfield's peculiar interest in law enforcement had nothing to do with upholding the privacy of radio communications.

War seemed imminent that fall when negotiations between Japan and the United States came to an impasse. The State Department insisted on terms that FDR and Secretary of State Cordell Hull knew would be unacceptable to the Japanese. For their part, the Japanese Foreign Ministry increased the number and severity of vague consequences should diplomatic efforts come to naught. The Army and the Fourteenth Naval District under Admiral Claude Bloch were responsible for the security of Pearl Harbor and the associated naval and army installations around the islands, and they took measures to increase security and war preparedness.

Admiral Thomas Withers was the ComSubPac at the time, and Jasper Holmes would likely have heard from his old sub force friends that they were drilling relentlessly with torpedo firing practice, crash dives, and airpower demonstrations. The skippers had assumed that their subs were invisible at a depth of sixty-five feet from the surface to the keel,* or periscope depth. Withers had Navy pilots drop "firecracker" bombs on all such subs, which harmed nothing but the skippers' confidence in the subs' stealth. Withers also held maneuvers where destroyers would use sonar to locate and make a mock attack on participating subs. One prewar destroyer division commander boasted that he could detect and depth-charge 70 percent of the submarines in a given area.

---

*Submarine depths are measured at the keel; at a periscope depth of sixty-five feet the shears, or structure around the periscope, might be only twenty-five feet under the surface.

Most of the sub skippers were older and had risen to command as a result of superior paperwork skills and adherence to sub fleet orthodoxy. If a destroyer or airplane caught the skippers while making an attack approach during fleet exercises, the staff officers were quick to reprimand them. The effect of the airplane, destroyer, and sonar approach drills was to scare the hell out of the already overcautious skippers, which among other things would cause serious harm to their effectiveness at the beginning of the war.

Holmes was also learning that his new job would soon have grave consequences for his friends in the sub force. Its proportions would extend to the breadth and depth of the U.S. Navy's entire war effort, and it would be no exaggeration to say that his work wasn't a matter of life or death but rather a matter of the lives and deaths of hundreds of thousands on both sides of the Pacific. Although he had no way of knowing that what he did would determine the outcome in the Pacific theater, he got his first hints about the job when his superiors detached him to the Combat Intelligence Center (or CIC), though what that entailed was never really clear. He moved his notes to the basement of the Administration Building, under the harbor director's office, in August 1941. It was a secure area, so he could put up the maps tracking the merchantmen. In the confusing bureaucratic scrum, he remained part of District Intelligence but was detached to the CIC's commander, Joe J. Rochefort.

Although there was much more to each man than met the eye, neither particularly impressed the other. Rochefort needed personnel, but a long-absent reservist whose background didn't suit his purposes might prove to be more of a hindrance. Holmes did have one thing going for him, though: the organizational title Combat Intelligence Center, a bureaucratic handle that Rochefort needed to conceal his activities. Still, he didn't know if Holmes could be trusted.

For his part, Holmes described Rochefort as "a tall, lean commander with a conciliatory smile that nullified his habit of caustic speech." And although Holmes's career had been cut short by physical infirmity, Rochefort and the officers who reported to him didn't have the rank that their classmates at the Naval Academy had attained; to Holmes this seemed to suggest that they might be second- or third-rate officers filling undesirable billets. His initial impression of them was that "there was no large outcropping of genius." But Holmes was mistaken, and would come to learn that their line of work required skill, dedication, and long periods of uninterrupted time, which came at the exclusion of sea duty. The selection boards held up their promotions because of their lack of experience aboard vessels.

Rochefort was at one time the intelligence officer to then Commander of the Pacific Fleet Admiral Joseph Reeves. Most of his time was spent doing background checks on the attendees of meetings with the admiral. He had also taken the Japanese language course and had studied radio intelligence, and when the spy case of Harry T. Thompson came up in the 1930s, he made arrangements that resulted in Thompson's conviction, as well as the identification of Thompson's handler, a Japanese naval attaché who was posing as a student. Thompson got fifteen years in the clink; his handler fled the country.

Before arriving to command the decryption shop, Rochefort's second-in-command, Lieutenant Commander Thomas H. Dyer, had actually set up Hypo, as it was called; Hypo was the real operation concealed behind the more innocuous-sounding

Combat Intelligence Center. Tommy had the air of a likable, absentminded professor with a good sense of humor. A photograph of him from that period shows him in uniform at his desk with wild hair, as though he'd just woken up. Given the long hours he worked, this wouldn't have been unusual. On the messy, cluttered desk are illustrations of hula girls, and behind him is a sign warding away any unnecessary cleaning help. His face is grim, almost despairing. Dyer's past in the Office of Naval Intelligence included an assignment to investigate a dead end in the Lindbergh baby kidnapping case. A woman had sent a collection of objects that might yield tantalizing clues, and though Dyer scrutinized every aspect in the gathering of junk, in the end he correctly concluded that the woman was delusional.

Heavy steel doors separated Holmes from Rochefort, Dyer, and the rest of their crew. They didn't talk to him about what they were doing, and he didn't inquire. His first clues about the organization came in dribs and drabs. They had unusual equipment: an IBM punch card machine and collators to sort the cards. Knowing that Holmes had a good assortment of resources, Signalman Anthony Ethier would sometimes pop out from behind the closed doors and ask Holmes bizarre cartographical questions about obscure coral atolls and place-names across the Pacific. Holmes probably learned from Ethier that the Coast Guard intercepted merchantman weather traffic—the very information he'd tried to get from the RCA station. He also learned that the weather codes had changed recently to deny the Japanese navy that information, and that the personnel behind the steel doors decrypted the signals, which would aid Holmes's ship plotting. And oh, by the way, Ethier was decrypting the much more complicated Japanese merchant marine weather codes, if he wanted the positions of their ships, too.

Holmes immediately realized that Ethier and his recently arrived assistant, Petty Officer William Livingston, were probably conversant in Japanese. Enough, at least, to crack codes. For Holmes, Hypo's activities were confirmed to him when Wesley "Ham" Wright, another of Rochefort's crew, found out that Holmes had taught mathematics at the University of Hawaii, and asked if Holmes could help create an equation to manipulate series of five-digit numbers. The solution, if one existed, was far beyond Holmes's capabilities.

Since Rochefort had an insatiable need for personnel, he took delivery of a handful of students from the Japanese language class in Japan. As war tensions increased, the Navy abandoned the school and started bringing personnel back to U.S. territory. In turn, the Japanese were also evacuating from the United States and its territories. Since the State Department was trying to find a diplomatic resolution of its tensions with Japan, the government loosened some of the restrictions on Japanese shipping. The *Tatsuta Maru*, a transpacific Japanese luxury liner, came to Honolulu to pick up Japanese expatriates. The Japanese naval officials took diplomatic packages to and from the consulate. These may have included instructions and specific questions for consulate chancellor Tadashi Morimura, whose true name was Ensign Takeo Yoshikawa. On October 20 or 21, 1941, he bought a ticket on a tourist plane and happily snapped photographs of the naval installations at Ford Island and the ships berthed in Pearl Harbor. Ensign Yoshikawa's activities would doubtless stop after the planned attack on Pearl Harbor, but the

Third Division of the Japanese Naval General Staff, for whom Yoshikawa worked, wanted an uninterrupted flow of intelligence after the attack. The ideal spy would be an inconspicuous Occidental. Their allies, the Germans and Italians, had already withdrawn their consular staff from Hawaii, however, and in any case, Germany and Italy would probably soon be at war with America. Luckily, they had already groomed Yoshikawa's replacement and his family during the past six years with tens of thousands of dollars. The naval officials aboard the *Tatsuta Maru* now carried thousands more in cash and instructions for Dr. Bernard Julius Kühn.

Kühn, as it turned out, had been a high-placed official in the Nazis' secret police apparatus. His station put him in the same circles as Joseph Göbbels, Hitler's grotesque propaganda minister, who along with his wife had raised Germany's "ideal family" of six children.* Göbbels liked children so much that he took Kühn's teenage daughter, Ruth, as a mistress. Since Kühn was too high on the Nazi Party pecking order to dispose of when the romance cooled, Göbbels needed to find a way to get rid of the entire family. In the mid-1930s, the Japanese were looking for a non-Japanese spy in Hawaii, and Göbbels suggested the junket to Kühn.

The doctor's travels around the islands, like Yoshikawa's, were reconnaissance missions. Even the trips to the docks with his son dressed as a sailor were a ruse; when the pair got back home, the tot's mother debriefed him about the speed, characteristics, and armament of the ships he'd boarded. Ruth's beauty parlor was likewise an elaborate scheme to pick up secondhand information

---

*At the end of the war, Magda Göbbels would poison all six children at the Führerbunker under the Reichstag, to spare them from life in a world without the Nazi Party.

about the composition of the fleet, the naval staff, and their war planning. Kühn devised a similarly elaborate scheme to transmit intelligence about the U.S. fleet after hostilities began. He bought a cottage at the beach with the money he received from the Japanese, and would communicate to Japanese submarines offshore with a predetermined set of signals by putting lights and sheets in the windows facing the ocean.

Rochefort's Hypo had watches around the clock to ensure that the station would be staffed in the event of an emergency. By mid-November, he included Holmes on some of the off-hour shifts, but since Holmes still wasn't officially "read into the program," Rochefort put Holmes on the distribution list for the daily traffic intelligence summary. This report wasn't put together from code cracking per se; rather, it was an analysis of Japanese navy radio signals. By identifying the originators and addressees, their location at port or at sea, and the amount of traffic between these nodes, Rochefort's analysts could infer the location of vessels and shore bases, how these vessels were organized into task forces, and the amount of coordination the naval General Staff was expending to move the Japanese fleet around the Pacific. Holmes learned that the Japanese had changed all the call signs, or the codes the radio operators used to identify one another, on November 1. This was a routine technique to discourage analysis of the fleet's traffic, and Rochefort's only remedy was to wait until the Japanese generated enough traffic in the new call signs for his analysts to reidentify the originators and addressees. The traffic was on the upswing, and Hypo had identified most of the 20,000 call signs by about mid-November.

Now that Holmes was reading the summaries, he could deliver them to Fleet Intelligence along with the maps he'd already been making. This was an important event because by delegating this task to Holmes, Rochefort was putting him in a position to act as an informal liaison between Hypo and the rest of the various naval organizations.

The Japanese were fully aware that the Americans were engaging in this sort of analysis, and on November 23, they started to generate traffic to indicate that most of their fleet was in the western portion of the Sea of Japan. But their subterfuge was revealed only after the war, because the signals were too weak to reach the U.S. Navy's listening stations in the Philippines, known as "Cast," or the Hypo station back at Pearl Harbor. Two days later, the Kido Butai, or "striking force," assembled near Etorofu, an island in the Kurile archipelago stretching from the northern Japanese island of Hokkaido to Kamchatka. The Kido Butai would maintain strict radio silence from that point on. The next day, Joe Rochefort presented a report to the Pacific Fleet commander, Rear Admiral Husband Kimmel, his intelligence officer, Edwin T. Layton, and others, about the strength and location of the Japanese fleet. The Japanese were generating enough traffic to determine that the largest components of the fleet were located around Indochina, near present-day Vietnam. Since the trade restrictions had severely curtailed Japan's access to oil reserves, the Japanese fleet's position there indicated an aggressive posture toward either the oil-rich Dutch East Indies or America's Asiatic Fleet. (Based in the Philippines, the Asiatic Fleet was separate from the Pacific Fleet.) It could also be interpreted as a threat to British-held Singapore. The traffic from the carriers had gone silent, however, and Rochefort noted this.

This almost always happened when the carriers were at port, but Rochefort knew that this wasn't conclusive evidence that the Kido Butai was actually at port. Curiously, there were also no messages *to* the carriers, which had sortied that day into the North Pacific in anticipation of an order to attack Pearl Harbor.

The passenger liner *Tatsuta Maru* probably left Honolulu on or around that day with diplomatic pouches filled with Ensign Takeo Yoshikawa's intelligence. It would be the last Japanese ship to visit Hawaii during peacetime, and would soon go into service as a troop transport and POW hell ship. At the same time, Secretary of State Cordell Hull delivered a proposal to the Japanese ambassador with terms that Japan would not accept. On November 30, the Japanese government resolved to make war on the United States. The next day, the Kido Butai and its carriers received the order to attack Pearl Harbor. They were already underway.

On December 1, the Japanese navy changed all 20,000 call signs in its communications network. This was only one month after the previous change, and represented a huge amount of coordination across all their holdings and ships. More ominously, they changed the code keys, which left U.S. Navy cryptographers in the dark. The next day, when Edwin Layton told Admiral Kimmel about this, and the fact that the carriers still had not been located, Kimmel is reported to have replied, "Do you mean to say they could be rounding Diamond Head and you wouldn't know it?"

"I hope they would have been spotted by now," he replied.

Also at this time, a messenger from Captain Irving Mayfield visited Joe Rochefort at Hypo. Mayfield was the District Intelligence officer who had warned Jasper Holmes away from the RCA offices; Holmes would soon find out why. Mayfield had been in delicate negotiations to get copies of the Japanese consular radio traffic when Holmes made his innocent, but poorly timed, inquiry. Still, Mayfield was unsuccessful until later, when RCA president David Sarnoff was vacationing in the Hawaiian Islands. Admiral Bloch had persuaded Sarnoff to dispatch the Japanese consular radio traffic going over RCA's network, and now Joe Rochefort was presented with a package of these messages. They were in the Japanese diplomatic code known as Purple, which had already been broken several years earlier. For the Americans, the decryption breakthrough was an incredibly powerful insight into the Japanese government's intentions as relayed through its Foreign Ministry; it trumped all. The British were especially sensitive to Purple's far-reaching powers in that messages in the code from the Japanese ambassador in Berlin offered up invaluable observations about Nazi Party decision making at the highest levels. But Washington had distributed the special Purple decryption machines almost everywhere but Pearl Harbor, so Rochefort couldn't read the decryptions to interpret Japanese intentions toward Pearl Harbor.

Shortly thereafter, the Japanese consulate wouldn't be able to read or transmit the Purple code either, because they began the process of destroying their Purple machines and burning the codebooks. Dr. Kühn sent his window-light communications scheme to the consulate at this time. Since most of the consulate's codes were now destroyed, Consul General Kita sent Kühn's details in a vulnerable code on December 6.

Eric Holmes's parents had given him the chore of preparing breakfast on Sundays so that he would be able to find his way around the kitchen later in life. As he went about his business in their home in the Black Point neighborhood of Honolulu, some fourteen miles from Pearl Harbor, on the morning of December 7, 1941, the eleven-year-old made one shocking discovery after another, some portending a state of war more so than others.

Jasper Holmes and his wife, Isabelle, got their first indication of the morning's momentous events when Eric burst into their bedroom with what would be the first, and arguably the most accurate, intelligence report of the day: "The [Honolulu] *Adver-tiser* didn't come, Mr. Herndon says to get up, the Japs are taking the island, and you have no coffee."

Thus alarmed, Eric's parents took care of first things first. "Call up the *Advertiser*," his mother replied. "There is a fresh can of coffee in the lower closet."

Holmes explained to his son with some authority that "The Japs aren't taking the island. They are thousands of miles away, taking an island in the Dutch East Indies." Soon afterward he got a panicky call from the office directing him to general quarters. He assumed it was just another drill, and that it was scheduled for Sunday out of sheer orneriness. He got dressed quickly and was backing out of the driveway in his Studebaker Champion when Izzy implored him to have some coffee and breakfast before he went. He decided to go to headquarters instead.

The many hills around Honolulu prevented Holmes from directly observing Pearl as he made his way to the base. It was a beautiful morning and his first glimpse of what transpired there came in the form of puffs of smoke above the harbor from anti-aircraft guns. He surmised that it must be a fairly realistic drill, because the shrapnel from the flak would fall back down on the harbor rather than on Honolulu. Also, conducting it on Sunday would cause less disruption among the populace. Admiral Husband Kimmel, the commander in chief of the Pacific Fleet, had orders not to cause undue alarm.

As he neared Pearl, Holmes's misapprehensions would be dispelled—as would everyone else's—in a cascade of confounding sights, smells, and sounds that initially were merely disturbing, then sickening, and finally pitiful. First he saw a column of thick, dark smoke rising up from the harbor. The Honolulu traffic seemed eerily absent, even for an early Sunday morning, although a traffic snarl had developed outside the base. Someone reported that a Japanese plane was strafing the road ahead. Cars roared out of Pearl, filled with the wounded like a blurry series of crimson-splattered snapshots.

Holmes eventually reached the front gate, where the security guard waved him in. He parked his car in a half-empty parking lot. All seemed calm but later he would realize that it was the eye of the storm between the first and second waves of the carrier-based Japanese aircraft.

Thirteen-year-old John Cromwell, Jr., was also anxious that the newspaper hadn't arrived at their home in Honolulu that morning; like most boys his age he was especially eager to read the funnies and the sports section. The Cromwell family was friendly with Jasper Holmes's family due to a shared connection with the U.S. Navy's submarine service. The relationship would prove to have dire consequences for both the Cromwells and the Holmeses.

John Jr. ("Jack") had plans with his family later that day to visit his father, John Philip Cromwell, who was at the Navy infirmary in Pearl Harbor, where he was recuperating from high blood pressure. Jack was eating breakfast with his five-year-old sister, Ann, and their mother, Margaret, on the lanai at the back of their home, watching the neighbors play tennis in their backyard tennis court, when the now familiar wail of the air raid sirens began to rise and fall. For the family, it was the first of many flashbulb moments that would be forever seared in their memory. Soon after the air raid sirens came the sounds and concussions of detonating bombs, which the family took to be war training exercises. In keeping with the completely surreal atmosphere in the early minutes of the attack, Jack would later recall that had it not been for the gentle *pong…pong…pong* of the neighbors playing tennis, the cascading crescendos of bombs would have sounded like London during the Blitz.

The phone rang. A friend had called to tell them to turn on the radio: Pearl Harbor was being attacked. Although they didn't have a direct line of sight to Pearl from the backyard, they could see downtown Honolulu. It was not yet clear whether the attack was by sea or air. As Jack scanned the horizon he noticed a plane flying over the city. It dove and dropped a bomb on an electric utility at the waterfront, pulled out of the dive, turned left, and flew up the valley toward the Cromwell family home. Watching in disbelief, the boy recognized its resemblance to the silhouettes of fighter planes and bombers printed on the cards that came with his bubble-gum. As the plane neared, he saw the "meatball"—the insignia of the rising sun—painted on the side of the plane. The pilot had flung the canopy open, and now Jack clearly saw the pilot in the cockpit. For Jack and everyone on Oahu, this was as unusual, as deeply unsettling, and as unexpected as witnessing a thunderbolt coil and strike from that morning's clear blue skies.

After the initial shock of the attack wore off, the neighbors organized an ad hoc civil defense council. A man in his eighties became the secretary of war, and Jack was deputized as his assistant. In their first task, the two shuffled off in a comical search for a suitable air raid shelter. After spending a considerable amount of time looking all over the neighborhood, they congratulated themselves after finding a concrete shed behind the Cromwells' house that reeked of gasoline for the tractors that plowed the nearby fields. Their first terror-filled night there would haunt Jack's sister, Ann, for the rest of her life.

# 3

## First Blood

Thousands of miles away, across several time zones, the USS *Sculpin* lay in harbor at the Navy Yard in Cavite (pronounced Ka-VEE-tee) in the Philippines. In the predawn hours, the urban glow from streetlights and all-night dance halls from nearby Manila lit up the night sky with comforting familiarity. The deck watch keeping the lonely vigil shortly after 3:00 A.M. on December 8, 1941, wouldn't have suspected that this would be the last time he would see this when an "All Stations Alert" signal light beamed out across the harbor from the signal tower. Anticipating a message, the signalman on watch called Quartermaster Art Jay to the deck to verify the broadcast that would follow. Although they had trained for the possibility of war, the dashes and dots beamed out to the ships in the harbor must have seemed preposterous: JAPAN HAS ATTACKED PEARL HARBOR X GOVERN YOURSELVES ACCORDINGLY.

Jay rushed down through the conning tower and into officer's country with the absurd message to wake up the executive officer—or XO—Lieutenant Charles Henderson. As second-in-command, Henderson made sure that the officers and enlisted men carried out Chappell's orders and tended to administrative details so that the skipper could focus his attention on the command of the ship. The crewmen never addressed him by his sardonic nickname because the tight-wound Henderson, or "Cheerful Charlie," was a capable officer and kept everything shipshape. But the sheer number of details and niggling problems burdened him to a point of near-constant disapproval and the occasional scowl. He was also difficult to wake up, and Jay finally had to read the dispatch in a loud voice to get Henderson out of bed.

As the seriousness of the situation dawned on Henderson, he drew in a long breath, raced out of his bunk, and padded barefoot on the linoleum tiles up and down the boat yelling, "Gunner's Mate! Gunner's Mate! Where the hell is that gunner?"

GM 1/c (Gunner's Mate First Class) Joe Caserio woke up and rushed to the control room to break out the machine guns and ammo boxes, and set them up on the forward deck and on the cigarette deck aft. Fifteen minutes after the first message, the fleet received another message that hinted at the ominous events at Pearl Harbor: CONDUCT UNRESTRICTED AIR, SURFACE, AND UNDERSEAS WARFARE AGAINST THE EMPIRE OF JAPAN.

In maritime law, "unrestricted warfare" was tantamount to piracy. The order effectively rescinded Marquis of Queensberry rules about the conduct of sea warfare. There was to be no quarter asked, no quarter given. Contradicting Winston Churchill's impassioned vilification of Hitler's U-boats, the U.S. submarines were now authorized to use the same tactic as the Germans; they would give no warning to enemy shipping or even allow them to evacuate. The skippers were instructed to simply sink the target ships and their sailors with them.

With the sense that unreality had become fact and that now

they were at war, the men of the *Sculpin* woke to the XO's yelling and spent the rest of the morning laying aboard stores and a full load of torpedoes for their first war patrol. So, too, did the rest of the ships of the Asiatic Fleet anchored there, including the *Sculpin*'s sister ship, the *Sailfish*. By 10:00 A.M. they were moored together along the tanker *Pecos* to fill up with fuel oil for the diesels and fresh water for the men and the batteries. Parked there like sitting ducks next to a potential inferno, the crewmen listened with dread as air raid sirens started in low and grew to a nerve-racking pitch. With just a few details about what had happened at Pearl Harbor, the anxious antiaircraft crews had overreacted in what proved to be a false alarm.

The skipper went to the base at four that afternoon for a briefing. In submarine parlance of the day, Lucius Chappell was the "old man," as were all skippers. Bucking maritime tradition, sailors seldom referred to submarines as "ships"; instead they were "boats." The personality of the skipper was so closely associated with the conduct of his boat that sailors referred to individual submarines with the words "he," "him," and "his." When entwined in the intensely psychological life-or-death struggle on the open sea, a wily enemy destroyer captain would become familiar to them; the matter was personal, and the men throughout the submarine fleet would also refer to the destroyer with the same pronouns.

The stereotypical submarine captain in print and on the silver screen is a flinty, resolute character with ice water running in his veins, but in truth there was a varied assortment of personality types. One captain was a holy roller who saw the hand of God in everything and rendered divine interpretations for even insignificant events. Some were colorful rascals, others were staid by-the-regulation men, and still others were tyrants who exasperated their men to within a couple of degrees of outright mutiny. None at this point had been tested in actual combat, and in truth, their backgrounds never seemed to give a reliable indication of whether they would be effective at leading aggressive patrols to sink enemy ships.

Lucius Chappell came about as close to the stereotype of the dauntless sub driver as any of the service's skippers. But he wasn't flinty, and ice water didn't course through his veins; rather, they ran warm and languid with a relaxed, Southern nonchalance, even in extreme peril. He was from a prominent and well-regarded Georgia family that went back to the beginning of the nation, and his gracious manners and trademark smile won friends among the officers in the submarine force and accolades from the enlisted men that would last for decades. He graduated from the Naval Academy in 1927, served aboard several ships, and went to New London in 1933 for sub school. He demonstrated above-average competence in subs, but it was probably his authoritative presence that led him up the ranks to command of his own submarine. The atmosphere aboard the *Sculpin* was free from unnecessary tension, and no one ever remembered hearing him raise his voice. However droll this pipe-smoking, soft-spoken Southern gentleman may have been, time would prove that he was no shrinking violet.

At the briefing with Captain John Wilkes, the task force sub commander of the Asiatic Fleet, Chappell learned some specifics about Pearl Harbor, his patrol area, and the secret new Mk VI torpedo exploder. Wilkes warned him not to divulge the patrol area until the ship had cleared Manila Bay. To evade surface and air patrols, the submarines would surface one hour after dusk and dive one hour before dawn, and remain submerged throughout the day. As for the top secret Mk VI, it was apparently a remarkable leap in technology, exploding when it detected a target ship's magnetic signature. Skippers would no longer have to worry about whether their torpedoes would pop harmlessly against the steel-reinforced sides of battleships. The Mk VI–equipped torpedo would run under the target ship, explode at the ship's soft underbelly, and break its keel with one shot. One shot, one ship: a battleship every time. According to the Bureau of Ordnance in Rhode Island, the Mk VI ate gunpowder and shat lightning. Tests had proved it. The device was infallible. And at the very reasonable price of $1,000 in 1941 dollars, each torpedo was surely a bargain. With the Mk VI, a handful of submarines would doubtless sink the entire Japanese navy.

The *Sculpin*'s first war patrol was nearly its last when it stood out to exit Manila Bay that evening. The night sky was dark; there were no navigation lights, and the familiar glow from the city was absent. To hamper nighttime air raids and enemy ships' navigation, nearly all of the Philippines observed blackout conditions. Along with the submarine USS *Seawolf* and the tankers *Pecos* and *Trinity*, the *Sculpin* followed the seaplane tender USS *Langley* toward Corregidor. As they passed through the minefields there, men in the after torpedo room heard a *bump-bump-bump* on the port side. The sound was probably coming from the propeller guard as it scraped against the rusty chains of a mine. Lieutenant Corwin "Mendy" Mendenhall went aft to reassure the nervous men.

Once they'd passed from Manila Bay into the South China

Sea, the *Sculpin* detached from the convoy and made an initial trim dive. They'd taken on new supplies, fuel, and fresh water, which had changed the weight of the boat. Although the diving officer could estimate the new weight and adjust how much water they'd have to take on in order to get compensation and trim, the only way to be sure was to make the initial trim dive. The officer of the deck cleared the bridge and gave two blasts of the diving alarm—*oo-OO-gah, oo-OO-gah.*

The control room crew opened the valves on top of the main ballast tanks. The air rushed out of the tanks with a roar as they filled with seawater from the vents below and the ship began to sink. The bow plane operator pushed a button to rig out the bow planes with hydraulic pressure, then stood by at the diving station wheel to steer them downward into a dive. Men in every compartment with a hatch to the outside dogged the latches to make them watertight. The maneuvering room shut a lever overhead that turned the diesel engines off. With the flip of another switch they connected the electric motors to the batteries. The engine room gang would shut flapper valves on the exhaust mufflers and on the main induction, a tube thirty-six inches wide and 100 feet long that sucked massive quantities of air into the ship for the diesels. If the ship dove with the induction valves open, it would be the equivalent of diving with a thirty-six-inch hole in the engine room, which in turn could flood the entire ship and kill all aboard.

In the control room, the diving officer and chief of the watch kept an eye on the Christmas Tree, an electrical panel with red and green lightbulbs. As the engines shut down and hatches shut, their corresponding red lightbulbs would glow green, indicating readiness for the dive. With the decks awash with seawater, the quartermaster would be the last down the bridge hatch, waiting carefully and holding the hatch open until the sucking action of the engines ceased. Everyone's lives were in his hands. If the diesels were still running while the induction was closed, the diesels would suck air through the compartments of the boat from any remaining openings. If the quartermaster closed that final hatch before the engines shut down, the diesels would suck every last atom of air from the crew's compartments. In such a vacuum, an officer would have no air with which to scream "Open the hatch," and in any event, the hatch would be held tight by the vacuum in the boat. The crew's eardrums might explode, and with no air pressure, their lung tissues would rip as their alveoli burst. The rapid reduction in pressure would cause the boat to fill with fog, the last thing they would see for about fifteen seconds before losing consciousness.

When all the lights on the Christmas Tree went green and the engines had stopped, the quartermaster hung on the lanyard on the deck hatch to keep it shut while a crewman dogged it tight. Then the chief bled air into the boat and watched the barometer. The crewmen's ears popped as the pressure went up in the compartments, and once assured that the boat was airtight, the chief would announce "Pressure in the boat!" The submarine would begin its descent in earnest. The diving officer took water in or pumped water out of the trim and auxiliary tanks to attain compensation and trim. Once the boat was as buoyant as the water around it, he'd note the amount of water they'd taken in for the next dive.

On each dive, every man had a job, and every job was crucial. If any one of them failed to accomplish even a single task in the crucial first thirty seconds of a dive—or during the war patrol—the entire crew of sixty-six souls could perish. There were no second chances, no mitigating factors. They would have to be able to do this and much more at a moment's notice, twenty-four hours a day.

The *Sculpin* headed south and east through the San Bernardino Strait to its patrol area, where they would guard Lamon Bay off the southeastern shore of Luzon Island. The Commander of Submarine Forces, Asiatic Fleet (CSAF), speculated that the Japanese might stage an invasion there. Unfortunately, only about twenty or so modern submarines, a handful of rusty old S-class submarines, a couple of cruisers, and an assortment of destroyers were available against the Japanese armada that would soon come. Since there was only one radio, the signalmen could copy only official Navy transmissions, and no one had a good idea of what had happened at Pearl, or even what was happening in the Philippines. They did, however, get snippets about preposterous Japanese claims of sinking several battleships and cruisers at Pearl Harbor, then Japanese landings on the western shore of Luzon, opposite their position. Despite radio jamming by the Japanese, they analyzed every broadcast for even the smallest scraps of information, and what they heard was disheartening.

General Douglas MacArthur lost all his bombers. The Japanese struck Cavite with an air raid. Over 200 of the sub force's torpedoes went up in smoke. A bomb destroyed Dick Voge's sub, USS *Sealion*, while it was in dry dock, and the submarine tender *Canopus* was a total loss. The submarines posted on the western side of Luzon had been ineffective in the face of landings there, and the U.S. Army was in retreat. There was also troubling news about the torpedoes: They ran much deeper than set, and either exploded soon after arming or not at all. Moreover, one torpedo was often not enough to sink a ship. Based on the information they were getting from the other submarines, Chappell changed the depth settings on the torpedoes shallower and shallower until they would practically run on the surface. The *Sculpin* also got word of Japanese landings at Aparri, on the northern tip of Luzon. CSAF sent a change of orders for them to go north and patrol there. A few days after they left, the Japanese landed at Lamon Bay, their previous patrol area. Nothing was going right for the Allies, and in conversations around the wardroom, the officers took to calling the fleet the RAF, for "Retreating Asiatic Fleet."

Since they were submerged all day, Chappell instituted what the men came to call the "Reversa" schedule, where most of them slept during the day and performed their duties at night. They had breakfast at dusk, lunch at midnight, and dinner at dawn. Some of the men didn't have lookout duty, and would never come out of the boat from the time they embarked on a war patrol till the day the *Sculpin* tied back up at the dock. Aside from periscope observations, none of them would see the light of day for a month or more.

The crew adjusted to the schedule and dug in for the long haul, keeping busy by operating the sub or doing maintenance work on the equipment. During off-hours they slept, ate, read magazines, and wrote letters, or they played cribbage, poker, and a Navy version of backgammon called acey-deucey. Strange as it seems, they also smoked inside the sub—at that time, people smoked in restaurants, buses, movie theaters, everywhere, and submarines were no exception. Each compartment had a smoking lamp to indicate whether they had the captain's permission to light up; at the end of a battery charge, the batteries gave off hydrogen gas, which was a fire hazard, so they kept the smoking lamp off at this time. Most skippers also didn't want to fill up the boat with cigarette smoke while submerged, though some would let the crew smoke during a particularly long depth charge attack to calm frayed nerves. After a sub had been submerged for twelve, eighteen, or twenty-four hours, sometimes there wasn't even enough oxygen to get a match lit, let alone smoke a cigarette.

Adding to the malodorous atmosphere was the short supply of water—there was enough to drink and to top off the batteries, but that was about all. As a result, the men wouldn't be able to shower for weeks at a time, and the sub took on a stale, musty stench. Some men took "French baths," while others resorted to using "pink lady," the alcohol fuel used to power the torpedoes. The *Sculpin* had also left in such haste that many of the men left their laundry back at Cavite and had to wear the same dirty clothes for weeks. In tropic climes this was usually a T-shirt and cutoff jeans, but sometimes even this was too much and on some boats the men went about their business completely naked. If this seems bizarre, it would be well to keep in mind that the subs were in equatorial waters with high humidity. When the sub dove for the day, the heat of the four massive diesel engines radiated throughout the boat. Even with air conditioning, the forward torpedo room—the coolest part of the boat—often went above 100 degrees. In the engine rooms, the temperature regularly went up to 140 degrees. There was nothing to be done about it but drink gallons of water and swallow handfuls of salt tablets. Under these conditions even the heartiest men would sweat off dozens of pounds by the time a patrol ended. As quoted in *Silent Victory* by Clay Blair Jr., one submariner wrote about the conditions while on patrol:

> The bunks beyond the wardroom are filled with torpid, skivvy-clad bodies, the sweat running off the white, rash-blistered skin in small rivulets. Metal fans are whirring everywhere—overhead, at the ends of the bunks, close to my ear....I am playing cribbage with the skipper, mainly because I don't like to wallow in a sweat-soaked bunk most of the day. I have my elbows on the table near the edge and I hold my cards with my arms at a slight angle so the sweat will stream down my bare arms...without further soaking the pile of cards in the center....Overhead is a fine net of gauze to catch the wayward cockroaches which prowl across the top of the wardroom and occasionally fall straight downward...they live in the cork insulation which lines the insides of the submarine's hull...we've killed over sixteen million cockroaches in one compartment alone....The deck in the control room is littered with towels, used to sponge up the water dripping off the men and the submarine itself.

Their only consolation was good food—probably the best in the Navy. The submariners got top cuts of meat and whatever frozen fruits were available, but any food became contemptible with routine. When the cook, or "Chief Stew Burner," dipped into the dreaded bologna they ate so often and grew to detest, they called it "horsecock." Chipped beef on toast was the slightly less appealing "shit on a shingle." Everyone and everything had a nickname. Just as the skipper was "the old man," the gunnery officer was always "Gunny," the pharmacist's mate "Doc." The motor machinists—or motormacs—were the "black crew," because the diesel fuel and crankcase oil covered their skin like black greasepaint, and electricians in the maneuvering room were "ampere hounds."

All of them developed "submarine ears." Whether it was a sudden change of course, or the engines suddenly stopped and the humming, pounding noise was replaced with an eerie silence, or the normal chitchat of the control room was replaced with terse, hushed tones, the implications of a sudden change gusted up and down the length of the boat with urgency. As it traveled, the men exchanged nods and knowing glances. Conversations stopped. Men who were seated stood up and crossed their arms or held themselves steady with one hand on a bulkhead or piece of equipment, tensed and ready for orders. The hundreds of polished knobs and indicator dials glowed with new intensity. Smokers checked the smoking light to see if they could get in one last cigarette before the action started, while others might watch a crewmate as he swallowed nervously, his Adam's apple rising, stopping, and falling. Even men sleeping in their bunks might take note of the quiet and wake up to the tension of those around them. The compartment talkers would adjust their headphones and the contraption perched on their chest that held an old-fashioned telephone receiver so that both hands were free to do work. Coming across the enemy—whether for the first time or the thirtieth—never became routine. Although it stretched the men's nerves taut, the shot of adrenaline had a curious stilling effect, as though they'd stumbled upon a tiger in the woods.

Mendy was the officer of the deck when they spotted their

first target. It was raining, and the wind howled and warbled as it licked around the antenna. The seas had kicked up with rough chops; one swell had flooded the deck and sent a torrent of water down the hatch into the conning tower. At 11:04 P.M., Cleland "Doc" Miller was standing lookout watch on the deck when he said, "Mr. Mendenhall, I think I see a ship ahead, slightly to port." He spoke quietly, Mendenhall would recall, "as if they could hear him if he talked louder."

Mendenhall quickly spotted the vessel through the rain gusts: a large, heavily laden cargo ship bobbing and heaving low in the water. He sounded the battle stations alarm and pushed the button on the 1MC to give orders: "Make ready bow tubes; come to course two-oh-eight." The crewmen on a submarine confirmed nearly every order to reduce errors or miscommunications, and the men in the forward torpedo room replied—"Make ready bow tubes, aye aye, sir"—while the helmsman (usually the quartermaster) barked, "Coming to course two-oh-eight, aye aye, sir!"

The skipper ran from his quarters to get to the deck and popped up the hatch, breathless. He grabbed a pair of binoculars and stared out into the darkness. "Mendy," Chappell said, "I don't see a thing." He had been reading when Mendenhall sounded the alarm, and his night vision couldn't adapt quickly enough to see the ship. Now the lookouts saw another ship farther out in the distance; it looked like a cargo ship, too. Chappell couldn't let the enemy ship get by—the standing order for all ships was to attack now that they were at war—so he made a snap decision: "It's all yours. Do your best," he told Mendenhall.

Mendenhall called the target's range, speed, bearing, and angle on the bow to the officer operating the Torpedo Data Computer (TDC) in the control room below. It was a large box with spinning dials and knobs to adjust the settings. Using inputs from the sub's gyrocompass and speedometer (the "bendix") as well as the target's information from observations on the deck or the periscope, the TDC would calculate the target's course over time. More observations made the TDC's calculations more accurate. While this was happening, the TDC adjusted the angle the torpedoes would take after they left their tubes. Each torpedo had a gyroscope, and as the TDC tracked the target, it calculated and adjusted the gyro angle in real time through a spindle inside the torpedo. When the TDC's predicted bearing, speed, and range matched what the crewmen observed on the deck or through the periscope, the TDC was said to have reached a "solution," and they could fire at any time. When the skipper gave the order to fire, the spindle would pop out of the torpedo. A gush of compressed air ejected the torpedo, and its alcohol-powered steam engine started. As the torpedo made its way to the target, the gyro adjusted the course until it reached the angle preset by the TDC. Simultaneously, a poppet valve opened on the torpedo tube. This allowed the seawater outside the sub to push the compressed air back into the torpedo tube, through the poppet valve, and back into the boat. When the seawater reached the poppet valve, it clamped the valve shut so that the sub wouldn't take on too much water. If the ship didn't take on the additional water through the torpedo tube, the loss of the torpedo's weight could alter the sub's compensation and make the ship broach.

Mendy called to the TDC operator: "Course two-nine-oh true. Speed, twelve knots. Range, two-five-oh-oh yards. Angle on the bow, seven-five degrees." They waited as the ship continued along its track; they were on an intersecting path and were coming closer and closer. Hopefully they could get their torpedoes off before the lookouts on the other ship saw the *Sculpin*'s low silhouette on the surface.

"Set depth ten feet."

"Set depth ten feet, aye aye, sir." They waited quietly in the warm rain, watching the target and the other ship for any signs that they might be aware of the sub's presence. The torpedoman reported: "Depth set, ten feet, sir."

"Set gyro angles three-oh degrees right."

"Set gyro angles three-oh degrees right, aye aye, sir. Gyro angles set three-oh degrees right, sir."

"Range, one-triple-oh yards."

"I have a solution . . . ready to fire."

"Fire one!" The *Sculpin* shuddered as the torpedo left the tube, then shuddered as the compressed air entered the torpedo room. From the slight shaking beneath their feet and the gust of air that went throughout the boat, the crewmen knew they'd fired their first war shot.

"One's away, sir."

"Fire two!"

"Two's away, sir." Still no sign that the target had spotted them.

Then from the soundman: "Both fish running hot, straight, and normal, sir."

They watched the target through the rain as it heaved on the heavy waves, waiting while the seconds seemed to turn into minutes. The cargo ship was coming closer and closer, oblivious to their presence. *Christ! When will they spot us? Why aren't the torpedoes exploding?*

When the torpedoes failed to explode, the skipper decided to fire two more. They were now so close that they could hardly miss.

"Set gyro angles four-five degrees right."

"Set gyro angle four-five degrees right, aye aye, sir. Gyro angles set four-five degrees right."

"Fire three."

"Three's away, sir."

"Fire four."

"Four's—"

They saw the sky light up a split second before the sound of the explosion hit them. A column of fire and smoke billowed upward. Four seconds later there was another explosion as the second torpedo hit.

The flash lit up everything around it—the target ship, the second cargo ship, even the *Sculpin*. The skipper decided to bring the aft torpedo tubes to bear against the second target and rang up a change in course. The helmsman spun the rudder and the aft torpedo room made ready the tubes. Pandemonium broke out on the cargo ship. It had slowed and was now starting to list. Through the rain, they could see pinholes of light on the target ship that lengthened into rays along the waterline and up and down the deck, contracting again into pinholes; the doomed sailors were running up and down the deck with flashlights. Sinking in rough seas like these, they were sure to drown. A gun crew on the target started to shoot wildly. One of the lookouts had spotted the *Sculpin* in the afterglow of the detonations and started directing the gunfire bursts toward the submarine. White-hot tracers whistled toward the *Sculpin* and splashed into the heaving sea swells next to the submarine. The cargo ship would be dangerous until it sank; even a single shot could hole the sub. Since they'd been spotted, the *Sculpin* lost the element of surprise. "Let's get out of here," the skipper said, and with two blasts of the diving alarm, they sank below the waves.

The ship's bobbing and heaving slowly subsided as the *Sculpin* went below the sea swells, then all was quiet. Below them was the Philippine Trench—one of the deepest holes in the world, 30,000 feet down.

"Rig for depth charge," Chappell said. The order was repeated throughout the boat. The watertight doors between the compartments slammed shut like bank vaults and made a fluttering sound as the men behind them spun the S-shaped wheels to dog the clamps shut. The battle talker listened to the compartments as they reported, then told the skipper, "Rigged for depth charge, sir."

"Rig for silent running." The men secured everything. In the control room they shut off the hydraulic pumps operating the planes and rudders—akin to power steering on a car—and shifted to quieter manual operation. In the oppressive heat and oxygen-poor atmosphere of the sub, the exhausting task of moving the planes and rudder by hand would quickly wear out the men. The maneuvering room lowered the speed of the electric motors to reduce the noise. "Rigged for silent running, sir."

The men settled down to wait. Their lives were now in the hands of the soundman, and they hung on his every word. He switched intermittently between the crippled cargo ship and the second ship, which was now circling around, possibly to drop depth charges. The screws on the ship they'd attacked slowed down, then stopped. The silence was replaced by breaking-up noises.

The sounds a ship makes as it breaks up are unbelievably

gruesome; more gut-wrenching somehow than actually watching it sink. As its compartments take on water, the ship lists and starts to tip over. As the angle of the floors become more acute, the objects inside it start to shift, then slide across the floor, just as the furniture in a house would if the house was slowly tipped over onto its side. The ship reverberates with thunderous booms when the cargo crashes into the walls, as though it were a steel kettle the size of a football field. The boilers and turbines jump their chassis and break through the collapsing bulkheads—the vertical walls between the compartments that hold the ship's structure together. As the angle of the ship's list increases, stresses start to push and pull on the metal plates. The inch-thick steel groans and cries as it gives under the stress until it rips like aluminum foil. When the cold water hits the boilers, they burst and hiss, throwing out enormous gusts of steam. Sometimes the screams of sailors scalded to death by the exploding boilers on a dying ship would travel through the water to the ears of an awestruck soundman. If the sub were close enough to the wreck, the submariners could also hear these horrifying sounds through the walls of the sub. Finally, the sea would cover the doomed sailors and extinguish their pitiful whimpers. Their final descent would take them through miles of water to the cold abyss that had not seen daylight since the time when the oceans formed, and would not see the sun again until the day it boils the oceans away from the face of the earth.

It wouldn't have been easy to turn their thoughts away from the unlucky sailors' fates unless the men of the *Sculpin* were not otherwise preoccupied with avoiding the same awful end. The soundman listened as the second ship charged around at high speed in a circle along the choppy waves above. Ten minutes after *Sculpin* had dived, the ship dropped a depth charge. It was far enough that they could hear the characteristic *click-click* of the detonator before the bomb went off. If it had been closer, there would be no warning, and if it had been farther away, it would have sounded like a distant rumble.

Chappell gave the order to take the sub deep and gave a course to evade. Over the next twelve minutes they heard two more depth charges, then they lost contact. Discretion, as they say, is the better part of valor, and the skipper exercised his by lying low for an hour. When the *Sculpin* surfaced ten minutes before 1:00 A.M., both ships were gone.

Over the next days, they continued to patrol and listen to the broadcasts. Because the Japanese jammed many of the frequencies, the Asiatic Fleet often rebroadcast messages to ensure reception. One day while decoding one of the messages, a hush came over the radio shack. They couldn't believe the message they were reading from their sister ship, the *Sailfish*:

ATTACKED ONE SHIP X

VIOLENT COUNTERATTACK X

COMMANDING OFFICER BREAKING DOWN X

URGENTLY REQUEST AUTHORITY TO RETURN TO TENDER X

# 4

---

# Hard Luck

The *Sculpin*'s sister ship, *Sailfish*, was built at the same time and in the same yard, but due to a disaster before the war that had killed half the crew, it became known as a hard-luck ship. The sinking had become a major spectacle in the press, and despite the loss in life, the survival of so many crewmen was in fact something of a miracle after so many other subs had gone down without so much as a single survivor. For the refitting crews assigned to clean out the ship, however, the salvaged hull was nothing less than a steel sarcophagus exhumed from the deep. Many sailors observe the ancient superstitions of the seas, and any such ship that had suffered that fate would be branded as cursed. The unenviable job of resurrecting the hapless sub and breaking it from its past fell to Morton C. Mumma, a taskmaster who did everything in his power to put the disaster out of the crew's minds, as well as his own. He drilled the crew mercilessly and frequently toured the boat to keep tabs on everything that was happening. If he found anything that wasn't strictly regulation, or deviated from his orders, he gave his officers hell and even earned the nickname "Summary Courts-Martial Mumma." Even as he was tough on his men, he was just as tough on himself, perhaps more so. Although the men never knew it until the crucial moment, despite his Herculean efforts, the ship's past weighed on him. As Admiral Charles A. Lockwood would discover, Mumma "never made a dive without thinking he was hearing water rushing in."

The *Sailfish* left Cavite on December 8, 1941, to patrol Lingayen Gulf on the western portion of Luzon, a potential landing site for the anticipated Japanese invasion. The *Sailfish* kept relatively close to the shore, surfacing at night and submerging at dawn like the *Sculpin* and the other subs. Large areas of the warm tropical waters would sometimes glow as the sub passed through, lighting up the sub with an eerie but unmistakable silhouette. It was caused by phosphorescent microorganisms in the water. When disturbed by moving objects like fish, dolphins, or submarines, it lit up and subsided. For a submarine relying on its low profile and stealthy night attacks, having the sea beam a spotlight on it was an unnerving phenomenon. Moreover, there was no guarantee that an enemy ship would be similarly lit up—the microorganisms appeared in unpredictable patches and avoiding them was like trying to move between raindrops.

Mumma's prewar habit of pacing up and down the boat only intensified now that they were at war. He kept everyone on pins and needles and had to know about every report, every reading, every nuance. Although it isn't clear whether he had standing orders to wake him up, or whether they went into a Reversa schedule, he likely didn't need to give such orders because his restless mind kept him awake at all hours as he strolled back and forth, tapping dials, looking at battery and $CO_2$ readings, asking questions about the equipment or why something hadn't been done. Mumma was driven by his responsibility, by his training, and by his will to succeed, and by all appearances he was making an extraordinary effort at superhuman endurance.

On the first and second nights they saw unescorted cargo ships charging south, which Mumma interpreted as friendly ships escaping from Hong Kong. The next evening, they spotted a destroyer or cruiser on a southerly course; the Japanese destroyers were so large that they were often mistaken for cruisers, especially early in the war. It was a disadvantageous setup for *Sailfish* because the moon was behind them, casting their relatively easily discernible silhouette along the horizon. The officer of the deck rang up battle stations, and Mumma once again came to investigate. The target was some miles out, but suddenly narrowed as it turned toward the *Sailfish*. Mumma immediately surmised that they had been spotted and decided to dive to periscope depth. The soundman began tracking the target, but its bearing seemed to wheel away north, and it was too dark and far away for Mumma to spot it in the periscope. As the cruiser moved faster on the surface than the sub could underwater, it left the area and they eventually lost contact, resulting in yet another sleepless night for the skipper. Since the Japanese had made diversionary landings on the northern tip of Luzon, the *Sailfish* received orders to patrol farther north.

By the time they spotted targets on the horizon at 2:30 in the morning on December 13, Mumma was exhausted, but girded himself for battle. Once again, the moon was disadvantageous, but this time they had spied the ships at a range of about 2,000 yards as they passed through the luminescent waters. They seemed to be fast-moving destroyers coming their way, and Mumma dove to periscope depth. One of the destroyers dropped three depth charges astern of the *Sailfish*, but they weren't close.

Following prewar doctrine, Mumma decided to make a torpedo attack on sound bearings alone.

The soundman, Dorrity, tracked the destroyer aft of the ship, moving from starboard to port. It was dead close—about 500 yards from the *Sailfish*, which was only 100 yards long. If they fired at it from any closer, the torpedo might not have time to arm itself before hitting the target. The ready lights on the aft torpedo tubes glowed in the control room.

"We'll fire two from tubes five and six," Mumma ordered, "three degree spread."

BANG! A depth charge exploded nearby.

"Set range five-oh-oh yards. Speed, sixteen knots."

"Torpedoes ready, Captain."

"Rigged for depth charge, Captain."

"We have a solution, Captain."

BANG!

"Fire five!"

The sailor at the control keyed the torpedo control panel and hit a lever. A gust of air filled the boat as the torpedo left. One of the crewmen clicked a stopwatch. Traveling at 46 knots at 500 yards, the torpedo should hit the target in only twenty seconds.

"Five's away, sir."

"Fire six!"

"Six's away, sir."

"Rig for depth charge!"

"Rig for depth charge, aye aye."

"Both fish running hot, straight, and normal." They waited and watched the hand of the stopwatch as it swept along its path: five...ten...fifteen...

*CRACK!* The boat shook. It didn't sound anything like the

depth charges. The soundman reported: "The screws on that bearing have stopped, sir." They waited for an explosion from the second torpedo.

BANG!—another depth charge.

The soundman came over the speaker again: "The torpedo hit, Captain. The torpedo has stopped." But why no explosion when the torpedo hit? Was the detonator defective?

BANG! BANG! BANG!

"They're pinging us, Captain."

Mumma's mind must have convulsed in horror: The Japanese didn't have sonar. Had he just sunk an American destroyer? Impossible! "Ask Dorrity what whiskey he's drinking!" Mumma said. "Up periscope!"

Mumma peered around at the destroyers nearby, even asked a second opinion. But they were far from displaying any signs of distress.

Dorrity, the soundman, reported again: They were definitely pinging up there—have a listen. He piped the signal through the intercom: It sounded like a baby spoon tinking a teacup.

Mumma was incredulous. He argued that it must be an American up there, but no, Dorrity replied. The pinging from American destroyers sounded different; they used a different pinging frequency.

All of Mumma's worst fears crystallized in that moment. No one had any idea that the Japanese had sonar. He realized from their training exercises that once a destroyer located a sub, the chances for sinking it were about 70 percent, and the destroyer directly above them had Mumma and the *Sailfish* in the crosshairs. If they acquired a target, they'd ping in rapid succession, called "short scale."

BANG!

The depth charges were getting closer.

Dorrity reported again: "Captain! They're shifting to short scale!"

"FULLSPEED! RIGHTFULLRUDDER! COME TO ONE-EIGHT-OH DEGREES! ONE-SEVEN-OH FEET!"

*BANG! shhh...* The concussion was so close it created bubbles in the superstructure of the boat that sizzled and hissed as they rose to the surface.

*"Full speed, aye aye!"—"Coming to right full rudder!"—*

*—BANG! SHHH—*

*—"One-seven-oh feet, aye aye, Captain!"*

"Mister Cassedy..." Mumma muttered to his XO.

"Yes, Captain?"

"I am going to my cabin."

"Yes... Captain?"

*BANG! SHHHH.*

Mumma walked past the men in the control room, opened the watertight door to the next compartment forward, shut it behind him, and sealed it tight.

The boat wasn't sinking fast enough because the warm water they'd taken on to come to periscope depth wasn't as dense as the cold water below. The diving officer took on another 15,000 gallons of ballast to get them down. They rigged for silent running and came to a new course away from the destroyers above. The depth charges continued as the *Sailfish* tried to evade under the waves, but as the sub sank deeper the explosions receded, then ceased altogether. Dorrity kept track of the screws above, which subsided, until he could hear only the pinging at some distance.

Mumma stayed in his cabin and asked Cassedy to request

that they return to Manila, resulting in the disconcerting radio broadcast that the other ships had intercepted. Although the rest of the fleet had some idea of what had happened, most of the crewmen on the *Sailfish* still didn't know about the state of their skipper. Many of his contemporaries might have guessed that Mumma was weak, but this simply wasn't true. He just wasn't cut out for submarines. He'd suppressed his concerns about subs in general, and the *Sailfish* in particular, and in a state of exhaustion a switch involuntarily flipped inside him. It could have happened to anyone, even the best of them—and it would. No one could determine what combination of stressors would lead to the overwhelming sense of dread that flooded over Mumma; it was something no one could determine beforehand. Rather than endanger the crewmen, he had to get off, and did.

The *Sailfish* stayed well offshore for the next three days and eventually crept into the wrecked Navy Yard in Cavite. In the pitch black of the dead of night, Mumma explained to the crew that he was leaving, and that they would be getting another captain, Lieutenant Commander Richard Voge.

They were getting Voge because his boat, the *Sealion*, lay scuttled in dry dock where a Japanese plane had dropped a bomb and killed several of the crewmen. They'd never had a chance.

The hard-luck *Sailfish* now had a hard-luck captain, and if the previous patrol had unnerved their former captain, there was no telling what he would have done on their next patrol.

# 5

## Live Ammo

A blizzard of events followed the sneak attack at Pearl Harbor that had implications for Rochefort's Station Hypo and, by extension, for the entire fleet. Up until December 7, 1941, Rochefort, Dyer, and the rest of the crew had been knocking their heads against the wall of the Japanese flag officer's code, an extraordinarily complex cipher that task force commanders used to communicate between themselves and headquarters back in Japan. Beyond the complexity of the code itself, the code breakers were further hampered by the fact that the Japanese seldom used the code. Without a sufficient amount of traffic, they didn't have enough examples to see patterns repeating, and as far as we know, the solution has never been solved.* After Pearl Harbor, the Navy department in charge of decryption, OP-20-G, directed Hypo to abandon the flag officer's code and start work on another code, JN-25. Unlike the flag officer's code, the Japanese used JN-25 frequently and had sufficient confidence in its

---

*It is possible that an enterprising soul at the National Security Agency has used computers in the years since World War II to crack the code, but it would probably be easier for a casual reader to crack the flag officer's code itself than to ascertain from the NSA whether this is the case.

security to transmit a huge amount of crucial information. By war's end, they had sent about 70 percent of their traffic in this code.

Another result of the sneak attack was a conspiratorial air of recrimination about who was responsible for the catastrophe. Although Japan's aircraft carriers effectively ruled the entire ocean long before they even lifted anchor on a course for Pearl Harbor, the prevailing attitude in the United States among sailors and civilians alike was that sufficient warning would have somehow averted the disaster. The Navy looked to radio intelligence with renewed interest, and when Rochefort requested more personnel and more space in the Administration Building to put them, he generally got whatever resources were available. When the USS *California* sank at Pearl Harbor, the ship's band no longer had a ship to play for—or any instruments to play with—so the district commandant assigned them to Hypo. Their abilities as musicians translated well into their new work as code breakers, and despite a wrongheaded attempt to wrest them from Hypo that went all the way to Admiral Kimmel's legendary replacement, Admiral Chester Nimitz, the unlikely "crippies" (cryptographers) stayed there and made significant contributions throughout the war.

Jasper Holmes had been delivering radio traffic summaries to the CincPac (Commander in Chief, Pacific) offices since November, and when subs began leaving for patrols in the mysterious Japanese-held Marshall and Caroline islands in December, the sub captains came to him for whatever little information he could provide for upcoming patrols. He was also briefing the submarine command about ship positions with his charts every morning. Now the collaboration with his old buddies in the sub force started to develop into what was perhaps the single most effective and devastating tactic against the Japanese navy. Since the onset of hostilities, Rochefort and Holmes had been watching the positions of Japanese submarines. The sub captains often betrayed their positions by shelling American land bases with their deck guns before the end of a patrol and were often very chatty in their radio broadcasts. In a technique called direction finding or DF, two or more Navy radio receivers at different locations would pick up the direction of these broadcasts, and determine their location by triangulation. Holmes tracked the Japanese sub *I-173* across the Pacific as it shelled San Diego, then Midway. ComSubPac Tommy Withers got word that a Japanese submarine would probably be intersecting the path of the submarine USS *Gudgeon* at a particular point on January 18, 1942, but Holmes almost certainly didn't tell Withers that they'd derived that from radio intelligence, or that the *I-173* had been broadcasting frequently along the way.

To his credit, Withers took the chance, and skipper Joe Grenfell of the *Gudgeon* described the ship when it miraculously came his way as "fat, dumb, and happy...the men were lounging on the upper deck, sunbathing and smoking." Grenfell fired three torpedoes, but this upset the trim of the boat and he was unable to see what happened while his periscope dipped under the water. He heard an explosion, then silence. When he was able to get another look, the *I-173* was gone, and he guessed that they may have dived with the ports open, sinking their own boat. Whether this was the case or the torpedo sank them was now academic, because their daily broadcast was never heard again, and the Japanese navy ceased references to the ship.

The code breakers had also broken a minor code that had major implications. The Japanese navy amassed at Truk in the Caroline Islands and so Truk came to be known as Japan's "Gibraltar of the Pacific." The port director there broadcast announcements about the departure of ships and convoys, as well as their noontime positions as they followed a strict, prescribed path to their destinations. Rochefort may not have believed his great fortune in discovering the names, destinations, and exact courses of enemy ships from this important port. Holmes immediately recognized that it would give the submarine skippers great chances for prize targets, instead of roaming the vast Pacific looking for opportunities. In this instance, however, there was no way for Holmes to conceal how they'd come by the information. There were no coast watchers that far into the Pacific. No spy could transmit the comings and goings of ships from Truk with sufficient broadcast strength to go undetected by the Japanese. The sub commanders would get the information firsthand if it had come from a stealthy submarine; they would naturally conclude that the only way for the deskbound oddballs in Hypo to have gotten such explicit information was for them to have broken a Japanese code. When Holmes caught wind that the heavy aircraft carrier *Shoho* was coming out of Truk, he had no doubt that the submariners could be trusted, but Rochefort was skeptical.

What Holmes proposed was extremely risky business. It was strictly forbidden by the guidelines for the use of radio decryption intelligence; it could not be used for minor tactical advantages, even if it was as significant as the aircraft carrier *Shoho*. The logic was that if the Japanese carriers suddenly had American submarines along their paths wherever they went, they would become suspicious, perhaps change the code, and leave the Americans in the dark when they most needed that source of intelligence. But as Tom Dyer said, battles are won on the basis of minor tactical advantages. Rochefort relented, but gave strict conditions: No paper was to leave the office, and Holmes would have to lie if the officers at ComSubPac questioned him closely.

In the first of a series of surreptitious intelligence tips, Holmes took a fountain pen and wrote on his palm the map coordinates where the paths of the carrier *Shoho* and the submarine USS *Grayling* would overlap. After divulging this to his old submariner friend Charles "Gin" Styer, Withers's chief of staff, he washed his hands thoroughly with soap and water. Styer took the information seriously and didn't inquire too closely about its provenance. The skipper on the *Grayling* went to the coordinates on February 18 and followed the orders to remain submerged during the day while his soundman monitored for the *Shoho*. Unfortunately, he stayed too deep for periscope observations, and neglected to load the tubes in time for an attack when he got a report of heavy screws. As a result, he watched the prized target slip away.

When ComSubPac read the skipper's patrol report, they recognized that the opportunity for a contact with such exacting detail would never have developed without Holmes's information, and came to think of the instance as a bird in the hand that had somehow gotten away. In his official reaction to the patrol report called "endorsements," Tommy Withers proceeded to figuratively flay the skipper alive.

While it's true that the *Grayling* may have had a better chance of firing on the *Shoho* if the skipper had taken different actions, the officers at Pearl who were disappointed when decryption possibilities didn't always translate into sinkings would discover that intercepting ships in the Pacific, as in this case, would always be a tricky business. The torpedoes had an effective range of about 2,500 yards; anything beyond that made the shot much more difficult. In order to get within 2,500 yards, the sub had to spot the target early and maneuver into position, often eluding dangerous destroyer escorts in their path. If they made contact during the day, the sub would have to do this underwater, where the subs were significantly slower. While a carrier or battleship regularly clipped along at 25 knots, a U.S. fleet boat could go only about 8 knots underwater for a half hour before its batteries were depleted. Usually it would lurk at about 2 to 3 knots to conserve its batteries for the time when it might get depth-charged—a certainty if it fired on a ship or convoy with escorts. Even the stars had to be aligned in order for any of these contacts to develop, because both navies navigated with celestial observations. If a storm was brewing up for a couple of days before a contact, the sub might not have a good celestial reference to fix its exact position. The same was true for the navigators on the target ships, and a navigation inaccuracy on the submarine compounded by an inaccuracy on the other ship could put the enemies so far away from each other at the appointed time that they might never see each other.

Despite the many frustrations, the submarine force recognized that what Holmes gave them was gold—wherever it came from—and coordinated their plans with him whenever possible.

During this time, the government was evacuating the dependents of military personnel from the Hawaiian Islands, just as they had in the Philippines before the war. For Rochefort's and Holmes's friend John Cromwell, as well as for countless others, it meant separation from their families, sometimes forever. Like many submarine families, the Cromwells moved to the familiar territory of Palo Alto, California. It was close enough to San Francisco to be accessible to the Mare Island Navy Yard, where the Navy built and overhauled submarines, but far enough to be—at that time—less expensive than San Francisco. For John Cromwell's son, Jack, and daughter, Ann, this meant new schools, a new neighborhood, and growing up without their father. Adding more strain to the situation was the presence of Margaret Cromwell's parents, who had moved in with them at their home in Palo Alto. Their grandparents had fallen on hard times during the Depression and, with the onset of old age, found it difficult to find jobs and support themselves.

While the family strained to hold itself together, Jack tried to take on the responsibility of being the man of the family—an unbidden role he tried his best to fulfill, for the time being anyway. Many of his new schoolmates found themselves in similar circumstances—an age of bubblegum and comic book heroes, of afternoon radio serials and matinees at the Bijou. Newsreels like *The March of Time* struck people differently in that time of intense patriotism; it seemed that those who had no family in the war thought of individuals' sacrifices with a detached, almost uncomprehending mien. Nevertheless, the propaganda spurred people on to join the armed services, buy war bonds, make Victory Gardens, and recycle war materials like steel cans and tires. They also swallowed tax increases as well as the rationing of nearly everything: gasoline, meat, butter, even bread. It didn't matter how much money you had—if you didn't have the coupons to buy certain commodities, you just couldn't buy them. The newsreels were persuasive, shocking, effective, and for those who did have family members on the front lines, they were frightening. Young Ann Cromwell frequently cried.

Back in Hawaii, the military couldn't enforce the evacuation among personnel with families classified as residents, who owned homes and paid mortgages, like Holmes and Dyer. The families who decided to stay found their social lives suddenly truncated as many of their civilian friends moved back stateside and the Navy built Pearl Harbor back, bigger even than anyone had ever imagined. Honolulu and the surrounding area also went through major changes as the Hawaiian Islands became the key staging area for fleet movements and invasions. Despite having the comforts of home, due to the nature of his decryption work Dyer would leave home with a lunchbox full of sandwiches his wife packed for him, and wouldn't return for days at a stretch, until he ran out of food or Rochefort ordered him to take a break and get lost for a couple of days.

All of them worked around the clock in the basement, sometimes sleeping fitfully on cots in the hallways for a few hours like college students cramming for a test. But the consequences of their test were literally a matter of life and death, and as the cryptographers grappled with the befuddling nuances of the JN-25 code, the cool, dank atmosphere in the basement of the Administration Building took its toll in the form of colds that often developed into pneumonia. Rochefort seldom left the building and took to wearing a red smoking jacket and carpet slippers, which gave rise to the legend that he was a bizarre eccentric. While this attire may not have been strictly Navy regulation and it was true that he had a strong personality that sometimes got him in trouble, he was by no means an eccentric. The mad professor aura created by the smoking jacket and carpet slippers was really just a pragmatic attempt to keep warm, but somehow it stuck and he is remembered that way in books and films. He was, on the other hand, a very dedicated commander who marshaled his forces to the point of exhaustion but no further. He gave them considerable latitude and loyally backed them up in bureaucratic dustups while he and his crew were accomplishing a half year's work in a matter of weeks.

The initial break on JN-25 came from Lieutenant Rudolph J. Fabian, a cryptologist at the Navy's radio intelligence unit at Corregidor (code name Cast) in the beseiged Philippines. The main OP-20-G headquarters in Washington, D.C., also called "Negat," worked on the codes as well, but it was Rochefort's group that was able to make most of the breaks.

Coding is the substitution of a letter, word, number, or concept with an unrelated signifier. For instance, we could *code* the letters a, b, c, t, and u as a=APPLE, b=BALL, c=CHARLIE, t=TOP, u=UNICORN. Working backward, the *decode* for BALL-APPLE-TOP would be the word "bat." If the coding is randomized, the code becomes more secure. For example, the sender and receiver of a code may agree to shift the letters in the code up a value of one on a predetermined day. In that case, a=BALL, b=CHARLIE, t=UNICORN, and the decode for CHARLIE-BALL-UNICORN would be the word "bat." This method is somewhat less intuitive than the original code, and would be slightly more difficult for an amateur. But it is susceptible to a trained cryptologist because of the similarity in values between "a" (apple/ball) and "b" (ball/Charlie). A skilled cryptologist will immediately recognize the pattern using innate skill, mathematical analysis, and intuition to "attack" such a code and break its secrets.

The way to get around this security problem is to use *encryption*, which is distinct from *encoding*. The simplest encryption is to substitute letters or words for numbers (encoding), then manipulate the numbers in some way to obscure their meaning (encryption). For instance, we might *encode* the alphabet thus: a=1, b=2, c=3, and so on. Then we might *encrypt* it by squaring the numbers in the code: $a=1^2=1$, $b=2^2=4$, $c=3^2=9$, and so on. Therefore, the *decrypt* of the cipher text 9-1-4 would be the square roots of the sequence, 3-1-2, and the *decode* of 3-1-2 would be the word "cab."

The encryption, or scrambling, of the numbers could be quite elaborate. However, given enough examples of a certain code, an astute cryptographer can divine even elaborate computations because they betray themselves by repeating a certain pattern. Overly complicated computations were also undesirable for two other reasons: In the days before computers, doing these calculations by hand would be more prone to error, and their unwieldiness made them too time-consuming. The Germans got around this by using a combination of electrical and mechanical randomness settings on a machine called Enigma. Enigma could be described as an analog computer to automate the encryption and decryption of signals, and used a series of rotors that rotated around a common axis. Essentially, it was a series of magic decoder rings, and each successive ring made the encryption exponentially more difficult to decrypt. A cryptographer trying to break the code would need not only an Enigma machine, but also the initial rotor settings and plugboard settings in order to read the same text as the recipient.

All of this increased the complexity of the encryption and the *apparent* randomness, and it decreased the amount of work to encrypt and decrypt. Enigma was, however, a machine that repeated certain patterns. Every rotor was wired to scramble in a certain, discrete way, and the Enigma machine's Achilles' heel was that the subsequent rotors relied on the motion of the first one, in what was a very predictable pattern. With initial help from expatriate Polish code breakers about the design of the Enigma machine, the British code breakers at Bletchley Park were able to discern those patterns. The British created a method to reduce the number of possible permutations, thereby eventually cracking the code. The Americans mechanized this attack method to determine the initial rotor and plugboard settings, and began decrypting Enigma transmissions in earnest.

In popular culture, the Germans get much credit for using such a diabolically clever device, and the British get even more for cracking its codes. It is interesting to note that the brilliant cryptographer William Friedman in the U.S. Army's Signals Intelligence Service (SIS), had a similar, though superior, concept at about the same time. Friedman added more rotors and also recognized the vulnerability of the rotor stepping mechanism, so he added a feature that stepped the rotors in a somewhat more random pattern.* The machine he created was called the SIGABA, and the Navy's version was called the ECM-2. At the beginning of the war, submarines like the *Sculpin* had to observe the "hundred fathom curve," a line they could not cross in enemy territory because if the sub sank in anything shallower than a hundred fathoms, or 600 feet, it could conceivably be salvaged, thereby compromising the ECM-2's secrecy. Fortunately,

---

*The Germans recognized Enigma's flaws and made improvements in 1939 and 1941—the SG-39 and SG-41, respectively—but were unable to get the new machines into production.

its code was never broken during the war, and was only retired in 1959, when faster alternatives became available.

In the 1930s, Friedman's team also cracked the Japanese diplomatic code they called Purple. Years before, the cryptologists went the simplest route when a rapid solution was desired: They cheated by stealing a copy. The SIS had the FBI perpetrate a black bag job—essentially cat burglary—at a Japanese diplomatic office to get the Japanese diplomatic codes. The FBI photographed the codebooks and replaced them without the diplomatic staff suspecting anything. A former missionary to Japan undertook the painstaking translation of the code, and while he did he kept it in a red binder, so the code became known as the Red code. The precedent having been set, subsequent codes were also referred to with color designations: Jade, Coral, and eventually Purple.

Like Germany's Enigma and America's ECM-2, Purple was transmitted by an encryption/decryption device that the Japanese called the Type 97. It used stepped rotors, but rather than using rotors with twenty-six steps for the twenty-six characters in the alphabet, it used two ten-step rotors for the consonants and a six-step rotor for the vowels A, E, I, O, U, and Y. This added a level of complexity that proved difficult to solve. Nevertheless, the underlying patterns betrayed the machine's vulnerability, and the code breakers at SIS were able to ascertain the patterns and break the code. Going one step further, and with the help of SIS cryptographer Leo Rosen, Friedman built a Purple machine so that they wouldn't have to decrypt each message by hand. To start with an unintelligible string of characters and end with a machine to turn them into intelligence gold was a remarkable achievement. Sadly, the strain and long hours of breaking Purple and making a machine took its toll on Friedman, and after having given so much to protect his country, he had a nervous collapse. He recuperated somewhat and would continue to contribute, but only in a reduced capacity for limited hours.

The Imperial Japanese Navy had a far more difficult system. JN-25, the code Rochefort's Hypo worked on after Pearl Harbor, was a *superenciphered* code. To send and receive messages, an operator needed three books. The first was an encoding book, which had up to 33,333 words, concepts, letters, numbers, names, and place-names. Next to each of these was a random five-digit number. All the five-digit numbers were divisible by three, so that if a telegrapher made an error, or the atmospheric conditions garbled the radio reception, a recipient could check to see if the code number corresponded to anything in the codebook.

Let's say for example that you wanted to *encode* the sentence "Sam went home." We would look for the three individual words in the *encoding* book and write down the five-digit numbers associated with those three words. For simplicity's sake, let's say those numbers are 00003, 00006, and 00009, so the encode of "Sam went home" would be 00003-00006-00009. We could broadcast that over the radio with Morse code to our intended recipient, and upon receipt, he would see that each of the three numbers is divisible by three—so it would appear that there are no garbles. The recipient would then take out his *decode* book, which was essentially the codebook arranged by number instead of by word, like a reverse phone directory. He would look up those three five-digit numbers, finding "Sam," "went," and "home."

Although there are 33,333 possible permutations in such a five-digit code, this was still a simple substitution *code*. Originators would find themselves using common words over and over again like "fleet," "destroyer," or a major port like "Yokohama." To make it more secure, the Japanese used an additional layer of *encryption*, making it superenciphered. In addition to the *encode* book and the *decode* book was an additive table book, or *encryption* book. Each page in the encryption book had a page number. On each page you would find several tables. Each table had its own number. Within each table there were numbered columns and numbered rows. In each cell was a random five-digit number.

The process started with a message. Let's continue with the "Sam went home" example. We would then go to the separate additive table book and randomly choose a starting point on a specific page, in a particular table, column, and row, where we would find a random five-digit number. Let's say there are ten tables on each page. We pick page 56, and settle on table 3, which looks like this:

## Table 3

|   | 0 | 1 | 2 | 3 | 4 | 5 | 6 | 7 | 8 | 9 |
|---|---|---|---|---|---|---|---|---|---|---|
| 0 | 61725 | 44177 | 58038 | 60558 | 50245 | 35279 | 75326 | 57152 | 60781 | 32871 |
| 1 | 24421 | 43472 | 19331 | 35161 | 35662 | 99586 | 05258 | 88009 | 65366 | 00706 |
| 2 | 33648 | 16881 | 87551 | 76998 | 56197 | 89418 | 25906 | 81003 | 12255 | 87165 |
| 3 | 00744 | 58399 | 69659 | 55314 | 02657 | 70861 | 92033 | 90658 | 02786 | 02896 |
| 4 | 82581 | 94488 | 31838 | 47703 | 50134 | 15460 | 98016 | 10639 | 68894 | 03714 |
| 5 | 81421 | 34784 | 71004 | 75008 | 17325 | 61126 | 93423 | 14128 | 58082 | 71472 |
| 6 | 42264 | 14891 | 47821 | 09803 | 59263 | 63155 | 24614 | 87610 | 21440 | 12120 |
| 7 | 59203 | 21153 | 78483 | 42214 | 03747 | 09652 | 75843 | 38765 | 47655 | 62315 |
| 8 | 00951 | 38126 | 88656 | 38976 | 59146 | 15086 | 24759 | 07842 | 61743 | 40173 |
| 9 | 40867 | 87881 | 66401 | 37593 | 23358 | 28619 | 50212 | 48193 | 78053 | 18233 |

Now we pick a random spot in the table, let's say column 0, row 3, where we see the number 00744. We subtract this from our first number using Fibonacci subtraction, where subtractions from numerals greater than 10 do not affect the next column. Thus, 00003 ("Sam") minus 00744 becomes 00369. We move to the next one in the column, 82581, and subtract that from 00006 ("went"), getting 28525. The next number in the column is 81421. We subtract that from our coded 00009 ("home") and get 29688. The result is 00369-28525-29688. We would send this superenciphered message to the recipient, along with the additive information they'll need to "strip" the additive from the original coded message (remember, page 56, table 3, column 0, row 3). You could transcribe this as 56303 perhaps, and to be really tricky you could prearrange to make the encryption key the third number in any message you send out, making the message 00369-28525-*56303*-29688.

The recipient would get this, look up page 56, table 3, column 0, row 3 in his additive book, and using Fibonacci addition (where sums in one column greater than or equal to 10 do not carry over into the next column) *add* the series of numbers he'd find there, resulting in 00003, 00006, 00009, which he would then look up in his decode book and again find that "Sam went home."

Any cryptographer, or crippie, getting far enough on his or her own to nail a meaningful number of keys would have to be inspired. It has been said that a good cryptographer either has the soul of a Beethoven and the mind of an accountant or, conversely, the mind of a Beethoven and the soul of an accountant. Making any sense of JN-25 required a breathtaking amount of work, a persevering spirit, and traces of genius. Beyond the thicket of additives and their underlying codes, however, was yet another barrier to understanding JN-25: the subtle intricacies of the Japanese language, and the refined nuances of the culture.

All languages are preliterate; that is, the words for nouns, verbs, adjectives, adverbs, conjunctions, articles, and so forth are conceived and operate in a governing grammar structure peculiar to that language before the language's users devise a graphical representation—writing, literacy—to actually write those words down. Westerners use alphabets with characters that represent individual sounds, for example the Roman and Cyrillic alphabets. Japanese, on the other hand, can be written with four different, complementary systems. Romaji was introduced by Portuguese missionaries, and is based on the Roman alphabet. The Purple machine used romaji to encrypt and decrypt messages. Katakana (or kana) and the complementary hiragana are both syllabary "alphabets," that is, each character signifies a syllable. If for example the Japanese language adopted the English word "imprecise," it would be written with three characters that represent the three syllables in that word: "im," "pre," and "cise." Kanji are characters that were adopted from Chinese ideographs, usually with the original Chinese meaning intact, but with a Japanese pronunciation that sometimes varied greatly from the Chinese; each ideograph represents a full word. Just as word placement or punctuation can alter the meaning of a sentence in the English language, kanji characters can have multiple meanings depending on the context within the sentence, how the characters are combined to create compounds, the character's placement in the sentence, and other factors.

Suffice it to say that the net effect of all these methods— romaji, katakana, hiragana, and kanji—as well as the intricate

rules governing them, and the fact that they are used to transcribe a complex, subtle, and refined language, makes Japanese
difficult in the extreme for the uninitiated Westerner. Super-
enciphering 33,333 terms in this language made JN-25 a howling conceptual wilderness for any cryptographer. It would be no
leap of the imagination to surmise that Joe Rochefort, Tommy
Dyer, and Ham Wright had photographic memories that could
recall the remotest clues of context and syntax in a stack of unrelated messages. It would appear to be the only way for them to
have linked the occurrence of one five-digit string of numbers to
another in different messages, and recognize the meaning of that
word as distinct from any of the other 33,332 words in the code.
In Japanese. This was their collective and individual genius.

We'll examine one final example to illustrate the daunt-
ing task that Rochefort's group undertook. One of the crippies
stripped the additive off a message, and its context suggested
what he thought might be a place-name. Jasper Holmes's merchant ship plotting had given him a thoroughgoing knowledge
of place-names from around the Pacific, and although he didn't
speak or learn Japanese, Holmes taught himself katakana. The
crippie gave him this (or something like this):

ウッ

ドゥ

ラ

ー

ク

Using a katakana table, Holmes learned that these syllables
were wou-du-ra-ku. Holmes stared at this for hours. Japanese
often place a long "u" sound at the end of foreign-sounding

words in the same way that English speakers naturally add an "n" at the end of the article "a" when the following word starts with a vowel, as in *a(n) orange*; it just sounds right to the Japanese ear. Removing the "u"s from wou-du-ra-ku gives you wo-d-ra-k. Japanese also simply does not have the letter "l," and native Japanese speakers sometimes pronounce "l" as "r," for instance the word "lollipop" might be mispronounced "rorripop." If we take wo-d-ra-k and change the *r* to an *l*, we have wo-d-l-ak. Further, if a Japanese language student studied English from a Briton, he might interpret "Woodlark" Island as "Woodl*ah*k," and pronounce it "WOUDu*rak*u."

It's important to keep in mind that this was only one term out of tens of thousands, representing hours of work in an understaffed unit that had the responsibility of informing the entire Pacific Fleet how to conduct the war in the Pacific. The task and responsibility was enormous; if Rochefort got even a minor but crucial detail wrong, the consequences would be catastrophic. If the Imperial Japanese Navy got conclusive evidence that the Americans had broken its codes, the Naval General Staff could have taken any number of steps, any one of which could have led to colossal losses of Allied ships, sailors, soldiers, even its forward bases such as Midway or Hawaii. They could change the additive tables or even the entire code, ruining months of work and leaving Rochefort, Layton, and Nimitz in the dark. The Japanese could also lay a trap. Before Pearl Harbor, the Naval General Staff had taken steps to transmit misinformation indicating that the Kido Butai was in the Sea of Japan, when in fact it was steaming eastward under radio silence with sealed orders to attack Hawaii. The Imperial Fleet by no means lacked the subtlety to lay a trap for the U.S. Navy's remaining carriers.

If the Allied losses piled up as quickly as they had in the war thus far—already with tens, perhaps hundreds of thousands of military and civilian casualties as well as POWs—the U.S. Navy would have no bases to fight from, and no ships or sailors to fight with. As Britain—the Allies' last toehold in Europe—fought for its very life, even a single defeat or succession of defeats such as the Allies had already endured in the Pacific could lead to Pearl Harbor–style attacks on the Australian mainland, or San Francisco and San Diego. The Allies would have no alternative but to sue for peace—not only with the Japanese, but also with the Germans.

The stakes were so high, the secret of JN-25 so important, that people would have given their lives to maintain its secrecy, and eventually would. The alternative in terms of human suffering and wasted lives was simply too appalling to contemplate.

Holmes's contribution in the example above was like a tiny tessera in the mosaic of intelligence that Rochefort's group was building, but it was significant nonetheless. When dealing with intelligence, more is always better, and in this case Hypo had discovered that the Japanese were monitoring the weather on Woodlark, an inconspicuous island in a tiny archipelago east of Papua New Guinea. Experience had proven that the advancing Japanese navy had an interest in the weather wherever they were, or would soon be. At about this time, Rochefort's group had also discovered an increasing number of references to a coded place-name called "MO." Although encoded—even within super-encrypted JN-25—Hypo had noticed patterns between these two-letter designators: They seemed to indicate the first two letters of the place-names, and if such was the case here, MO stood for Port Moresby, a possible invasion site on the southern coast of Papua New Guinea. The Solomon Islands were nearby, and just across the Coral Sea was Australia. If the Allies lost Port Moresby, they would lose all of New Guinea. If the Japanese took the Solomons, they would establish not only a choke hold on Australia, but also a defense against their eastern flank, and multiple staging sites for invasions in any direction.

Working against time, the men of Hypo coasted slowly up and down the cool, clammy halls like wraiths. They had bags under their bloodshot eyes, their expressions crazed with exhaustion and the effects of Benzedrine, an amphetamine that Dyer kept on his desk like breath mints, and that they popped into their mouths every so often like candy to stave off sleep, to postpone eating, to keep their minds on that elusive thread, that hunch, that euphoric state of fixation buzzing about their heads that nagged them even in fitful bouts of sleep on their cots like a gambler's favorite long shot. The sunless flicker of the fluorescent lights, the sound of shuffling papers and clacking Teletype keys, the smell of stale cigarette smoke and the manila-colored punch cards as they were fanned out and stacked up, comprised a weird amalgamation of human aspiration and the efficiencies and horrors of modern technological war, like a ghost heaving and clattering in the guise of a war machine.

The *machina ex deo* worked relentlessly to create what would be, for a time, the Japanese fighting man's worst nightmare. In a mysterious series of events that flowed from bad luck into some accursed fate, it frustrated his every move, turned his food to maggots if he ever got it, denied his comrades bullets and bandages, seeming to turn the sun's very face away inexorably from him by degrees until he faced starvation, defeat, death, and over-whelming batteries of hostile guns. Ultimately, with nowhere to turn and nothing to lose but his dignity, he would very often face his own rifle barrel.

The intelligence derived from decrypted radio transmissions was so secret that the U.S. government created a new security level beyond top secret to describe it: ULTRA. The British had a more fitting code name, Magic.

For Jasper Holmes, the omniscience would prove a Faustian bargain.

# 6

## Damn the Torpedoes

After the crewmen of the *Sculpin* had dusted themselves off
from the severe depth-charging of February during their second
patrol, they went to Fremantle in Western Australia for a brief
refit. While they were there they learned the full extent of the
catastrophe at Pearl Harbor as well as the losses of Wake Island,
Guam, Saipan, Hong Kong, Singapore, and most of Malaysia. It
didn't stop there, though. With several capital ships now at the
bottom of the sea, the combined forces of Britain, the Nether-
lands, Australia, and America were in full retreat all across the
Pacific. They now stood to lose Luzon and the entire Philippines, New Guinea, and the Solomon Islands. After that there
would be only Australia left for the Japanese to conquer, then
the island outposts at Midway, Johnston, and Hawaii. The next
recipients of Japanese military might were justified in their new-
found anxiety; the Japanese juggernaut seemed unstoppable, and
to make matters worse, most of New Zealand's and Australia's
fighting men were in Great Britain or in North Africa fighting
Erwin Rommel's Afrika Korps.

The submarine force was effectively all that the Asiatic Fleet
had left to throw at the Japanese, and during *Sculpin*'s refit at the

Australian port of Fremantle, the crewmen were hailed by the locals as heroes, their last line of defense. The men enjoyed the relative luxury of showers, sleeping on beds they didn't have to share, fresh fruits and vegetables, and the attention of the Australian beauties. But the respite was all too brief, and the harried sub commanders had little time to establish a truly effective rest and relaxation base for submariners coming off the grueling war patrols. After ten days and a refit, the *Sculpin* put out to sea again, bound for the Molucca Strait, where they had taken their first serious depth charges.

Not long after leaving Fremantle, they noticed that the exhaust from the engines was running black, and soon after that one of the pistons seized. They discovered that some of the fuel they'd taken aboard was dirty and was clogging the fuel filters. They also received a message from CSAF that a Japanese aircraft carrier would be in Staring Bay on March 26. The motormacs worked on the broken engine as the *Sculpin* tried to limp into position to intercept the carrier, but the day before it was due to arrive the entire ship unexpectedly jolted, as though something had hit it.

There was a general commotion—everyone wanted to know what had happened. Had they run aground? Did they hit a mine? The torpedomen in the forward room had been doing maintenance on the tubes by shooting "slugs" of seawater, but this was entirely different. When the officers got to that compartment, they discovered that a torpedoman had fired a live torpedo while the inner door and shutter had been closed. The supervisor, Torpedoman First Class Bill Dowell, had turned his back while looking for a tool when it happened. After confirming that a live torpedo wasn't protruding from *Sculpin*'s bow, they did their best to repair the damage to the tube, but the tube was out of commission just hours before they would be going into battle.

Half past ten the next night, the *Sculpin*'s diesels started to speed up. The men shifted slightly in their bunks and at their stations as the ship changed course and the crewmen in the control room went silent. The skipper went up the ladder to the deck. The men knew something was up and wondered what the lookouts had seen as they went about their business. Chappell started barking orders. The annunciators rang up a new speed and the helmsman swung the boat around to a new course. The men waited anxiously, tensing up, until finally they heard the sound they had all been expecting: general quarters. They took off like racehorses, running to their battle stations if they weren't there already. In each compartment, all eyes were on the battle talkers—any command would be relayed through them, and any command hinted at what was happening. The battle talkers also eavesdropped on whatever else was going on in the ship and gave the men a blow-by-blow account of the orders as they came.

The moon was high and bright, and the lookouts had seen a cargo ship, zigzagging and unescorted. Once they determined the base course, the skipper steered the ship to an attack position where they would meet, and went below to attend to some business. The cargo ship zigged again while he was away so the exec set a new course, but it was wrong, and when Chappell got back the target had peeled away and was putting some distance between them. Rather than begin the process of making an "end around," where they would steer clear in a large arc around the target at high speed and submerge just ahead of the target's plotted course, they decided to submerge and take a long-range shot.

The skipper had the periscope up when they came to depth. Lieutenant Mendenhall was at the TDC and plugged in the information as Chappell called it out: speed, 10 knots; range, 3,700 yards. They were at the outside edge of the torpedoes' capabilities, but fired three fish at four-second intervals. Once again the stopwatches came out as they waited to hear the results. Chappell raised the periscope again to see the torpedo wakes streak out from the ship, confirming the soundman's report that they were running hot, straight, and normal. While he was watching, the target made another change of course, and the stopwatches pegged out well past the time when the torpedoes should have hit the ship.

Chappell reloaded the tubes and surfaced to try to make an end-around before dawn, but the target ship was still too far away by daybreak. It was useless to try to beat it to Staring Bay because the sub would surely be spotted on the surface during the daylight hours. They swallowed their disappointment and submerged to continue the search for the aircraft carrier or any other ships that might come their way.

The next day they chased two contacts that didn't develop into attacks, and were submerged at about 4:00 P.M. when *Sculpin* spotted a pair of ships on the periscope. They were a heavily laden cargo ship with a destroyer escort, bearing down on them as though wandering straight into a trap. Chappell called battle stations and slowed the ship down to make occasional periscope observations. If the *Sculpin* was going too fast, the periscope would trail a long, white wake behind it—what they called a "feather"—as the skipper watched the ships. The ships were coming along at a pretty good clip—Chappell estimated about 12 knots—and soon came within range to have a good look at them. The destroyer's guns and torpedo tubes were missing. Chappell thought the ship may have been damaged in a previous battle and converted to the less glamorous task of escorting convoys. The cargo ship, however, was a good size, 7,500 tons maybe, and so loaded down that the water practically came over her freeboard.

"Bearing, mark!" he called to Mendenhall on the TDC, who made note of the reading and entered it into the machine.

"Range, one-five-oh-oh yards. Angle on the bow, nine-five degrees. Set torpedo depth ten feet. Down scope."

"Torpedo depth ten feet, aye aye."

"Down scope, aye aye, sir."

Chappell had them dead to rights and everyone knew it. This was no long-range shot, and the ships above still had no idea what was coming to them.

"Up scope."

"Up scope, aye aye."

Chappell rode the scope up and watched as it peeped up above the water so that he wouldn't have too much of it exposed. Even though the tip was about as thick as a broom handle, alert lookouts would spot it on a clear bright day.

"We'll fire three torpedoes, at four-second intervals. Spread, two degrees."

"Two degree spread, aye aye, sir," Mendy replied as he dialed in the numbers. The first torpedo would go to the middle of the target, and the other two would go 2 degrees left and 2 degrees right, so that if they misjudged the speed of the target, at least two of the torpedoes would meet the mark.

"Bearing...mark! Range, one-three-five-oh yards. Down scope."

"Down scope, aye aye, sir."

Mendy checked the spinning dials on the TDC: They matched perfectly with Chappell's figures.

"It checks out, Captain. You can fire when ready."

The men in the control room tensed.

"Fire one!"

The ship shuddered, and some of the men's ears popped as the air impulse shot the torpedo out, then the water shoved it back into the boat through the poppet valve. They heard the engine on the torpedo sing and start to fade before the second and third torpedoes left.

"Torpedoes running hot, straight, and normal, sir," the sound-man reported.

"Up scope!"

It was a beauty. Chappell watched as all three torpedo wakes drew toward the cargo ship. They were now so close that he could see individuals on the deck. They'd spotted the torpedoes! They were running back and forth, yelling. The torpedo wakes were lining up perfectly; they were so close now, the ship was so big it was like hitting the broad side of a barn. The ship was just too big to evade the torpedoes, and now they were hailing the destroyer with their signal lights. The men on the destroyer evidently saw the torpedo wakes as well and followed them back to their source, and now the destroyer sped up and turned in the *Sculpin*'s direction. One last look at the cargo ship: There was pandemonium as men came out and ran around on the deck. There was nothing they could do now—stop, turn, go full reverse. They were doomed.

"Down scope! Take her down!"

Chappell glimpsed the quartermaster holding the stopwatch.

"Come to two-oh-oh feet. Rig for depth charge."

"Two-oh-oh feet, aye aye, sir."

All along the length of the boat the watertight doors banged shut.

"Left full rudder. Come to one-oh-oh degrees."

Some of the men heard two distant explosions, but the skipper hadn't heard them. Neither did the soundman or the other men in the forward torpedo room. It couldn't have been the torpedoes detonating—that would have been unmistakably loud. Had the torpedoes failed again? The soundman tracked the destroyer going across the *Sculpin*'s wake, but it didn't drop any depth charges. The cargo ship's screws seemed to stop, and the soundman never heard the ship again, but he didn't hear breaking-up noises either. When they surfaced, neither ship was anywhere in sight.

The *Sculpin* patrolled uneventfully for the next few days. Having come this far beyond enemy lines with no success, the men's nerves were fraying. The torpedomen redoubled their maintenance efforts on the fish by opening them up, checking measurements, and overhauling them day after day. The strain was telling on all of them but mostly on Bill Dowell, who had been supervising the tests when one of the torpedomen sent the torpedo through the closed tube. At precisely midnight on April Fool's Day 1942, the lookouts spotted a smudge of smoke northward on the horizon and Chappell once again began the painstaking process of determining the course of the target while maneuvering them into position. Luckily, the moon was in their favor, backlighting the target's silhouette while obscuring the *Sculpin*'s low profile.

It was another supply ship, this time a little smaller at about

5,000 tons. Chappell got the *Sculpin* in position 1,000 yards away. The data on the TDC matched closely with his observations. He had a solution and fired three torpedoes: the first at the middle of the target, the other two at 3 degrees on either side. It would be difficult to have more favorable conditions short of rowing out to the target with the torpedo and detonating it in the captain's quarters. Chappell watched in anticipation as the torpedo wakes lined up perfectly with the target's track. The soundman noted that the screws' speed hadn't changed. Chappell saw that the target didn't change course. Fifty seconds after firing, they lost trim and the periscope dunked. When they got back up for a look, the cargo ship was chugging merrily along, though with a change in course. The lookouts had probably come to their senses and seen the torpedo wakes, though they were so close that they probably would have heard them as well. But there were no explosions.

Chappell gulped and looked at the men around him. He'd led them thousands of miles, deep into enemy territory, and survived depth charge attacks with them, only to fire nine duds in a row. It made him sick at heart that he and the rest of them could do everything in their power to put their lives on the line and make a textbook-perfect attack approach only to have the torpedoes fail, and he wrote in his report:

> It would have been impossible to gain position ahead of enemy for a second attack before enemy fetched Staring Bay and, if the truth must be told, the Commanding Officer was so completely demoralized and disheartened by repeated misses that he had little stomach for further action until an analysis could be made, the finger put on the

deficiency or deficiencies responsible, and corrective action taken.

Chappell went over the firing data over and over again, rubbed his eyes, checked the torpedo tubes and equipment. The torpedoes met the target. He saw it with his own eyes. Only two things could have happened: Either the torpedoes ran too deep, or the Mk VI exploders didn't work.

Whereas the *Sculpin* dealt with engine failures and torpedo troubles, fortune shifted favorably for a time to the *Sailfish* under Dick Voge, though at first it didn't seem so. Like the previous captain, Voge, whose name rhymed with "Yogi," was straight as a ruler. But the day-to-day sense of tension and anxiety throughout the boat was notably absent.

Just as the *Sculpin* had, they refueled in the Dutch East Indies and went directly on patrol after a brief rest period while the rest of the combined navies retreated under the relentless Japanese assault. Their patrol area was north of a string of islands—Java, Bali, Lombok, Sumbawa, Flores, and Timor—that formed a natural barrier between Australia and the rapidly expanding Japanese sphere of influence. Between the islands were straits that formed a series of bottlenecks where the American subs could set up ambushes for the Japanese ships passing through.

On March 2, twelve days out, they were at the northern entrance to Lombok Strait between Lombok and Bali when a mid-morning periscope sweep showed a destroyer seven miles out and closing fast. Voge gave the order for battle stations and called up the periscope. The sea was as calm as glass. In these conditions, with no waves or whitecaps to distract the eye, their periscope would be like a flag in the middle of a golf green, and if they got shots off, the torpedo wakes would be even more conspicuous. If he tried to press home an attack, he would have to get so close that the destroyer wouldn't be able to avoid the torpedoes. If they missed at that range, they would be sitting ducks.

Voge decided to take the risk and maneuvered to get closer to the destroyer, making infrequent periscope observations.

"Up scope!"

"Up scope, aye aye, sir."

"Bearing, mark! Range, four-five-oh-oh yards. Speed, sixteen knots. Angle on the bow…"

The TDC operator began tracking the destroyer by dialing the measurements into the machine. The black dials with white numbers and increments started rotating like the gears of a watch.

"The superstructure's pretty far forward. Two stacks with a big rake. First one has three white stripes."

They waited as the skipper got sonar reports from the soundman. If he heard the destroyer's screws change speed or start off on another direction, they knew the speed and bearing would change, but the destroyer charged on, seemingly oblivious. The closer the range, the greater the danger of having their scope spotted. They consulted their ship identification charts. According to the skipper's observations, it was a *Shigure-* or *Hatsuharu-* class destroyer bearing down on them. Although their curiosity was killing them, Voge waited until he thought they were so close now that he would be firing on the ship practically point-blank, and told them they would be firing two fish, depth six feet. There was a torpedo shortage, and by firing this close they should need only two torpedoes anyway.

In the control room, everything was silent, aside from the occasional report in hushed, clipped tones. The men sweated as the heat from the diesels radiated throughout the boat, and listened as a curious hiss slowly became louder and louder. Like a coming freight train, they heard the destroyer as it cut through the water, its screws pounding out behind it with a furious, frothy churning sound, gradually getting louder and louder. With the smooth water and the bright daylight sun, the submarine might appear like a shadow in the water as the destroyer approached. If the destroyer's lookouts had even the slightest idea that they were there, it could turn to ram the *Sailfish*. Voge wouldn't know until he made another observation. The anticipation was unbearable, but still Voge persisted. If he waited too long, the destroyer might get by.

"Up scope! Final bearing and shoot!"

"Up scope, aye aye, sir."

Voge bent down to ride the periscope as it rose and flipped the ears down as soon as it came out of the periscope well. He rotated it as he crouched down.

"Bearing, mark!" he called as he pushed a button on the scope. A buzzer sounded as the reading went to the TDC.

"Range, one-one-oh-oh yards."

The officer watched as the new measurements sent the dials on the TDC spinning wildly; the destroyer must have changed course or the skipper's measurements must have been wrong.

"Down scope!"

"Down scope, aye aye, sir!"

The TDC operator called out to the skipper: "Captain, the bearing is off by thirty degrees!"

Then the TDC suddenly stopped.

"Captain, the gyro setting overload tripped."

"Well...set the gyros by hand."

"Setting gyros by hand, aye aye, sir."

Precious seconds slipped by as they calculated the correct angles. If they missed they were as good as dead.

"Recommend thirty degrees left, sir."

"Make it so. Fire when ready."

The men in the forward torpedo room changed the gyro setting by hand.

"Ready to fire, sir."

"Fire one!"

The *Sailfish* jerked and filled with air as the torpedo left the tube. The TDC operator busily worked on the angle for the next torpedo. They waited anxiously—this shouldn't be taking so long. Usually there was five seconds between torpedoes. Maybe fifteen, twenty at the most. Nearly a full minute went by before they had the angle.

"Recommend gyro angle six-four degrees left, sir."

"Yes, make it so!"

*Tick.*

*Tock.*

*Tick.*

"Gyro angles adjus—"

"—Fire two!"

"—adjusted, sir...Two's away, sir!"

They listened as the torpedoes chattered away toward the target, which by now was so loud it seemed that the props were beating against the sides of the hull. By this time the first tor-pedo should already have hit. The enemy must have seen the first torpedo. There was no way they could have missed it. And if they saw the first one, they would be ready for the second one.

"Rig for depth charge."

"Rig for depth charge, aye aye, sir."

"Up scope!"

"Up scope, aye aye, sir."

The destroyer was zigging and zagging wildly from one place to the next. There was no way the torpedoes would hit now. But it didn't seem to be closing on the *Sailfish*. Hoping they could get in another shot, Voge kept the scope up—they were as good as spotted anyhow—and called out the bearings as they changed. If they zigged to a new course and stayed still long enough for him to get a shot off, the *Sailfish* might survive.

"Bearing, mark! Range, nine-oh-oh yards…"

*BANG!*

An explosion rippled through the *Sailfish*. Voge was dumb-founded. The destroyer wasn't close enough for depth charges…It didn't fire one of its guns…He chased the periscope all around the horizon; there were no other ships in the vicinity. That must mean…

"TAKE HER DOWN FAST!"

*BANG!*

"Take her to two-three-oh feet. Fifteen degrees down bubble."

"Two-three-oh feet, aye aye, sir."

*BANG!* From the interval of the explosions, there must have been at least two planes above, maybe more. Voge didn't wait to find out. The *Sailfish* dove for the cover of the deep. Fortunately, the destroyer didn't start pinging, relying instead, perhaps, on the airplanes. While they'd been at periscope depth, the *Sailfish* must have stood out as clear as if they'd been on the surface. They heard another bomb go off but it sounded farther away at that depth. The soundman tracked the destroyer as it left the scene, and four hours later they came back to periscope depth—there was nothing to be seen.

There was some minor damage to the *Sailfish*; the force of the bomb had pushed the wires from the torpedo firing circuit on the deck into the conning tower, and they were leaking around the edges. The starboard screw shaft squealed under certain conditions, but otherwise everything was fine. They made repairs and did normal maintenance until it would be dark enough for them to surface at twenty past seven that evening. Shortly after they came up, the deck lookouts saw a large ship on the horizon, moving slowly in the path of the moon. Voge came to the deck and got a rough bearing before pulling the plug.

Like the destroyer they'd tangled with before, this ship was coming in their general direction, but luckily it was going slowly enough—about 8 knots—for the sub to maneuver into position. As it came closer and closer, the image they saw in the moonlight seemed to split apart into four separate ships. Voge still couldn't get a definitive glimpse at them, but what he saw floating out there on the moon-dappled waves made his heart leap. The biggest ship was completely flat along the top deck, with a small island superstructure: an aircraft carrier. The other ships looked like destroyer escorts, one out in front and another two on either side of the bow. But why were they going so slowly?

Voge tentatively identified the ship as the vaunted Japanese carrier *Kaga*, which had participated in the attack on Pearl Harbor. He also guessed that they must have been alerted to the *Sailfish*'s presence by the attack that morning. The enemy formation would be much safer from subs if they went faster with a radical zigzag course, but at that speed their hydrophones wouldn't be able to detect anything beyond the sound of the water rushing past their hulls. Perhaps they were taking a different tack by proceeding slowly and cautiously, listening all the while. If that were the case, getting past the screen of destroyers would be especially tricky, but Voge simply couldn't give up the opportunity for a crack at one of their flattops. Japan had an estimated eight carriers, the United States only three; knocking out even one of them or sinking it could level the playing field considerably. He had to take a chance, and rang up a new course and speed to take the *Sailfish* somewhat outside the vanguard.

The torpedoes had two speed settings: The first was 46 knots with a nominal range of about 4,500 yards, and the second was at 31½ knots and 9,000 yards. Practical experience during the war would dictate that they use only the fast setting and at targets only within 2,500 yards, the closer the better. But at this point they'd been at war less than three months, and Voge opted to fire all four torpedoes at a great distance with the slower setting.

The *Sailfish* went northwest under the waves and sidled into the path of the formation, then made a 180 degree turn to bring the stern tubes to bear, waiting for the flattop to wander into his firing zone. With his tail to the carrier, Voge also hoped to be able to slip away quickly from the hornet's nest he'd stir up. The *Sailfish* would need all the help it could get going against no fewer than three destroyers. Voge made periscope observations and chatted with the TDC officer until it seemed like they could get no closer before firing. He called for the scope, made the bearings, and shot the fish at twenty-second intervals. As he watched the torpedo wakes recede into the inky water toward the carrier, he decided to shoot the last torpedo slightly ahead of the bow.

"What's the track?"

"Four-five-oh-oh yards, sir. Three minutes till the first one hits."

They were accustomed to waiting a minute, maybe two. It was a curious feeling to have, like waiting for a terrible car accident they'd set into motion but could not, and would not, do anything to stop. They also knew the odds against them when the game was up. Unless they hit the carrier with the first salvo, there would be no second chances; it would increase speed beyond their ability to keep up under the surface. If they surfaced, the carrier and destroyers could outrun them. The only thing they could do was hope that that first salvo sent it to the bottom and wait for a shellacking from the destroyers, maybe creep out of there in one piece. The control room was deathly silent, as though any comment now might jinx the torpedoes. It was already a long shot.

"Up periscope."

"Up periscope, aye aye, sir."

Voge looked at the formation. If they'd spotted the torpedoes, they hadn't done anything about it. As the seconds wound down, the men in the submarine heard a *CRACK*, then a distant rumble. Voge saw flames shoot up 150 feet into the air along the side of the carrier.

A cheer went up throughout the boat.

"Four minutes, nine seconds, sir. That was probably the first torpedo."

After they'd shot the torpedoes at twenty-second intervals they counted down the seconds, waiting for the others to hit—five, ten, fifteen, twenty—nothing—twenty-five, thirty, thirty-five, forty—nothing—forty-five, fifty, fifty-five, sixty—nothing. Could the last three have missed completely?

"Down scope."

"Down scope, aye aye, sir."

*CRACK!*

"Up scope!"

"Up scope, aye aye, sir."

"That was four minutes, nineteen seconds after the last shot, sir."

Voge watched, transfixed, as the destroyers started to belch smoke when they fired up their turbines for more speed. Soon they were crisscrossing the water madly around the crippled ship, which had slowed and taken on a list. Then they heard the first depth charge, far away: *clickclick BANG.*

"Down scope. Come to course one-one-oh, depth two-five-oh feet. Rig for silent running. Rig for depth charge."

The control room barked the commands back to him and went about coming to the new course and depth as the destroyers tore the water above, stopping altogether from time to time to ping. Water is a better conductor of sound waves than air; the soft *tinks* traveled faster and clearer toward the submarine than if it were on the surface, eerily bending and distorting until it reached the steel walls of the *Sailfish*, where the men strained their ears in complete silence to hear it.

*Tink...tink tink tink...tink...tink tink...*

The men interpreted the number and frequency of the pings, trying to divine what was going through the minds of the men who were trying to detect them. Each ping was a revelation: Was it louder than the last? Were they closer? Farther? Were there more pings now than before? Was that an echo? Did the destroyer pick it up?

From the time they heard the first depth charge they would have had a shot of adrenaline, and with it the seemingly super-human sharp vision, the coordination of movement, the burst of energy. But when rigged for silent running, there was nowhere to put that exertion, and as the excitement receded the tension piled up. Their bodies involuntarily reacted to the stress as their hearts pounded and they gasped for breath. Their skins tingled as their pores opened with little pinpricks and bead after bead of ticklish sweat slowly rolled down their bodies in the relentless heat. As a reaction to the stress, even their guts would stop the normal process of digestion, and their bladders would seize up, seemingly turning into solid rocks.

*Tink...tink...tink tink...TINK TINK TINK...*

The men sat with their hearts in their throats. Mundane sounds—a cough, a sniffle, even a nervous man grinding his teeth—became maddening distractions, but there was nothing, nothing they could say. If a man dropped something, a cup or a tool perhaps, all of the sailors wanted to yell at the top of their lungs for him to *shut the fuck up*, but all they could do was sit absolutely still in frustrated, mute horror and cast murderous glances at the offending seaman.

*Tink...TINK TINK...tink...*

The pinging stopped. The crewmen let out a long breath. Had they given up? They waited, listened. The screws of the destroyer picked up speed. They realized with dread that it was going to make a run and lay a pattern of depth charges. The men looked to the walls of the sub as though they could see through them, straining to try and track the movement of the ship trying to kill them as it crawled along the surface. They heard faint splashes—distinct from the sound of the water rushing against the destroyer's hull. Depth charges. Suddenly the floor below them seemed to drop away and the ship all around them tilted down at the bow. The skipper must have heard them, too. They weren't falling after all. He must be taking them deeper. If a depth gauge were handy they might take a look to see...250 feet...260...270...how far was the old man going to take them? They were already below test depth. The shipyard wouldn't make any guarantees beyond that. With the additional pressure coming from a depth charge, well. Only time would tell.

*Clickclick bang... clickclick* BANG *click* BANG *click*BANG BANG BANG.

They flinched, the muscles in their faces frozen with anxiety. It was like trying to stand stock-still in the dark and hold your breath while a blind man nearby blasted away with a shotgun. Even a blind man gets lucky sometimes. To take their minds off it they counted the charges. That was seven so far. Eight... nine...We're all right so far! *BANG BANG BANG BANG.*

Even yet they sat stock-still. There was nothing to be done. Waiting between explosions they might wonder how they got here: What have I done? This was a terrible mistake. Why was it I got into submarines in the first place? The money? What if I *die* here? Should've gone to the surface fleet. Why didn't I listen to my brother? What was it the guys at boot camp said? At least you can swim away from a sinking destroyer fer chrissakes.

*Tink...tink...tink tink...*

The sub started to level off...290...295...297...301. They glanced at the walls beyond the wires and tubes, wondering if they would hold. All around them were their comrades' pale white faces. What would it be like to die here? With all these men? Jesus Christ, do I look like a goddamn sissy? Buck up, sailor.

*Tink...tink...tink tink* TINK TINK *TINK TINK* TINK TINK *tink...tink.*

Splashes.

Come on you stupid bastard. Take your best shot.

*Clickclick* BANG... *clickclick bang...bang...bang...*

Twenty-seven, twenty-eight, twenty-nine. *Jesus, will it ever stop?* Thirty...

The stifling heat took its toll. The men strained to get a breath as the compartments filled with $CO_2$. Each depth charge filled them with new outrage upon outrage, anger, fury; they wanted to scream, to run, to hit something, but the body's normal reaction to mortal danger—fight or flight—was utterly snuffed out, repressed to the very deepest recesses inside them. It was unnatural. They couldn't run—there was no place to go. They couldn't fight—they would surely die up there on the surface. They couldn't lift a finger, move a muscle, or even make a peep for fear of being heard. It was like a nightmare of being strapped into an electric chair. Their palpable fury had nowhere to go but inward. They sat there, clenching their jaws. Clenching their fists. Crossing their arms. Uncrossing them. Twitching. *Hit the bulkhead with your fist!* No, no, no. *Breathe.* Your heart's pounding.

Take a deep breath.

Get up.

No, sit down.

*Clickclick bang...click* BANG... *BANG BANG...clickclick bang.*

Close your eyes. Clamp shut!

Breathe.

Just as their nerves had unconsciously strained taut, one by one their bodies could do no more. Eventually they sagged, limp with perspiration, utterly exhausted from merely sitting and listening. The air was hot—over 100 degrees—and the boat was moist. It felt like the compartment had filled up with hot gravy and they were drowning in it. They felt beaten up, listless. Still, their guts clenched with every explosion. *BANG*...thirty-seven... *BANG*...thirty-eight...*BANG*...thirty-nine...*BANG*...forty...

Finally it stopped, though they couldn't believe it at first. The sounds of the destroyers' screws faded away to nothing. They became aware of the silence, the utter, blissful silence all around. Ten minutes passed, then twenty. The skipper was still keeping the boat down. Despite the heat, they felt that they could all breathe easier. They'd get out of here yet. It would be easy street from here on out. The skipper probably sank a carrier out there tonight. Won't have to do another damn thing to make this patrol a success. Maybe we'll haul clear and take a couple days off, have some depth charge medicine. Maybe some cheap-ass rum. Or brandy. Mumma never would have stashed that stuff.

But it was at precisely midnight when it happened.

They never heard the destroyer coming—maybe it had been up there all along, just listening...listening. They didn't hear the eight splashes up above, either. If what had happened before was like a nightmare, the eight explosions that ripped the sea all around them was like waking up to find that the nightmare was real.

They crept away, nerves strained to the breaking point, wondering if they would ever be safe. They would be on patrol another sixteen grueling days to wonder, and just as the bottleneck of Lombok Strait funneled ships toward the *Sailfish*, the ship's patrol assignment made it vulnerable to the Japanese destroyers that seemed to harass them twenty-four hours a day, sometimes before they could even get an effective battery charge in for the night. Before they would leave for Australia, many of the men would wonder if they'd gone mad.

The stresses were compounding on the *Sculpin*, too. In addition to the depth-chargings, the officers and crew were demoralized by the futility of their faulty torpedoes and the danger they presented. One man came to Lieutenant Mendenhall to complain about serial headaches and fatigue, and in the middle of their conversation he collapsed from sheer nervous exhaustion. He was taken to his bunk and spent the rest of the patrol there, limping out from time to time. He was not the only one however. As Chappell would write in his report:

> The physical and, to a greater extent, the psychological well-being of the men is deteriorating at an accelerated rate. Manifestations are sleeplessness, chronic headaches, general lassitude, loss of appetite, marked decrease in mental alertness, emotional instability, and increasing nervousness…any radical change in the ship's course or speed, particularly at night, would cause noticeable tension to develop…the slightest physical ailment would affect the men out of all proportion and it was therefore necessary to make rather free use of sedatives.

# 7

## Minazuki

Like the men in the submarines, the code breakers at Hypo were putting in thirty-hour shifts to accomplish their important work. Although they realized that the Benzedrine was causing side effects and health problems that could shorten their lives, they rationalized its use as necessary to getting the job done and almost certainly not as dangerous as facing bullets, shells, and depth charges. As Holmes would later write, "There is no justice in a war that sends one man to safe duty in a basement while thousands of his comrades are dying in desperate battle."

Hypo's chief, Joe Rochefort, and the chief intelligence officer for the Pacific Fleet, Edwin Layton, were especially aware of the intelligence failures leading to Pearl Harbor and vowed never to let it happen again. In the early months of 1942 they would confer with each other on a direct telephone line up to forty times a day. To ensure security, the phone wasn't even wired into the switchboard system and relied on a hand-crank magneto to make it ring.

Rochefort's team started to break through the JN-25 code in earnest. Each decrypt—though incomplete—added tantalizing clues about the Japanese navy's capabilities, movements, and plans. It was like reading the enemy's mind, but with every third or fourth word blanked out. When the same string of five numbers cropped up in multiple radio intercepts, the code breakers had to rely on their photographic memories to recall certain instances where they'd last seen that five-digit code, as well as its context, in order to infer what that code meant. Sometimes the last use of those five numbers had occurred days, weeks, or even months ago. Luckily as the Japanese kicked their complicated offensive operations into high gear, the code breakers had more than enough examples to start making sense of how the Naval General Staff and the Combined Fleet were moving the Japanese navy across the vast chessboard of the Pacific. The Naval General Staff was roughly analogous to the U.S. Navy Department, and the Combined Fleet under Admiral Isoroku Yamamoto was the counterpart to the American Pacific Fleet under Admiral Chester Nimitz.

With a staff of only about fifty men, Rochefort's team started by prioritizing the messages; obviously a message from a task force commander promised better information than the message of a supply ship skipper. Then the cryptographers stripped the messages of additives. The ex–USS *California* band members began the laborious process of hand-punching the tabulator cards for the IBM machines, while Tom Dyer's assistant Ham Wright supervised the machine's operation twenty-four hours a day. Most messages took about sixty or seventy punch cards, sometimes more.

The resulting code groups—the strings of five-digit numbers stripped of their additive numbers—would go to cryptographer/linguists, the most specialized and highly trained of the lot. These included Rochefort and his assistant Dyer, as well as

Joseph Finnegan and Alva Lasswell. All had attended Japanese language instruction in Japan and had special abilities for the task, which, as Layton put it, was like putting a puzzle together without all the pieces. Finnegan was an intuitive code breaker who made broad, but calculated and logical, leaps based on the associations of disparate messages, whereas Lasswell made meticulous and conservative estimations drawn only from what could be demonstrated. Rochefort recognized a good pairing when he saw one, and as Holmes recounted, when Finnegan had an impressive hunch, Rochefort would pretend not to believe him. Finnegan would then enlist Lasswell's complementary skills to fill in the gaps between what seemed to be Finnegan's flights of fancy. The result was an inspired, but solid, intelligence product. Even this result had gaps, however, and Rochefort and Dyer would spend hours trying to fill in blanks for 100 to 150 messages a day. The result of several hours on one message that had seemed at first to be a major breakthrough might eventually reveal itself to be only a mundane report about the water supply on some godforsaken coral outpost in the middle of nowhere. But even that new information was grist for the mill, useful in that its codes were no longer unknown entities; Rochefort's exquisitely compartmentalized mind would file it away for possible use someday.

Finnegan learned that the Japanese radio operators on newly captured Wake Island in the Central Pacific were recording American call signs to analyze radio traffic between the U.S. Navy's ships and outposts, as well as listening to commercial broadcasts from Honolulu for possible intelligence information. Since this represented an opportunity to compare the Japanese reports of what the Americans were broadcasting, if Finnegan could get his hands on broadcast transcripts he might be able to identify several valuable code groups. Holmes had recently transferred his plotting duties to other offices in the Navy Yard and had taken on whatever administrative tasks would lighten Rochefort's load, so he volunteered to try to get transcripts of the Honolulu broadcasts. Unfortunately, he discovered that the radio stations didn't keep such records. Stumped, Finnegan reasoned that the broadcasts were based on reporting from the local newspapers, and asked for a complete copy of both local newspapers since December 7.

Rochefort also learned about the *Kamikawa Maru*—a seaplane tender or mother ship that could launch and service several seaplanes—located around the Woodlark Island area that Holmes had decoded. This suggested that the Japanese were conducting reconnaissance in the 500-mile radius of the seaplane tender and setting up for an offensive action. Finnegan discovered the presence of a new mystery ship he dubbed the *"Ryukaku"* based on the information he had available. It had land-based planes associated with it instead of seaplanes, and they surmised that it was a new, smaller aircraft carrier capable of supporting invasions. As more pieces of the puzzle dribbled in, they came to find out that the Japanese navy's Fourth Fleet—a collection of cruisers and destroyers suitable for protecting a landing operation—was assembling in Rabaul, a Japanese stronghold that was within striking distance of northeastern Australia, the Solomon Islands, and New Guinea. The kicker came when they started getting traffic about a geographical location code-named "MO."

The Japanese code names followed a pattern—Rabaul was "RR," and the code names for the islands around Rabaul started with R; Palau was "PP", and its associated islands began with P.

Rochefort guessed that the Japanese were assembling an invasion fleet to take Port Moresby—MO—on Papua New Guinea and perhaps establishing new bases farther into the Pacific in order to cut off and invade Australia. Thus advised, Admiral Nimitz and Layton realized that if they were able to get a task force down to thwart the invasion of Port Moresby, not only would they save Australia from the encroaching Japanese stranglehold, but they might be able to isolate part of the Kido Butai's carrier force and defeat it in detail.

For their part, the Japanese offensive plan for the war had gone off so successfully and with so few losses that they were scrambling to determine what to do next. Although they knew there would be much fighting ahead, with their initial missions accomplished, a triumphal mentality set in that would become known as "*shōribyō*," or victory disease. The Naval General Staff in Tokyo made plans to invade Australia, but dropped the idea when it became clear that the Japanese army wouldn't spring ten divisions from the occupation of Manchuria. So they developed more modest plans to invade New Guinea, Fiji, New Caledonia, and the Solomons, starting with Port Moresby, where they could set up bases to raid convoys supplying Australia and stage long-range bombing patrols on enemy warships and the Australian mainland.

In contrast, the Combined Fleet officers' priority was to create a ring of mutually supporting defensive positions out of the various island chains—unsinkable aircraft carriers—spread throughout the vast ocean. Their argument was that concentrating naval power in the south would leave the Japanese mainland open to carrier raids from the central and barren North Pacific—just as they had attacked Pearl Harbor. But if the Japanese were able to make a base in the Aleutians and take Midway Island, then

Oahu, they would rule the Pacific. Since the Combined Fleet's planners had gained almost insurmountable credibility with the raid on Pearl Harbor, the Naval General Staff acceded to their demands. The seeming necessity for taking Midway was punctuated with new urgency when Captain Jimmy Doolittle led his famous bomber raid on Tokyo and other parts of the Japanese mainland on April 18, 1942. When FDR was asked whether the bombers came from an island in the Pacific or from mainland China, he merely answered "Shangri-La." But Doolittle's ordinarily land-based B-25 bombers had taken off from the aircraft carrier *Hornet* in a task force led by Admiral William "Bull" Halsey hundreds of miles from the Japanese coastline.

The Japanese public was shocked that American bombers could somehow reach across thousands of miles, and that the Americans would have the audacity to make war on their sacred homeland. Even though the raid destroyed little of Japan's war-making infrastructure, the effects loomed far out of proportion. The supremely confident militarists had egg on their face, and took steps to recall pilots and their airplanes back to the homeland. All available Japanese navy ships went on a wild-goose chase for the carriers, burning precious fuel and wasting valuable time. The raid also had the effect of making the high command shift resources away from where they would be most valuable, and delayed their other offensive operations, which gave the Americans invaluable breathing space. During this time, the Kido Butai was occupied with British targets in the Indian Ocean, and Nimitz's carriers *Enterprise* and *Lexington* were able to stage hit-and-run raids against the Marshall Islands with relative impunity. This caused much consternation among the upper echelons of the Japanese navy, upsetting their offensive plans even further.

Rochefort now told Layton that after the Kido Butai's successful Indian Ocean campaign, the aircraft carriers *Shokaku* and *Zuikaku* would be going to Truk instead of Japan. This suggested that after becoming aware of the presence of *Enterprise* and *Lexington* in the Marshalls, the Japanese might reinforce the MO invasion force and its escort carrier "*Ryukaku*" with the *Shokaku* and *Zuikaku*. The odds then would be against the Americans three to two. For a force with a total of four aircraft carriers in the Pacific* versus an estimated eight for the Japanese, the loss of even one aircraft carrier would be a serious blow. But the Allies couldn't afford to lose Port Moresby or let the Japanese control shipping to Australia, and so the stage was set for the historic Battle of the Coral Sea. The tidings for the Americans were not good the night before battle as they received a radio transmission from the U.S. Navy radiomen in Corregidor:

ONE HUNDRED AND SEVENTY-THREE OFFICERS AND TWENTY-THREE HUNDRED AND SEVENTEEN MEN OF THE NAVY REAFFIRM THEIR LOYALTY AND DEVOTION TO COUNTRY, FAMILIES, AND FRIENDS.

It was Corregidor's final transmission before the Philippines finally capitulated to the Japanese.

If the stakes hadn't been so high, the Battle of the Coral Sea would have been characterized as a comedy of errors. The U.S. task force commander Vice Admiral Frank Jack Fletcher

---

*Saratoga*, the fourth, was out of commission in overhaul at this time.

chased false leads, split up his forces, and repeatedly ignored the radio intelligence officer on board his own ship. When a reconnaissance plane gave a contact report with a faulty code, Fletcher prematurely launched all the aircraft from his two carriers, *Yorktown* and *Lexington*. If Japanese land- or carrier-based planes found them, they would have no defense. When Fletcher discovered the error, he flew into a rage. Luckily, MacArthur's bombers reported a carrier sighting not far off from the original contact report, and Fletcher broke radio silence to redirect them to the new coordinates. They found and sank the *"Ryukaku"*—in actuality, the smaller escort carrier *Shoho*—and triumphantly radioed, "Scratch one flattop!" For their part, the Japanese had no radio intelligence to speak of, and although they were nearly within striking distance of the American carriers, their reconnaissance flights were hampered by a fortuitous rainsquall that appeared between the forces. Fletcher's radio intelligence officer told him exactly where he'd find the *Shokaku* and *Zuikaku*, but Fletcher refused to believe him until Japanese planes bombed into oblivion an oiler and destroyer that Fletcher had left behind. Rear Admiral Chuichi Hara, the Japanese commander of Carrier Division Five, discovered Fletcher's location from the destruction of the *Shoho* and later by a floatplane report. After expending all their bombs on the hapless American oiler and destroyer, Hara's planes harmlessly circled the *Yorktown* and *Lexington* for a friendly visit. After returning from the attack on the *Shoho*, the planes of the *Yorktown* and *Lexington* refueled and rearmed. Inexplicably, despite the fact that both Fletcher and Hara had a very good idea of where the other was, neither launched an attack until the next morning.

Hara's planes made an attack on both the *Lexington* and the

*Yorktown.* The "Lady Lex" was older, larger, and less maneuverable, and the Japanese bombers found their mark as the *Lexington* slowly turned to evade the bombs. The *Yorktown* was also heavily damaged, but the *Lexington* had so many fires that sections of its inch-thick plating actually glowed cherry red in the noonday sun. To keep her from the Japanese, Fletcher sank the ship with torpedoes launched by a destroyer. The Japanese were luckier, but not by much. Although the *Shokaku* and *Zuikaku* survived the battle, they were both so damaged that they would need extensive repairs, keeping them out of action for months.

At the outset, it looked as though the Japanese had won yet again, but this time the margins were closer. They had exchanged the smaller escort carrier *Shoho* for the heavy carrier *Lexington*. For a navy with an estimated carrier superiority of ten to four, the results favored the Japanese.

There were other, more important developments that threatened the United States fleet, however. The Australian prime minister received Hypo's weekly intelligence summaries through the Australian navy's coordination with the Americans. In an effort to quell the fear of a Japanese invasion, he prematurely announced that the invasion of Port Moresby had been called off, and that Australia would have plenty of warning if the Japanese attempted another invasion. How he could have known this so soon after the battle came perilously close to leaking Hypo's secrets. With an inferior naval force, Nimitz and the Allies had only their superior intelligence to avoid catastrophic ambushes and forewarning of invasions, and if the ill-timed words aroused any suspicion that the Japanese code was compromised, now or in the future, it would likely have changed the outcome of the war.

Although the Battle of the Coral Sea didn't seem like a victory at the time, the results turned out to be advantageous for the Americans. The *Shokaku* was so damaged as to be put out of action for several months—long enough for the Americans to get some breathing space after so many defeats. In addition, a large number of the *Zuikaku*'s highly trained and battle-hardened pilots, as well as their planes, were now lost forever, making that ship ineffective until it could get replacements. Another benefit of the Coral Sea engagement was that the Japanese flooded the airwaves with messages encoded in JN-25, which gave Hypo, the Cast team relocated to Melbourne, and Negat in Washington, more examples of the code than they could reasonably handle. More important, it gave Nimitz the confidence he needed to trust the radio intelligence he was getting from Layton, and by extension Joe Rochefort. This confidence would be crucial in the month to come, when on May 11, Rochefort discovered that the Japanese were assembling a massive armada in Saipan. The message specified particular anchorages for the Japanese Second Fleet. Two days later, the term "MI" was associated with an invasion force. The day after that, logistical details turned up when the Japanese navy authorized maps of the Hawaiian Islands chain to be sent to Saipan, as well as another message describing a Koryaku Butai—invasion force—participating in a forthcoming "AF" campaign. From what they could gather, AF served as a submarine base that sent out long-range reconnaissance patrols. This suggested Pearl; Midway, west of Pearl; or Johnston Island, southwest of Pearl. Rochefort also noted messages about the Aleutian Islands chain off Alaska, specifically Attu, Kiska, and Dutch Harbor. Rochefort was convinced that Yamamoto was building up a fantastically elaborate operation, and that the main target was Midway Island.

Back in Washington, Navy Department head Admiral Ernest King expressed doubts, and wanted Nimitz to have Halsey cover the southwest Pacific area in the event that the Japanese continued with their intentions to threaten Australia by taking Fiji, Samoa, and New Caledonia. King was being advised by the ambitious Redman brothers, Joseph and John, who had restructured OP-20-G, the department overseeing the code breakers at Negat, Hypo, and Cast.* As Hypo was part of their fiefdom, they wanted Rochefort to conform to nice organizational charts and do as he was instructed, regardless of whether that marshaled his—or Hypo's—considerable talents in the most productive way. Their bureaucratic reorganization scheme had its merits in that it geared up OP-20-G to produce intelligence on a massive wartime scale, but it shunted aside Laurance Safford, one of the Navy's most gifted cryptographers. It also severed several informal personal connections between Negat and Hypo, causing friction and morale problems. The most serious problem was that without Safford, Negat started to misinterpret the radio intelligence about whether AF was Midway.

One of Negat's objections was that it was entirely too coincidental that the Japanese code for Midway—AF—was suspiciously similar to the Americans'. When they read a Rochefort report that a Japanese unit had requested that their mail be forwarded to their new address at Midway, Negat suggested that Rochefort was falling for Japanese deception and misinformation. They claimed that the A in AF stood for the Aleutians. Then they said it might be Australia. To cover all their bases,

---

*Cast's sensitive operations moved to Australia shortly before the fall of Corregidor and was subsequently known as Belconnen.

they started warning that the West Coast might be the target. With recriminations about the Pearl Harbor disaster running rampant, Admiral King had a knee-jerk reaction to every possible threat, no matter how negligible, and sent Nimitz scrambling with several attack warnings. In addition to the backbreaking work of trying to crack enough of JN-25 to confirm that AF was Midway, determine the Japanese order of battle, and discover when and where they would attack, Rochefort had to do the painstaking task of going over Negat's many mistakes and misinterpretations to determine where their solutions had gone wrong. The disagreements ignited in what could be called a 1940s flame war until someone pointed out the errors to Admiral King and he finally conceded that AF was Midway. The younger Redman was doubtless humiliated to have his competence called into question. Undaunted, Negat and the Redmans then insisted that the Midway invasion was most likely scheduled for mid-June, and proceeded to fight tooth and nail over *that* interpretation.

But it was Nimitz's call, and according to Layton, he was convinced that Rochefort was right from May 14 onward. The problem was that if Rochefort were right, then Negat—and Nimitz's superior, King—were wrong. Nimitz had to find a way to get Halsey's task force back to Hawaii for the Midway battle, which was coming soon. Nimitz relied on sleight-of-hand, and sent an "eyes only" message to Halsey hinting that he should somehow get sighted on a course toward Ocean and Noumea islands, where the Japanese were planning an invasion. A seaplane spotted the task force, Halsey got clean away, and once more the Japanese got the jitters about their invasion plans for Ocean and Noumea in New Caledonia, off the Coral Sea.

Rochefort was able to confirm all of this by radio interception and decryption.

Since the invasion plans for Ocean and Noumea were now off, and King was finally convinced that Midway was the new target—albeit at a much later time—Nimitz was able to convince King to bring Halsey's carriers back to Pearl in time for the Midway invasion. Incredibly, Negat backtracked and started making more ominous warnings that AF may yet be a target in Alaska. Rochefort knew that the Aleutians were also a target, and that to head off any more interference from Washington he needed to prove beyond doubt that AF was Midway. A massive Japanese task force was heading to one of America's last Pacific outposts while bureaucrats in Washington dithered with inconsequential, vague, and contradictory intelligence assessments.

At this time, Rochefort, Holmes, Finnegan, and Dyer were discussing the Midway problem around one of the Hypo desks when Holmes offhandedly remarked that he'd gone there while he was teaching engineering at the University of Hawaii. They'd done studies to determine what effect saltwater had on mixing concrete for the buildings there, since they made all their precious fresh water with massive evaporation tanks. If the evaporators broke down, there would be serious problems. Finnegan caught on to this and said that if the Japanese knew there were problems with the fresh water evaporators, their listening post on Wake Island would be sure to report it. Rochefort sat there quietly, the permutations of code groups clicking away in his mind as he reached back to the code groups they'd broken. *Water*, he thought. *Midway. AF.*

"That's all right, Joe," he said to Finnegan. He got up and left. Holmes wouldn't learn until years later that the thousands of tumblers in Rochefort's mind clicked in unison at that moment and unlocked the key to proving AF's identity.

In the succeeding days, they got bits and bobs of tantalizing information. Admiral Chuichi Nagumo would lead the Kido Butai to be in position northwest of AF by N-2 day for the attack on N-day. What was N-day? they wondered. From their many decrypts, they had only three examples of how the Japanese coded dates: three kana characters. This was further encrypted beyond the additives and codes. It was truly a riddle wrapped in a mystery inside an enigma. Rochefort's group realized that in order to get all the dates to snap into place, they would have to solve this riddle.

While they were working the date-time code, Yamamoto flashed the Combined Fleet's order of battle—the roster of ships he intended to use—as well as detailed instructions for the campaign against AF and the Aleutians. Finnegan recognized it for what it was straightaway and started to decode it with help from Ham Wright and Joe Rochefort. That left Lasswell with the date-month code.

Amid all the piles of intel, a decrypt came across Tom Dyer's desk from the Japanese stronghold of Kwajalein:

The AF air unit sent following radio message to commandant 14th Naval district. AK (Pearl Harbor) of 20th. With reference to this unit's report dated 19th. At present time we have only enough water for two weeks. Please supply us immediately.

Dyer correctly interpreted that Midway—AF—had sent a plain-language message to Admiral Bloch at Pearl Harbor—AK—

thereby giving the Japanese vital information. He snorted and waved the message at Rochefort. "Those stupid bastards on Midway. What do they ever mean by sending out a message like this in plain language?"

Rochefort was uncharacteristically placid about the affair because it was a devious bit of radio intelligence deception he'd played—not only on the Japanese but also on Washington. The ruse wouldn't be revealed for years, but when Holmes had remembered the water distillers on Midway, and that Finnegan was reading Japanese intelligence reports out of Wake, Rochefort realized that he knew enough of JN-25 to get the Japanese to inadvertently show their hand. There was at that time an underwater cable between Hawaii and Midway for secure communications. He asked for, and received, permission to send a message over the secure line to Midway requesting that they send a plain-language radio broadcast stating that their water distillers had broken. They elaborated by also sending it in a strip-cipher code that was known to have been captured at Wake Island. Bloch kept the deception going by acknowledging receipt and saying that he'd send barges with fresh water. The Japanese were listening, too, of course, wrote a coded report, and sent it out—thereby conclusively confirming that AF *was* Midway. Rochefort—and likely Bloch, Layton, and Nimitz—kept the secret for years.

For their part, Washington warned Rochefort not to be taken in by Japanese radio deception.

On May 25, the Japanese changed the additive tables for JN-25, just as they had before their last major offensive, Pearl Harbor. It was a blow for Hypo and the rest of the code breakers, but by that time Finnegan, Wright, and Rochefort had decoded 90 percent of Yamamoto's May 20 directive. After the Combined

Fleet assembled at Saipan, the commanders would parley on May 26 and depart for their destination on May 27. Given the distances involved and the speed they would travel, it would put the massive Japanese armada close to Midway by June 1 or June 2.

Late on May 26, Lasswell finally made a breakthrough on the date code: It was a simple grid with the twelve months listed as columns and thirty-one kana characters as rows, with alternating kana characters in the cross references providing a garble check. Having solved the all-important date code, Hypo could reread the many decrypts about the invasion plans within the context of when the invasion would happen. The Japanese decreed that the battle for Midway would occur on the second or third day of Minazuki, the "low water month" of June. It was also apparently the code name for their anticipated new mailing address.

Rochefort worked around the clock to make sure everything checked out; he had a meeting the next morning with Nimitz, Layton, and the top commanders of the Pacific Fleet. He was fully aware that the Pacific command would be setting sail on his advice and would make momentous decisions based on his assemblage of details great and small. If he misinterpreted even a small aspect of the jumbled pile of decrypted messages scattered on his desk and throughout the basement, the task force commanders could easily make mistakes that would cost lives, ships, maybe even the war. There were no second chances. Running late, Rochefort put on his coat and hat, tucked some charts and papers under his elbow, and ran out the door for the most important meeting of his life.

Nimitz's ordinarily bright blue eyes fixed on him with withering disapproval. Rochefort was late, disheveled, and unshaved, shifting uneasily before the assembled group of high-ranking

Navy officials. Exhausted, Rochefort peered at them with bloodshot eyes; he could see that was more than enough scrambled eggs for a buffet, and that everyone was cleared for what he was about to divulge.

He told them that the Japanese would attack Alaska, and although they intended to keep the Aleutian Islands strongholds, that the timing was a ruse to lure the Pacific Fleet. At Midway, the fleet could expect to face the first and second carrier divisions, including the Kido Butai's *Akagi*, *Kaga*, *Soryu*, and *Hiryu*, along with elements of other fleets as escorts, and a main body invasion force. The *Shokaku* and *Zuikaku* would not be there due to the damage they received at the Battle of the Coral Sea. The Japanese had sortied from Saipan that very day and would attack Midway from the northwest on June 2 or 3 to soften up the island for the invasion force that would follow. The staff marveled at the value of what he was telling them; Nimitz asked some questions, including those about the source, to which Rochefort replied that the source was very good. One of the men gathered there commented that Rochefort's spy in Tokyo was worth every penny, but neither Rochefort, Layton, nor Nimitz tried to dissuade him from believing that the intelligence came from a mole in the enemy's camp.

After the meeting, Nimitz famously asked Layton for his opinion on where and when they would find the Kido Butai. Layton demurred, saying that it wasn't possible to give a precise location or time, but Nimitz insisted. As Layton recalled later in his book, "I knew that I would have to stick my neck out, but that was clearly what he wanted. Summarizing all my data, I told Nimitz that the carriers would probably attack on the morning of 4 June, from the northwest on a bearing of 325 degrees.

They could be sighted at about 175 miles from Midway at around 0700 local time."

For Nimitz, there was never any question about what to do. Thousands of miles southwest of Pearl, the *Tangier* and the *Salt Lake City* started to send radio broadcasts intended to resemble carrier task forces. On May 28 the carriers *Enterprise* and *Hornet* steamed out of Pearl for a point 350 miles northeast of Midway to ambush the Kido Butai, while all available dockworkers worked night and day to shore up and repair the crippled *Yorktown*. While the rest of Honolulu was blacked out, the oxyacetylene torches and arc welders swarming over the ship cast a weird glow across the nighttime harbor. The workmen used so much electricity trying to cram three months of repairs into three days that blackouts were reported across the island. Where the workmen couldn't make structural iron repairs in the bombed-out ship, they shored up plates and bulkheads with ordinary lumber. They simply had to do everything in their power to get the ship back into fighting order; even if they repaired the ship in time, the odds would be three to four in favor of the Japanese. If the *Shokaku* and *Zuikaku* hadn't been knocked out of commission at the Coral Sea, the Kido Butai would have been invincible. As it was, with the element of surprise provided only by Hypo, Nimitz's task force commanders had a good chance of winning an upset victory. Whatever the outcome, Nimitz appreciated that this was perhaps the most momentous battle of the war, and may well decide the war's outcome. It was arguably the most important naval battle in history, and it would be determined by Joe Rochefort and the group at Hypo.

Miraculously, the dockworkers repaired *Yorktown* enough for it to accompany the other two carriers. It left Pearl Harbor on

Saturday, May 30, and not a day too soon. Japanese submarines arrived on that day to form a reconnaissance picket around the Hawaiian Islands to report aircraft carriers and attack targets of opportunity. Their arrival had been delayed by the hasty redrawing of plans caused by the Coral Sea battle, Doolittle's bombing of Tokyo, and raids on Japanese strongholds in the Pacific. Had they gotten there in time to report the carriers, Nimitz would have lost the element of surprise. An intelligence coup also prevented Japanese plans for a reconnaissance flight over Pearl before the battle. Nimitz's forces escaped detection by the very narrowest of margins, but the Japanese had one last chance to discover the ambush. Somehow a Japanese radio intelligence unit at Owada in Japan discovered that there were carriers in the Hawaiian area—not in the southwest Pacific as they had previously assumed. They transmitted their intelligence to Yamamoto's flagship in the main force, the *Yamato*, as well as to Admiral Nagumo, who was commanding the four carriers in the Kido Butai. Nagumo never received the report, and Yamamoto refused to break radio silence to amplify the warning; he assumed that Nagumo had received it and read it. Nagumo's first confirmation of the presence of American carriers would come at a time when he would be least able to do anything about it.

The battle started when a U.S. Navy PBY flying boat located the invasion fleet and radioed a report. Nimitz reiterated to his task force commanders that the invasion fleet was not the striking force with the Kido Butai's estimated four or five carriers. The next day, Nagumo launched an attack on Midway with nearly all his planes. The ground-based forces on Midway mustered up some bombers to locate and attack the Japanese carriers, but they were ineffective. Midway's obsolete fighter planes were likewise swatted from the sky, although the antiaircraft guns made a good account of themselves and shot down several of the attacking Japanese planes. After assessing the effectiveness of their attack on the island, the Japanese flight commanders recommended that they come back to finish off the job.

While the Japanese were returning from bombing Midway, task force commanders Admirals Fletcher and Raymond A. Spruance launched their own attacks—and their timing couldn't have been better. Although the Japanese had learned of one American carrier through a floatplane reconnaissance report, they didn't have nearly as much information as Fletcher and Spruance. Nagumo was caught on the horns of a dilemma: His pilots were low on fuel and he'd already started outfitting a second wave with bombs suitable for attacks on land targets. He was committed to getting the pilots back, then wasted precious time refitting the available planes with ordnance to go after the one carrier they knew about. Then they spotted the first American torpedo bomber.

The top-of-the-line Japanese Zero fighter planes made quick work of the obsolete American Devastator planes as they came in flat and slow in order to launch their torpedoes. Of forty-one such planes launched in the raid, only four would come back, and of the thirty-seven crews who were shot down, only one man survived. Despite the signal failure to damage even a single Japanese ship, the torpedo bombers had accomplished at least one thing: The Zeroes were now low to the water and would not be able to gain sufficient altitude in time to have an effect on the American dive bombers, which came in squadron by squadron to drop a series of devastating bombs on the *Soryu*, the *Kaga*, and the *Akagi*. Only the *Hiryu* escaped unscathed to launch its own attack on the American carriers. Each of the Japanese carriers that had been hit were doomed because they received the bomb hits when their hangars were filled with highly inflammable aviation fuel and munitions. The remaining pilots from these ships landed on the *Hiryu* as its own pilots searched for the American carriers and found the *Yorktown*.

The hastily repaired veteran of the Coral Sea battle took several hits and lost power. The order to abandon ship went over the PA system, and the crew made its escape. When the stubborn old carrier didn't sink, some crewmen went back to see if it could be saved and started to pump some of the seawater out of the bilge. But no one could account for the *I-168*, a Japanese submarine lurking off the slow-moving carrier. A salvo of four torpedoes blew new holes into the *Yorktown* and sank the destroyer assisting her. With the massive amounts of new water cascading into the ship, and the loss of the pump power from the destroyer, she finally sank.

The sorties from the remaining carriers, *Hornet* and *Enterprise*, found and sank the final Japanese carrier, *Hiryu*, and with it the last of Japan's most seasoned naval pilots. The defeat was so surprising, so total, that it threw Yamamoto and the rest of the Japanese invasion forces into disarray. After a few feints to try to draw Spruance toward the Combined Fleet's battleships in a night engagement Spruance was sure to lose, Yamamoto conceded defeat and called off the invasion. He turned back the mighty Combined Fleet—an armada whose cumulative deck area was larger than the twenty acres of the island they'd been sent to capture.

Despite the fact that many of their officers realized the proportions of their defeat, for the Japanese, their case of victory disease acquired peculiar symptoms. Speaking through their propaganda organs, Midway and every other defeat was either downplayed or became a victory, and by some strange logic the massacre of thousands of their troops and sailors became signs of progress. The state of the armed forces was strong—and getting stronger. Pilots claiming to have shot down a plane and skippers claiming to sink an American ship were given credit for cumulatively sinking whole American armadas, even on the scantest of evidence. Victory would only take more time—and more sacrifice. As loss after loss piled up and the traditional wooden boxes containing the cremated remains of fallen sailors and soldiers came home, many refused to acknowledge the inevitability of defeat. Even later when Japan's major cities were firebombed into cinders, wide swaths of the population still thought that they were winning the war, because that was what they were told by their leaders. Toward the end of the war, the many Japanese who read the writing on the wall had to consider whether national defeat might be preferable to the peculiar present state of starving in supposed victory.

The U.S. Navy was ecstatic. When the location of the Japanese carriers came through to Nimitz, he recalled Layton's prediction of where and when they would find them, and told him, "Well, you were only five minutes, five degrees, and five miles out." Although they were down to three carriers in the Pacific—the *Hornet* and the *Enterprise*, along with the *Saratoga*, which was being refitted on the West Coast—they had destroyed four of Japan's six largest aircraft carriers and rendered the other two incapable of fighting. The Japanese navy could no longer range around the Pacific and project its power at will. The American public was heartened to have good news after so many months of defeat and retreat, but just as they'd wondered where Pearl Harbor was on December 7, 1941, they puzzled at the significance of the flyspeck of Midway on a map of the Pacific and wondered how the Navy had conducted a major naval engagement without any of the ships actually spotting one another.

Unfortunately a *Chicago Tribune* reporter with special knowledge of Navy operations thought everyone should know more. His front-page headline was a huge scoop, straight out of the Navy's hide:


JAP FLEET SMASHED BY U.S.—
2 CARRIERS SUNK AT MIDWAY
Navy Had Word of Jap Plan to Strike at Sea—
Knew Dutch Harbor Was a Feint


The article went on to describe the Japanese ships in such detail that the only logical conclusion was that the Americans knew about the invasions at Midway and the Aleutians because they had broken the enemy's code. Japanese naval attachés at neutral consulates and embassies around the world read American publications for intelligence—and this was a whopper. It was only the first of a string of security breaches, near misses, and self-inflicted wounds that would plague the Navy well into the next year.

# 8

## The Slot

By September, the *Sculpin* plied the Pacific in search of enemy shipping and men-of-war. A tour in the East China Sea yielded little but danger because the daytime submergence doctrine and unreliable torpedoes made for dangerous but unsuccessful encounters. They were taking extraordinary measures to travel thousands of miles so that they could risk their lives to fire faulty torpedoes at the enemy, then take a depth-charging that in some cases was fatal to the boats and all within. In what was to be the longest-running and wholly unnecessary scandal of the war beneath the waves, the torpedoes' occasional hits and sinkings covered up its flaws.

But the magnetic exploder had been tested only once before the war. In a trial against a ship that was going to be scrapped—oddly, a submarine—the first of two torpedoes made its way harmlessly underneath the target. When the second torpedo worked as designed and exploded underneath the submarine, breaking its keel and sinking it, the Bureau of Ordnance satisfied itself with the 50 percent success rate and moved the Mk XIV torpedo into production with the Mk VI exploder. When it came to actual war, when men's lives were on the line, the skippers found that the torpedoes weren't the miracle weapons breath-lessly described to them with utmost secrecy.

The first fault they discovered was that the torpedoes ran too deep. Admiral Lockwood, who was commander of Subs, South-west Pacific, took his skippers' advice to heart and on June 20, 1942, he ran tests by firing the torpedoes into fishing nets. He found that the depth settings were off by an astounding eleven feet. A torpedo like that would never stand a chance against a ship with a shallow draught, such as the dangerous destroyers that specialized in hunting and killing the submarines. Lock-wood wrote to the Bureau of Ordnance, but their response was that his tests weren't conducted properly and were therefore inconclusive. Infuriated with the lack of cooperation, Lockwood conducted them again, and finally forced the bureau's hands into recognizing that there was a problem, and they finally took steps to address the depth setting.

What most skippers suspected but what the Navy wouldn't acknowledge for another year—about eighteen months into the war—was that contrary to the bureau's assurances, the Mk VI magnetic influence detonator was worse than useless, it was pos-itively dangerous. The detonator was supposed to be triggered by a rapid change in magnetic flux caused when the torpedo went under the large iron mass of a ship. If the trigger wasn't sensitive enough, the torpedo would pass underneath a target ship, fail to recognize the sudden magnetic change, and keep churning past the target. Fully alerted to the easily spotted torpedo wakes, the ship that should have been doomed now charged the submarine or alerted a sub killer. Even worse than this were the occasions when the magnetic exploder was *too* sensitive. A safety precau-tion armed the torpedo only after its engine had completed a certain number of turns, so that it could explode only after it had traveled about 400 yards—a little over one boat length—thus preventing a premature explosion too near the submarine. But many skippers were discovering that the torpedoes exploded as soon as they armed—thus giving their position away to the enemy before they could even make evasive maneuvers, a situation much worse than if the exploder never went off at all. The torpedoes also had a contact detonator but the skippers were under orders not to use it. The result was that the Bureau of Ordnance was able to put the torpedoes' faults onto the skippers, claiming that they weren't giving the torpedoes proper maintenance, were making inaccurate observations, or that junior officers were making mistakes on the Torpedo Data Computers. More often than not the sub commanders at headquarters inexplicably concurred with the "Gun Clubbers," as the Bureau of Ordnance was called, and criticized the skippers for their inability to hit targets as well as for a lack of aggressiveness. To make matters worse, many of the skippers deactivated the magnetic influence detonators in favor of the contact detonators, which buttressed the false impression that the magnetic detonators were working more consistently than they were.

It was true that some skippers were avoiding risk at all costs, preferring to patrol far from anywhere they were likely to run into trouble. They were usually older, more cautious captains who had risen up the ranks on the basis of how well they did paperwork, followed Navy doctrine, and how clean their boats were. Most notably, the really aggressive skippers had been sacked before the war because they were detected by destroyer escorts during exercises. After the war started, though, the overcautious skippers came back with too many torpedoes, too many excuses, and outraged junior officers. After the submarine high command sniffed out the overcautious skippers and replaced them, the average age of a submarine skipper was around thirty years.

In Lucius Chappell the men of the *Sculpin* had the benefit of an aggressive and seasoned skipper. After proving the faulty depth settings on the torpedoes, Admiral Lockwood started off the *Sculpin*'s fifth war patrol by accompanying it on a trip from Fremantle to the port of Albany on Australia's southern coast. Lockwood would have dearly loved to have gone out on a true war patrol—many of the older officers derisively called "staffies" also wanted to go out as well—but Lockwood's superiors reminded him of the consequences if he were to be lost or, worse, captured. As a commander who was sympathetic to the skippers under him, however, Lockwood saw the benefit of sending senior staff out into the field to see what his boys were up against on war patrols. For their part, the men under the capable Lockwood affectionately called him "Uncle Charlie."

It broke his heart to see the submariners as they came back pale, tired, and frightened. Despite having the best food in the Navy, most of them were reduced to skin and bones from patrols in the tropics, where the heat from the engines made the interiors of the boats feel like a blast furnace. They'd also endured several bizarre and painful maladies while on patrol. Because of the need to conserve water for drinking and for the batteries, the hygienic conditions deteriorated, and many of the officers and crew developed painful "Guam blisters," a pernicious skin infection also known as impetigo, which was caused by a contagious staph infection. They also developed "Catarrhal fever," which was essentially a very bad sinus infection. Anyone who has been laid low by sinusitis can attest to the discomfort caused by slight pressure changes caused by the weather; in the submarine environment where each dive caused severe pressure changes several times a day, the effect caused searing, exquisitely excruciating headaches that reduced grown men to bedridden wrecks. There were even cases of life-threatening appendicitis. In these situations, the less-than-qualified pharmacist's mates set up impromptu surgical suites and performed appendectomies with scalpels fashioned from the cook's carving knives and muscle retractors made from stainless steel kitchen spoons. Despite the medieval conditions, the men survived the operations.

For many of the men, the damage went beyond the physical. The intensely psychological nature of the submarine war began to take its toll as many of the combat-stressed men developed panic attacks and shell shock, a term that would come to be known as post-traumatic stress disorder. The stresses were especially telling on the skippers, on whose shoulders everything rested. They were often called upon to undergo the Herculean task of attacking and evading, staying on their feet for twenty-four, forty-eight, even seventy-two hours at a stretch. After reading other skippers' patrol reports, they realized that in order to stay effective and clearheaded, they would have to trust their executive officers—their second-in-command—to act in their absence. Some refused to delegate responsibility and set up cots in the conning tower so they could be ready at a moment's notice, but being notified for every bump, every inconsequential repair or bird sighting quickly wore them down. Between patrols, most turned to drink, to varying degrees. In *Silent Running* by James Calvert, one officer recalled the appalling effects of stress on a skipper he chanced to see while delivering official documents:

Through an interior door I could see into the dining room. Sitting at the table and leaning over it was a skipper of one of the new submarines just reporting in. He was dressed only in his underwear and needed a shave badly.

He didn't see me in the living room, as he was entirely preoccupied. On the table was an open bottle of scotch and a tumbler full of what looked like straight whisky. A towel was draped around his neck. He had grasped each end of it and, in his right hand, also the tumbler of scotch. To get this up to his mouth without spilling it, he was pulling on the left end of the towel. His attempts were not succeeding. He was trembling so violently that, even with support from the towel, half the whisky was being spilled before the tumbler reached his mouth.

Lockwood did everything in his power to make shore leave better than simply being off the boat. Bands playing patriotic or humorous tunes greeted them as they came in from patrol. On the dock, they automatically got their mail, as well as fresh fruits and ice cream. The sailors and technicians on the submarine tenders took over the boat while the submariners went to the best hotels the area had to offer, where they drank and caroused like sailors do.

After dropping off Lockwood in Albany, the *Sculpin* underwent repairs. The ship and its men were showing signs of wear after several months of hard-pounding war patrols. The electrical motors were starting to short out and blow fuses—a catastrophic failure if they were caught dead in the water while trying to slink away from a depth-charging. The battle for Guadalcanal was raging while they waited to get back out on patrol. Guadalcanal was a heretofore unknown island off Papua New Guinea with a hastily built airstrip. Land-based Japanese planes would be able to bomb the Australian mainland and strangle shipping to the western ports, forcing cargo and war matériel to go through the much more dangerous Antarctic route. The Japanese were staging landings and reinforcements from the port city of Rabaul on the nearby island of New Britain. The situation on Guadalcanal was desperate for both sides, and the commanders sent *Sculpin* to do what it could to sink troop transports, supply ships, and men-of-war slipping in and out of the Vitiaz Strait. The ships were using the waterway to support the Japanese effort on Guadalcanal and resupply the Japanese landings on the northern shores of New Guinea.

After a false start and further repairs to the motors, the *Sculpin* finally made its way into the patrol region, and went nearly a month without spotting a ship. They bided their time by conducting reconnaissance on Thilenius and Montagu harbors, where they thought they might find ships, but they weren't able to come closer than a single sighting at 13,000 yards. Finally on the morning of September 28, they spotted a seaplane tender making 18 knots off Cape Lambert, New Britain. That was almost *Sculpin*'s best speed on the surface, however. Since it was now daytime they had to lurk submerged at slow speed, and watched the plum target speed away. Fortunately, the Japanese seemed to be conducting operations in the area, and an hour later a periscope sweep revealed masts on a southeasterly course; they would be able to position themselves in time to get a shot and shortly went to battle stations.

Chappell watched closely on the periscope as the ship came closer, an oil tanker zigzagging widely, he guessed at about

60 degrees with each turn. It was escorted by a small antisubmarine patrol boat the likes of which Chappell hadn't seen before. The soundman caught the ship with his hydrophones and started tracking it at about 10,000 yards. By listening to the screws and counting the number of turns per minute—in this case, 62—he would be able to alert the skipper if it put on steam to speed up long before Chappell would be able to observe the ship going faster. Time ticked by as Chappell popped up and down with the periscope, trying to determine the tanker's shifting base course so that he could predict whether it would zig toward one side of the *Sculpin* or zag to the other.

"Bearing, mark!"

"Sixty degrees relative, Captain."

"Distance to track?"

"One-five-double-oh yards. Track, niner-oh degrees."

Chappell had lined up the *Sculpin* to take a shot from the stern tubes.

"Final bearing and shoot." Chappell paused, leaning into the scope, his forearms draped over the ears. He rotated the scope back and forth, stopping on the escort.

"The escort's coming directly at us. He's got a bone in his teeth. He's seen us. Down scope."

"Down scope, aye aye."

The crewmen shifted uneasily. When an antisubmarine boat had a bone in its teeth, its bow wake loomed high and white as it cut through the water. The soundman tracked it, however, and assured Chappell that it hadn't changed speed, and was now changing course. Maybe he hadn't seen the periscope after all.

"Up scope!"

"Up scope, aye aye."

"It's about thirty degrees to the left of the tanker. I think they're going to make another zig."

If the tanker changed course again, it would change all the TDC's calculations and they would have to start all over again with new observations.

"She's zigging toward us. Down scope."

"Down scope, aye aye."

"If he goes sixty degrees again, toward us, he'll come too close for us to get a shot." Chappell reversed course and rang up full speed on the annunciators. The *Sculpin* shifted slightly as the boat swung around to the new course. Chappell hoped it would put them right on the money. Then he slowed down the boat so that when he raised the scope it wouldn't make a feather on the surface. The sub was so quiet with anticipation they could have heard a pin drop.

"Up scope."

"Up scope, aye aye."

Chappell watched the tanker complete its zig. As he'd suspected, the escort hadn't seen them. He called out the speed and angle on the bow to Mendenhall below in the control room so he could input the new information into the TDC, then put the periscope down again.

"Set depth six feet. Two degree spread. We'll shoot four fish."

"Depth set six feet, sir."

"Two degree spread, sir."

"Up scope. Final bearing and shoot."

"Bearing, mark! Angle on the bow, seven-three degrees. Range, one-eight-six-oh. Down scope."

The red indicator light on the TDC labeled SOLUTION flickered, then glowed brightly. They were ready to shoot. Mendenhall called out: "Set!"

"Fire five!"

The boat heaved. Their ears popped with the inrush of air. They waited until the proper amount of time elapsed before they fired another fish.

"Fire six!"

"Fire seven!"

"Fire eight!"

"All fish running hot, straight, and normal," the soundman reported.

Chappell waited a few seconds after the last torpedo left, then raised the periscope again. All was as he'd left it: The tanker was doing nothing to evade. Chappell watched the first torpedo hit the stern of the tanker. A split second later, the explosion shook the boat, letting all aboard know that their torpedo had met its mark. A small cheer went up. He watched the second torpedo hit seconds later amidships on the port side.

"The target's screws have stopped, Captain," said the soundman.

The men heard another explosion, which seemed to come from far astern.

Black smoke billowed from the wrecked tanker as it started to list heavily to port. Chappell swung the scope around to see the escort bearing down on them, fast. It was already tossing ash cans over the sides.

"Take her down quick. Two-five-oh feet. Rig for depth charge. Full speed. Come to course oh-four-five."

The boat tilted downward by the bow. They braced themselves gently on the bulkheads or whatever was handy while the floor shifted underneath amid the sound of a series of explosions. They were strongly reminiscent of bombs dropped from airplanes. Had the escort called in an air patrol? Next came a string of depth charges that seemed to come from far astern: *tik tik boom, tik tik boom.* They were probably the ash cans the skipper had seen. He decided to use the racket as a sonic screen to get some distance from the patrol boat; the escort wouldn't be able to use his hydrophones while the depth charges were banging around.

"Full speed," he said.

"Full speed, aye aye," said the helmsman as he rang it up on the annunciators. Ten minutes crept by, punctuated by an occasional depth charge, then there were none. They were probably listening up there; it was time to employ stealth. The escort was no closer to getting them; they'd probably be able to slink away.

"Rig for silent running."

"Rig for silent running, aye aye, sir."

They shifted to manual control of the helm and the planes so that the noisy hydraulic pump wouldn't give them away. The quiet electric motors slowed to the slightest whisper—just fast enough for them to be underway and adjust their depth if necessary. The quiet minutes ticking by confirmed that the escort was probably searching in an unproductive quarter, far away.

"Secure crew from battle stations," said Chappell, relieved that they'd gotten away without taking too much of a beating.

Mendenhall had been on duty for a long time and looked forward to hitting his bunk. He was elated that they'd finally been able to guide the torpedoes with his TDC skills, but if two and possibly three torpedoes had hit, why hadn't all four? Too much spread? He may also have thought about the next class for his school of the boat. To get the coveted patch with two dolphinfish facing a submarine in the middle, their "dolphins," they had to be qualified in submarines. This included detailed drawings of the ship's dozens of intricate systems: air lines, tanks, electrical wires, everything. To be qualified in submarines, they also had to demonstrate that they knew how to use every single piece of equipment on the boat, no matter if it wasn't their specialty or even in their compartment. They had to work the diving planes, demonstrate how to load a torpedo and fire it, start the engines, close hatches and valves in every compartment for a dive or to surface, move the gigantic switches and levers in the maneuvering room. The dolphins were no mere merit badges; they represented complete mastery over the most complicated vessel in the Navy, with the implication that they could all rely on one another to do any job on the boat if the circumstances came to that.

While Mendenhall was trying to relax and get some shut-eye, the soundman reported from the forward torpedo room: "They're pinging, sir. Bearing, about two-seven-oh degrees."

The soundman revolved the hydrophone through the points of the compass and heard screws coming in from the south. "There's a second one, sir. Moving in."

He moved back to the pinging escort for a few tense minutes. The bearing wasn't changing, but...

"He's shifted to short scale, Captain. I think he may have something. The second one's getting closer. I think the first one's guiding him in."

Some of the men could hear something that sounded like a tap running somewhere in a distant room that was growing louder.

"Coming in from one-three-oh degrees."

The sound grew louder so that all the men could hear it, like steam coming from the mouth of a boiling kettle, growing louder until they had the peculiar sensation of hearing a steam locomotive as it crossed a bridge above them, hissing away. The men looked blankly at the tops of their compartments, their imaginations giving form to the sound. They cast glances toward one another, half expecting the enemy's ship gliding above them to cast a spectral shadow through the compartment.

"Take her to two-seven-oh feet."

"Two-seven-oh feet, aye aye."

Then came a sound like a child happily splashing his hand in a full bathtub...bubbles rising...more splashes.

"Depth charges, sir."

They could hear the ship above so clearly, it must have been right over them. There was no way to tell how close until the depth charges went off, and they tensed, waiting for the barrels of high explosive to sink.

*BAM!*

Everything went dark as lightbulbs all over the boat shattered and tinkled onto the green linoleum of the deck. Mendenhall was nearly shaken clean off his bunk, as though he were on a train that had sustained a head-on collision. He heard the unmistakable sound of...*drip...drip...drip drip drip...ssssshhh ssshhh SSSHHHH*. He went into the hallway and ran straight into a quickly growing puddle. Men were shouting all over the boat. He traced the sound of the water coming into the officers' lavatory. A stream of high-pressure water was coming out of the toilet: A connection to the sea had sprung a leak and it was quickly filling up the boat and letting tons of water into the officers' quarters. If the saltwater pooled up and got to the compartment below, it would hit the batteries.

They were now in mortal danger.

Mixing saltwater with the sulfuric acid in the batteries would create a billowing green cloud of toxic chlorine gas that would burn their eyes, snuffing them out one by one in an unbelievably horrible death by chemical asphyxiation. If enough water got into the battery compartment, the batteries would start an irreversible chemical reaction and begin to boil, culminating in a massive explosion of battery acid.

Men threw down bedding, pillows, anything to build a dam around the hatch leading to the batteries below. Mendenhall called for help and leaned over the toilet, trying to stop the seawater from coming in from the quarter-inch tube, but it was coming in like the blast from a pressure washer, threatening to pull the skin off his hands.

Charlie Henderson, the exec, was running up and down the boat getting damage reports. There were leaks in the forward torpedo room, where plugs in the hull were pushed in, admitting water into the compartment like sprinklers. Then the motors cut out; they wouldn't be able to maneuver or change depth. After ten tense seconds that seemed like an eternity, the maneuvering room found some switches that had been jarred open and were able to start up the motors again.

*BANG!*

The men saw the outer hull push inward between the rib structure of the submarine's walls, as though it were an aluminum can reacting to a firecracker. The disturbed water coursed through the superstructure, making a rushing roar of effervescence as millions of tiny bubbles rushed up through the deck plates and around the handrails. In the conning tower, the depth gauge reacted to the sudden increase in water pressure by pegging out—the needle indicator flew off the pin—and the gasket on the door to the exterior of the ship bulged inward and was starting to cut. A locker sprang off its welded foundation on the bulkhead and crashed on the floor of the conning tower, spilling its contents all over.

*BANG!*

The men in the forward torpedo room watched with horror as the valves in their compartment spun open with every explosion, as though turned by unseen hands. The water pressure from the depth charges was actually forcing the watertight valves open—from the other side.

"Sir, the stern planes are jammed!" said the planesman. They were at 280 feet, taking on water, and going deeper. Jack Turner, the engineering officer, got another man on the plane wheel and together they were able to budge the wheel, but only barely. Meanwhile Mendenhall was just outside, sitting on a chair in the yeoman's tiny office, passing water forward in the bucket brigade through the control room. Turner got the boat to two thirds speed and gradually got the boat on a 10 degree up angle. They couldn't use the noisy pumps or they'd give their position away. The water in officer's country sloshed aft to keep it away from the battery hatch. It pooled up against the bulkhead to about twelve inches, where the bucket brigade dipped it up and passed it forward. They still hadn't fixed the leak in the head.

*BANG!*

"Sir! The Christmas Tree—"

Two of the green lights now flashed red—some of the valves leading to the outside of the boat were now open. It was the outboard vents for the batteries—special tubes that drained hydrogen gas away and out of the boat when they charged the batteries on the surface. If those didn't hold, water would siphon directly into the batteries themselves, causing the chlorine gas and explosion they all dreaded. The skipper guided the boat away from the scene as quietly and quickly as he could as they ascertained the damage all around the boat. It was a mess: The water distiller had broken loose, the pump room was flooded, there were electrical shorts throughout the boat. The drain pump wouldn't work, hydraulic fluid was in the bilge, but still the *Sculpin* held, and despite the high anxiety of seeing the hull open up on the Christmas Tree, the valves didn't leak seawater to the batteries. After an hour and a half they were able to shake their pursuers and finally stop the leak in the officers' head. Mendenhall gave his report that the bucket brigade had moved the water forward and secured the leak, and when he turned to go Chappell noticed a dark splotch on the seat of his pants. The skipper asked him what he'd been sitting in, and Mendenhall realized that for nearly two hours he'd been sitting in glass shards from a broken lightbulb. Steward Eugenio Apostol was on his first patrol and had helped in the bucket brigade. He asked the exec, "Now we go up and shoot the destroyer, maybe?"

When they got back to periscope depth two hours after the initial attack, there was thankfully nothing on the surface. They stayed down because it was daylight now and spent the next couple of days repairing everything. It was the worst beating *Sculpin* had ever taken, extensive but manageable. One of the two periscopes was damaged. The fridge had shorted and spoiled 500 pounds of meat, and they lost sugar, flour, and coffee when it was submerged in the saltwater. To top it off, the labels on the canned food had gotten wet and slipped off, which made for an odd smorgasbord at meals. Despite all the destruction, Chappell determined that with repairs they could continue their patrol, and after a couple of days' rest and repair, they were ready to go back on the hunt.

During the next week *Sculpin* drifted eastward toward the bottleneck approaches of the Japanese fortress of Rabaul, which the quartermasters had taken to calling the Slot. Most of the Japanese shipping in the area funneled down to this point before going through the strait leading to the operations at Guadalcanal. They were able to spot several distant ships on the horizon, and even get in close enough to a troop transport to set up an attack, but this was foiled by a nervous destroyer captain who started dropping depth charges on what they could only assume was a school of fish. The destroyer was too far away to hit them, but even a blind dog gets lucky sometimes and finds a bone. While Chappell tried to determine how best to attack, the transport got away.

Days went by before a periscope sweep revealed smoke on the horizon again—the sign of approaching ships—and Chappell laid a course for a convoy. Although *Sculpin* was submerged, they were able to close on three ships, which quickly developed into a destroyer, then a small transport, and a large transport going about 14 knots. Incredibly, despite the submarine attack just a few days ago, the convoy wasn't zigzagging. Chappell rang up two thirds speed on the annunciator and put on a track to intercept the three ships. During his periscope observations, he was careful to look for planes so that he wouldn't have any nasty surprises as on the previous attack.

At three minutes past one, the skipper rang up general quarters. The approach was developing nicely, and he even had a shot at the destroyer leading the pack. Though he was sorely tempted to have a go at it, the troop transport was the more valuable target and he held off until they got to within 1,200 yards. Once again he had the ship in his crosshairs, dead to rights, if only the torpedoes would work properly. He also hoped that the destroyer wouldn't give them too much of a working over; the conning tower door was still leaking and he didn't know if it could take much of a shock. At twenty past one he fired all four fish from the bow and raised the periscope to track their progress when the diving officer took on too much ballast to compensate for the loss of the torpedoes' wake.

"Depth! Keep your depth!"

Jack Turner, the diving officer at the time, slowly and carefully planed them back up to periscope depth. Meanwhile, they heard three explosions—it seemed like the torpedoes had done their job. Seconds later, Chappell was able to get the scope back up through the surface of the water. The transport was sinking. The soundman reported that it had stopped and that he was hearing breaking-up noises. They would soon come close enough for the crew to hear them for themselves, but now they had to evade; the destroyer was charging up to where the torpedo wakes had started, and the other target ship had swung wide to avoid the catastrophe.

Chappell followed the torpedo wakes to just aft of the target's stern and gave the order to go to deep submergence. Despite the fact that they hadn't seen any airplanes, the crew heard the rumbling of an explosion aft of the boat. They made their way to the sinking transport and heard the popping, tearing noises of the sinking ship as they passed nearby, then made a course of about 60 degrees away from the target's original course.

*Tik-tik* BOOM. *Tik-tik* BOOM.

They were relieved to hear that the depth charges were well

Lt. Commander Fred Connaway.
*Naval Historical Center*

Captain John Philip Cromwell.
*Naval Historical Center*

Admiral Isoroko Yamamoto,
commander of Japan's
Combined Fleet.
*Naval Historical Center*

Commander Lucius H. Chappell.
*Courtesy of Randy Chappell*

Captain Edward T. Layton.
*Wenger Command Display*

Lt. Wilfred "Jasper" Holmes.
*Wenger Command Display*

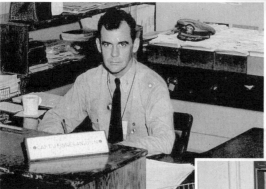

Captain Joseph Finnegan.
*Wenger Command Display*

Lt. Commander Thomas Dyer.
*Wenger Command Display*

Fleet Radio Unit Pacific
(FRUPAC) Section GZ-Y
decoding room.
*Wenger Command Display*

FRUPAC Information Section, where "crippies" came to check obscure cross-references to ships, geographical place names, and anything else that seemed important.
*Wenger Command Display*

Survivors of the USS *Squalus* disaster.
*Naval Historical Center*

The raising of the USS *Squalus*, to be later rechristened USS *Sailfish*.
*Naval Historical Center*

HIJMS *Chuyo*.
*U.S. Navy photo*

George "Moon" Rocek (right) on leave in Cicero, Illinois, with his brother Rudolph and sister Sylvia.
*Courtesy of George Rocek*

Bill "Billie" Cooper.
*U.S. Navy photo*

USS *Squalus* under construction at the
Portsmouth Navy Yard.
*National Archives*

Bow photo of the USS *Sculpin* after its
radical refit in 1943.
*National Archives*

Stern photo of the USS *Sculpin.*
*National Archives*

A photo documenting the many changes to the USS *Sculpin* after its refit in 1943.
*National Archives*

The *Sculpin* as she appeared during the *Squalus* disaster.
*National Archives*

Planesmen at the diving station of a WW II-era submarine.
*National Archives*

Awaiting orders to surface in the engine room of a WW II-era submarine.
*National Archives*

Diving control station in the control room of a typical fleet boat. *From* The Fleet Type Submarine

Though cramped, the galleys and mess halls in WW II submarines turned out some of the best food in the Navy.
*National Archives*

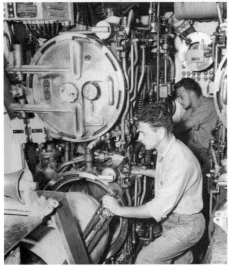

Torpedomen loading a "fish" into a forward torpedo tube using pulleys.
*National Archives*

A skipper in the conning tower flipping down the periscope "ears" after ordering "up periscope." Note the sailor on the right, who wore battle phones to relay the skipper's orders as well as to confirm that sailors in other compartments had accomplished the orders. Note also the intentional doctoring of the photo on the depth gauge above the skipper's head.
*National Archives*

A Japanese merchantman in the crosshairs of a submarine's periscope. Skippers used the horizontal gradations along with a device called a stadimeter to determine the height of the masts, and therefore the range of the target ship.
*National Archives*

A page from the JN-25 codebook used to encode secret Japanese navy transmissions.
*National Archives*

### R—T

| 11271 | Ranger (少空) [R] | 55791 | San Francisco (甲重) [S] |
|---|---|---|---|
| 27786 | Rapidan (给油) | 26034 | San Juan (乙軽) |
| 47995 | Rasher (潜) | 62121 | San Pablo (水機母) |
| 01710 | Rathburne (113) (駆) | 71298 | Sanderling (掃) |
| 20553 | Raton (潜) | 57120 | Sandpiper (水機母) |
| 03915 | Raven (掃) | 66714 | Sands (243) (掃) |
| 38568 | Ray (潜) | 55506 | Sangamon (给油) |
| 72807 | Redfin (潜) | 29379 | Santa Fe (乙軽) |
| 34314 | Reed Bird (掃) | 15303 | Santee (给油) |
| 18597 | Regulus (潜貨) | 38007 | |
| 73893 | Reid (395) (駆) | 02292 | Sapelo (给油) |
| 32376 | Relief (病) | 19440 | Sargo (潜) |
| 22482 | Reno (乙軽) | 09351 | Saufley (駆) |
| 15376 | Renshaw (駆) | 66816 | Saury (潜) |
| 63162 | Rind (404) (駆) | 03243 | Savannah (乙軽) |
| 71013 | Richmond (乙軽) | 42906 | Sawfish (潜) |
| 37122 | Rigel (给水) | 24141 | Scamp (潜) |
| 01839 | | 74895 | Schenck (159) (駆) |
| 26007 | Road Runner (掃) | 06468 | Schley (103) (駆) |
| 07734 | Robalo (潜) | 67299 | Schroedar (駆) |
| 23469 | Robin (掃) | 72468 | Scorpion (潜) |
| 65?64 | Rochester (甲巡) | 27240 | Sculpin (潜) |
| 57165 | Rock (潜) | 61623 | Seadragon (潜) |
| 74376 | Rockway (水機母) | 03471 | Seagull (掃) |
| | an (駆) | 46089 | Seal (潜) |
| | 18) (駆) | 50160 | Searaven (潜) |
| | r (347) (駆) | 43704 | Seawolf (潜) |
| | (駆) | 36330 | Selfridge (357) (駆駆) |
| | n (405) (駆) | 21681 | Sepulga (给油) |
| | (駆) | 14229 | Shad (潜) |
| | er (潜) | 22041 | Shaw (373) (駆) |

| ○○○ | | | (留壹) | | | |
|---|---|---|---|---|---|---|
| | 0 | 1 | 2 | 3 | 4 | 5 | 6 |
| 0 | 20609 | 60170 | 84038 | 45960 | 28875 | 68173 | 1120 |
| 1 | 61054 | 85469 | 27480 | 62373 | 81562 | 03079 | 4831 |
| 2 | 12433 | 05392 | 62535 | 90664 | 13459 | 57628 | 6449 |
| 3 | 91971 | 76617 | 45278 | 14839 | 74566 | 27636 | 0486 |
| 4 | 19415 | 33740 | 97941 | 60062 | 45981 | 95410 | 4152 |
| 5 | 69251 | 91369 | 59805 | 25185 | 04358 | 67139 | 2185 |

An additive table used to further scramble secret communications after encoding.
*National Archives*

USS *Sculpin* stands off the Isle of Shoals as Navy salvage ships prepare to raise her sister ship, USS *Squalus*.
*National Archives*

Fleet Admiral Chester W. Nimitz.
*Naval Historical Center*

Example of an actual JN-25 message
blank as filled out by a radio clerk.
*Wenger Command Display*

ULTRA decode of a Japanese radio
transmission giving the details of the
catastrophe.
*National Archives*

Crew of the USS *Sculpin*, late 1943. Front:
Cook Carlos Tulao, Lt. Corwin Mendenhall,
Chief Weldon E. "Dinty" Moore, Lt. John
Turner. Rear: Chief Electrician's Mate John
Pepersack, Quartermaster 3/c Alvin Coulter,
Signalman 2/c Keith Waidelich, Electrician's
Mate 2/c John Swift, Machinist's Mate 1/c
John "Gus" Hollenbach, Motor Machinist's
Mate 2/c Ralph Austin, Chief Electrician's
Mate Frank J. Dyboski, Chief Motor
Machinist Chesley DeArmond.
*Courtesy of George Rocek*

away from them, far enough to hear the characteristic *tik-tik* of the detonators before the explosion, but soon another ship had come to the scene—perhaps one of the small, quick sub hunters they'd been encountering on this patrol. There were more depth charges, some so far away that they sounded faint. The second ship started the search over the next hour, and both escorts came quite close above the *Sculpin*. The men waited in anticipation as they listened once again to the sounds of the ships above them. There was no pinging, but then they heard a queer, unsettling sound; it was the same sound they heard the day they'd left Cavite: a chain rubbing, scraping against the side of the hull. This time it wasn't a mine, though. The escorts above were fishing for them with a grapnel attached to a heavy chain, hoping to snag on some vent or bit of superstructure that would drag them up to the surface or at least betray their position. The crew listened intently to the horrible sound as the links clinked and slid, bumping against their sanctuary, hoping against hope that the sailors above didn't detect anything. Finally the chain drew away from them, and the ships circled overhead for over an hour, then seemed to give up.

At half past five they went to the surface and raised the periscope, but the convoy had gone on, and their victim lay at the bottom of the sea. They had gotten away scot-free.

A week later, *Sculpin* received a radio message that required decryption. It seemed to be an unbelievable bit of straight dope about the noontime position of a Japanese supply ship on its way from Rabaul to Kavieng, a port on the island of New Ireland. Although Chappell could only guess how anyone could know about the convoy's position in time with such precision, he set a course to put them on the path of the unsuspecting ships and in the early hours before dawn on October 14, the lookouts saw another large transport, then a smaller transport, and finally a destroyer leading them all.

The weather conditions had been patchy, with overcast and occasional rainsqualls. Since they'd only just spotted the target, and dawn was coming, Chappell decided to set up fast and make a surface attack rather than submerge. They quickly made observations and sent the speed and bearings down to the control room, where the TDC operator punched them up. When the moment came, they fired all four bow torpedoes and started to pull away. Chappell watched in disgust as all four torpedo tracks went ahead of the transport's bow. They'd set up the attack too quickly, he'd gotten the speed wrong, and now the destroyer was running around pell-mell, dropping depth charges left and right. The mere sound of the depth charges was as impressive on the surface as it was while taking them down below, but it didn't appear that the destroyer had seen the *Sculpin*, and for some reason it didn't follow the torpedo tracks back to the sub. When the torpedoes reached the end of their runs, they exploded, and Chappell thought this may have confused the destroyer's skipper further. Another rainsquall came on, soaking the deck watch, at the same time providing ample cover for the small silhouette of the *Sculpin* to peel away into the gray morning rain showers pelting the sea. Chappell felt bad that he'd gotten the speed wrong—it seemed to be a recurring problem—and he would write later with his characteristic humor not often found in war patrol reports that "like a relative in jail this attack makes a painful subject for discussion."

Given that they often went days without seeing hide nor hair of the enemy, the crew was probably relieved that they would have a productive patrol when they spotted more ships a little after four that very afternoon. Unfortunately they were still submerged due to daylight and weren't able to close to less than seven miles. But a couple of hours later, near twilight, they spotted more smoke on the horizon, crawling east. Chappell moved the *Sculpin* in a general direction intended to intercept, impatient for dusk and its protective cloak of darkness to set in, and a little after seven that evening they blew the klaxon three times to surface. The *Sculpin*'s diesels roared to life while the blower's noisy air compressors rattled away to store air in the tanks for the next dive. Chappell plotted the classic submarine end-around, racing the *Sculpin* at high speed in a wide arc just at the periphery of the target's line of sight. With any luck, the curvature of the earth would hide the *Sculpin*'s hull and most of the conning tower's small silhouette from view. When night fell, the convoy of three ships—an escort, a transport, and a tanker—suddenly made a turn to starboard and took a southerly direction. The convoy had anticipated the likes of the *Sculpin* and intended to throw any lurkers off their path with the radical change in course.

Chappell decided on a surface night attack. If the sub got spotted, it could still submerge quickly, and if not it could maneuver at high speed and possibly make another end-around to get in a subsequent shot at a second ship in the convoy. Chappell and the officer of the deck noted the moon—it was half full but overcast—and they decided that all things being equal, it was more important to get into position quickly than to hide their silhouette. As the *Sculpin* drew closer, the ships drew in and out of low-lying clouds and rainsqualls that hid and revealed them.

The first ship was likely an escort, the second a large transport. The last one was a medium-sized tanker. It seemed the easiest to pick off, and Chappell knew that the oil it contained was more crucial than the troops on the transport. Just as he signaled his intention to target the tanker, the sub's lookouts noted a shape drawing out of the fog and becoming solid, moving astern of the tanker: another sub chaser.

Chappell kept a wary eye on this new development while continuing to pursue the tanker. Eventually, the sub chaser swept away to the other side of the tanker, giving him a lucky break and a straight shot. The hapless ship crawled along the horizon at about 10 knots, making no attempt to evade. When it reached the perfectly perpendicular point with the *Sculpin*'s nose at about 1,500 yards, Chappell gave the signal to fire. The torpedoes roared out with a burst of compressed air, raced off under the surface with their harsh metallic sewing-machine sound, and made a slight right turn to intercept. The men on deck watched with grim satisfaction as the lengthening wakes made by the torpedoes' steam motors led straight to the tanker's path. One of the attack party crewmen counted the time from his stopwatch.

"...fifty-five...sixty...sixty-five...seventy—"

An enormous explosion deep under the water heaved waves and smoke into the air along the starboard side of the tanker.

"Sir, that was probably the third torpedo."

"...seventy-five..."

Bang! Another hit, this time just short of the bow.

"...eighty...eighty-five...ninety...ninety-five..."

It became apparent that Chappell had overestimated the speed again, or perhaps two of the torpedoes were duds. The only difference it would have made was in the amount of time it would take for the tanker to sink. The ship was holed badly, with smoke pouring out into the overcast night.

More ships that they hadn't seen before appeared in the convoy. Two destroyers got a full head of steam and started charging around the formation, randomly casting depth charges as they went, then firing their guns. Chappell decided to change course and hightail it on the surface, and soon a welcome rainsquall enveloped them, sealing them out of sight from the advancing destroyers. Although everything had gone their way, the shifting weather could just as easily have revealed them to the wily sub chasers, and rather than making another end-around to intercept the convoy again, Chappell decided to evade for another hour. It was late by now anyhow—they'd been plotting ships since early in the morning and were exhausted. *Sculpin* hadn't fully charged the batteries yet and Chappell didn't want to make another attack where they might have to dive on low battery power, so he ordered two engines put on line to charge and the other two to maneuver.

The men were glad to have only four torpedoes left. After firing them they could count on going back to Brisbane, in Australia, and receive a hero's welcome for sinking so many ships. Chappell continued to patrol back and forth, waiting for another ship, until four days later Emmett "Middie" Mills spotted smoke on the horizon during a routine periscope sweep. Chappell was able to steal toward what he described as a strange ship. The Japanese had been refitting old ships to plug gaps in their naval forces, and many had unusual configurations. The "odd-looking affair" seemed to have "started life as a small, coal-burning tramp." Chappell observed that it now had guns on forecastle and deck wells, as well as a seaplane and rack upon rack of depth charges. The officers agreed that it was probably an ill-disguised Q-ship, or decoy, to lure unsuspecting submariners.

Chappell decided to go after the zigzagging ship and got into position for a stern shot. If they didn't sink it straightaway, it would have a chance to bring its formidable number of depth charges on them. An hour and a half after first spotting the ship, the crew went to battle stations. Chappell made quick periscope observations—at two in the afternoon, they couldn't afford to be spotted with nighttime so far away—and waited for the Q-ship to complete a right zig before he was able to set up a shot. At a range of 1,900 yards Chappell shot three torpedoes and pulled down the scope. Sound reported no change in course, and after about a minute he put the scope up again, watching as the wakes streaked toward the unsuspecting ship. The first torpedo exploded about twenty-five feet behind the ship, then, seconds later, another torpedo hit forward of the bridge. The ship started to make a drastic turn—the pilot must have seen the wake of the third torpedo—as men scurried back and forth on the deck, manning the guns. The sailors quickly loaded the deck gun on the forecastle and one of the other deck guns, and started lobbing shells where the torpedo wakes began. The *Sculpin* was already well away from that position, but close enough to hear the concussion of the shells as they hit the water. The shells were unlikely to hurt much of anything after splashing down, and as the Q-ship got closer, Chappell decided to fire his last torpedo at the ship. If it had been hit by the first two torpedoes, it didn't appear to be heavily damaged, and was even speeding up.

"Up periscope."

"Up periscope, aye aye."

*Bang, splash.* Another shell hit the surface of the water.

"Range, one-seven-oh-oh yards. Speed, eleven knots. Angle on the bow... Bearing, mark! Down scope."

"Down scope, aye aye."

"We'll fire this last one and go deep."

*Bang, splash.*

The men in the conning tower nodded, waiting for the time to pass for Chappell to make another observation.

"Up scope."

"Up scope, aye aye."

"Final bearing and shoot. Range, one-six-double-oh yards. Angle on the bow, five-four degrees. Speed, eleven knots. Bearing, mark!"

"Set!"

Chappell gave the order to fire and watched the torpedo momentarily to make sure it wasn't making a circular run; it seemed to be going right, and the soundman reported that it was running hot, straight, and normal.

"Down scope!"

"Down scope, aye aye."

*Bang, splash!*

"Take her down, two-oh-oh feet."

"Two-oh-oh feet, aye aye, sir."

Chappell changed course—if the torpedo missed and didn't sink the tub, at least they might chase the torpedo wake again.

"One-oh-oh feet," said the diving officer. "One-one-oh feet... One-two-oh feet."

*Click-click BANG.* Depth charge, but not close.

*Click-click BANG.* That one seemed even farther away.

*Click-click bang.* The Q-ship was throwing ash cans in the wrong direction.

*BANG!* Coming sixty seconds after firing their last torpedo, they hoped that it had found its mark and sunk the Q-ship. They waited to hear from the soundman... nope, the ship was still up there. Seemed slower though.

"Come to course one-two-oh."

"One-two-oh, aye aye, Captain."

*Click-click bang.* Still throwing depth charges, but not many, and then the sound stopped altogether. The crew listened as the sound of the Q-ship's screws slowly receded until late afternoon, when they ventured a peek to see what was going on up there and saw heavy smoke on the horizon. It was possible that the Q-ship was heavily damaged; they probably would have heard the screws stop and the sounds of a ship breaking up if it had gone to Davy Jones's locker. Chappell surfaced amid heavy, intermittent rainsqualls, and the Q-ship was nowhere to be found. It was just as well because the only way to finish it off would have been to engage in gun action using the *Sculpin*'s 3-inch deck gun—a lopsided fight considering the Q-ship's armament. Chappell was content to radio his results and the intention to head back to base. He was hoping that the submarine high command might finally give the crew a long period of well-deserved R&R.

# 9

## The Silent Service

At Station Hypo, the summer and fall brought in few decrypts. The leak leading to the *Chicago Tribune* story suggesting a break in the Japanese codes caused consternation throughout the Navy. Especially incensed were the Redman brothers, who encouraged prosecution of the parties involved. When it seemed that a sensational public trial would air all of the Navy's most precious secrets, the anti-Roosevelt publisher of the *Tribune* needed no further incitement to make a big stink. As the case drew nearer, the government's seriousness in pursuing criminal charges seemed to confirm that they had actually broken the code. Finally, cooler heads prevailed and the case was dropped. The Japanese intelligence apparatus in neutral countries probably read of the developments with interest, however, because after only three months in service, JN-25 was hastily changed in August.

Hypo had to drop all work on the old version and start yet again. Fortunately, the sudden expansion of the unwieldy Japanese empire created problems in codebook distribution. Many ships and far-flung installations across the Pacific didn't receive new codebooks in time, but still needed to be informed about fleet movements and receive instructions and orders. As a result, duplicate messages were sent in the new JN-25, the previous version of JN-25, and other minor codes for a few weeks, offering the code breakers a Rosetta stone of sorts that gave brief glimpses into JN-25's latest iteration.

For Hypo, there was never a good time for the Japanese navy to make a radical change in JN-25, but the August changeover was particularly ill-timed due to the Marine landings at Guadalcanal and Tulagi on August 7. Two days later, a Japanese task force surprised the American landing force. Without benefit of advance warning provided by radio intelligence, the Allies were no match for Japan's superior ships, and suffered a humiliating defeat at the battle of Savo Island. The Australian heavy cruiser HMAS *Canberra* sank, with 193 lives lost. The U.S. cruisers *Vincennes*, *Astoria*, and *Quincy* also went down, each having a complement of 800 to 900 men. The marines on Guadalcanal were now as effectively isolated on the island as their Japanese counterparts, and the battle would rage for several excruciating months as each side sought to reinforce and resupply their troops. The fighting at sea was no less savage than on the island itself, and during the several naval battles that ensued, dozens of ships sank. So many went down in the channel between the islands around Guadalcanal that it became known as Ironbottom Sound. The men at Hypo felt anguish at each loss, and despite the extraordinarily complex and labor-intensive task of cracking JN-25, they took each sinking as evidence of personal and professional failure. Many of the officers in the sunken ships were classmates and friends from the Naval Academy, dead and gone forever.

At about this time, Rochefort's intransigent enemies in Washington spun plots to remove and humiliate him. First they sent officials to send back scathing reports about his suitability for command using an illegal code under Nimitz's nose. When Nimitz discovered that messages had been going back and forth under his command and without his knowledge he was furious, but the code went inexplicably missing and he was left in the dark. The powers that were also denied Rochefort any acknowledgment for his contribution in cracking JN-25 in time for Midway. When his replacement arrived and he was assigned for temporary duty in Washington, he could see the writing on the wall. Nimitz was confronted by a fait accompli when notice that Rochefort's temporary duty was now permanent came by mail, conveniently arriving too late for Nimitz to protest to the Bureau of Personnel. Frustrated by the command in Washington, Rochefort's irascible temperament reared up and he requested sea duty. In yet another breathtaking example of convenient self-contradiction, the bureaucratic conspiracy of dunces shamelessly backtracked to opine that what Rochefort knew was too valuable to put him in a command where he might be captured. Rochefort, the oracle of Midway, ended up in charge of a floating dry dock in San Francisco.

In one of his last communications to Jasper Holmes, Rochefort asked that he and Hypo give as much loyalty to their new boss as they had given to Rochefort. Though the surprise appointment of a new boss and the doldrums associated with their struggle to crack the new version of JN-25 were demoralizing, Dyer, Finnegan, Lasswell, Wright, and the rest met the challenge with equanimity and, if anything, worked harder than before. The nature of the war was changing, and the organization of Hypo in relation to the other pieces of the intelligence puzzle was changing, too.

Offensive operations like Guadalcanal required a much larger and broader intelligence apparatus across all services, and Holmes's Combat Intelligence Center—the desk Rochefort had used to hide the activities of Hypo—mushroomed into a bewildering number of acronyms, as well as an infusion of men and resources. The Joint Chiefs of Staff were drawing up plans to roll back Japan's defense structure of island rings, and these plans required not only radio intelligence but also photo reconnaissance and interpretation, prisoner interrogation, and rapid translation of captured documents. After an unfortunate incident where a friendly ship struck a mine outside one of the Allies' bases, the new Joint Intelligence Center, Pacific Ocean Area (JICPOA), even got the task of gathering and distributing intelligence about American bases as well as Japanese strongholds.

Despite the need for intelligence from all sources, radio intelligence still represented the best opportunity to determine the Japanese navy's strength, composition, and distribution. While the cryptographers worked to regain their footing on the new JN-25, they were still able to read the Truk port director's messages dispatching ships into and out of that important fortress. Early in 1943—despite a warning from OP-20-G in Washington that it was impossible—Hypo was also able to crack what would become known as the Maru Code. Like JN-25, it was a superenciphered code, but had only four digits instead of five, making it much less complicated. It revealed the comings and goings of Japan's merchant marine: the Maru-class cargo ships bringing iron, tin, rubber, and other war matériel to the homeland, as well as the invaluable oil tankers and military supply ships that kept Japanese outposts stocked and fed.

The Maru Code was obviously most useful to the submariners, the only ships in the Navy that could sneak into enemy-held waters and sink the Marus that fed the Japanese war machine. Along with decrypts of Japanese sailors' messages telling of submarine sightings, torpedo attacks, and detection of American submarines by DF—direction finding—Holmes started serving up the exact location and noontime positions of important convoys. When Admiral Lockwood became Commander Submarines, Pacific (ComSubPac), he brought on *Sailfish* skipper Dick Voge as his chief of staff. Voge came to Holmes every morning to go over the decrypts relevant to the submariners and brought a thin Pacific overlay map to update information about the location and direction of enemy convoys as well as the location of his own subs. Since the submarine skippers generally preferred to maintain radio silence so as not to give away their position to the Japanese, sometimes Holmes's *Japanese* eyewitness accounts were the only clues as to the submarines' locations.

Voge got high marks for his administration of submarine business at Pearl Harbor. On the nightly "fox" broadcast to submariners,* he often included small personal remarks, such as the announcement of sailors' new babies. For the first time, someone who'd actually seen the undersea war had their backs, and the submariners felt that someone actually cared about them while on patrol.

One of the first things they'd noticed—long before Dick Voge came on the scene—was that the skippers' war damage estimates were often inflated. In fact, Hypo had determined that the carrier Dick Voge sank in the *Sailfish* was an important ship—a

---

*Broadcast on the "F" or "fox" channel.

seaplane tender—but not a carrier as they'd hoped. There were many other letdowns for other skippers, but it was best to have an accurate account of the enemy's strength. Another discovery was that the Japanese convoy escorts often claimed that they'd sunk a submarine after a perfunctory counterattack. This happened so often that in the aggregate the Japanese high command had the idea that more American submarines were sunk than actually participated in the war. Unfortunately for the Japanese, they didn't have decryption to verify these sinkings, and while their antisubmarine tactics were terrifying and even sometimes effective, the false reports and the old initial victory disease misled them into not making improvements until a serious gaffe was made by a high-ranking U.S. politician.

Perhaps the most unsettling discovery was the steadily accumulating evidence that even after Lockwood had settled the dispute about torpedoes running too deep, the Japanese radio transmissions were now confirming the submarine skippers' long-suffering observation that the detonators were blowing up prematurely or not at all. In an odd mirror image of the victory disease afflicting the Japanese navy, the Bureau of Ordnance and their representatives at the sub bases continued to blame the skippers for the dud torpedoes and refused to consider for a moment that the Mk VI detonator was anything less than a paradigm of perfection. But contrary evidence was mounting. The Japanese noted the prematures, thus alerting them to the presence of American submarines, as well as the heart-attack-inducing sight of ghostly torpedo wakes running toward their ships, then under them, then harmlessly past them. The Japanese broadcast all of these contact reports on the radio, secure in the knowledge that it was absolutely safe to do so.

The submariners, Hypo, and perhaps especially the Japanese were able to acknowledge that the Mk VI exploder didn't work. Everyone except the Bureau of Ordnance and its apologists on the sub bases knew. Holmes was finally able to confirm it personally when in late January 1943, the Australian corvette *Kiwi* used sonar to acquire the Japanese submarine *I-1* as a target off the coast of Guadalcanal. The *Kiwi* proceeded to lay down depth charges that exploded underneath the submarine; the rapidly expanding gases displaced the water ballast in the sub's tanks, upset its compensation, and heaved it violently up to the surface. The *Kiwi* then set upon its prey, methodically ramming the stranded sub three times and shooting the men popping out of the hatches. When the sub captain made a courageous but ill-fated samurai sword attack on the corvette, he was shot down. The *I-1* ran aground but sank by the stern, and in the confusion of the gathering night, several of the Japanese submariners made a daring escape to Japanese-held lines, taking with them valuable intelligence documents.

They didn't secure all of the documents, however. Salvagers were able to secure an original copy of the JN-25 code, and although it was out of date and Hypo had already cracked most of it, Holmes would write that the discovery was for the code breakers "as precious as moon rock to an astronomer." They were able to confirm old hunches, correct long-standing errors, and glean seldom-used code groups they'd never been able to crack. In addition to this was a codebook listing all the two- and three-digit codes signifying geographical areas, including confirmation of their old favorite, AF for Midway. The Aussies were also able to take the wounded navigation officer as a prisoner for interrogation back at Pearl. Despite the animosity of war, Holmes was able to sympathize with him as he recounted his experience on the doomed sub. Having reached a certain rapport with the officer, submariner-to-submariner, Holmes asked the question he'd wanted to ask most: Were the Japanese having trouble with their torpedoes?

The officer answered in Japanese and smiled while a translator told Holmes the answer.

"No," he said. "But you are."

That confirmation and the rest of the intelligence materials came at a steep price. The crew of the *I-1* who were able to get away reported the possible loss of some of the codebooks. Although they buried or destroyed some of the books, they couldn't recover them and couldn't account for what was left on the submarine. The Japanese realized they had a major security breach on their hands and tried desperately to scuttle the *I-1*—the bow was still sticking grotesquely out of the water near the beach—but the Allies beat back the ships sent to sink the submarine. Two weeks after the *I-1* went down, the Japanese navy went through the laborious process of changing their codebooks once again, but as there were no fewer than 200,000 copies scattered throughout the Pacific theater, they had to transmit signals in new codes for those who had received new codebooks, and then retransmit them for those who had not. The result was a headache for security and even more openings for the code breakers to attack the Japanese codes. Within a month of the code change, Hypo was able to read enough traffic in the new codes to produce actionable intelligence.

One of the most important breaks in the war came on April 13, when Alva Lasswell came across a short message with huge consequences. It was Admiral Yamamoto's itinerary for a personal inspection of bases around Bougainville, near Guadalcanal, where Japanese forces were gearing up for a major aerial offensive against the Americans. Holmes and Lasswell took the decrypt to Nimitz's intelligence chief, Ed Layton. Yamamoto had spent time in the United States before the war attending the Naval Academy and Harvard University, as well as a posting as a naval attaché in Washington, D.C. Several high-ranking Navy officers remembered him well. His dossier probably included the information that Yamamoto was exceedingly punctual in his appointments. The question was whether they should intercept Yamamoto's plane and shoot it down. Brilliant tactician though he was, Yamamoto was becoming a familiar adversary, and knowledge of this particular enemy's capable imagination and his inspired use of carrier-based planes was an asset in itself. But in the end, Yamamoto's abilities outweighed Nimitz's appreciation of those abilities, and Nimitz concluded that even if Yamamoto's replacement was a devil they didn't know, the great Japanese admiral's death would be a debilitating blow to the Combined Fleet's morale. What they proposed was nothing less than an attempt at assassination that might not work, and that had the added possibility of tipping off the Japanese about Hypo's success. Nimitz went up the chain of command all the way to President Roosevelt, who weighed the evidence and concluded that the benefits of having Yamamoto out of the picture outweighed the risks.

Nimitz coordinated a plan with Admiral Halsey and the Army air commander on Guadalcanal, and on April 18, a group of long-range P-38 Lightning fighters shot down the plane carrying the admiral of the Japanese Combined Fleet, Isoroku Yamamoto.

Yamamoto's chief of staff, Captain Yasuji Watanabe, was beside himself with anger and frustration, not only because of the admiral's death, but also because radio operators did not carry out his explicit orders to transmit the admiral's itinerary using only JN-25. He was convinced that the army's code was compromised, and that the American code breakers read the army version of the itinerary. Nor were the Japanese the only ones who were furious. British prime minister Winston Churchill instantly surmised what had happened and was reportedly filled with righteous fury that his great friend FDR had risked everything on a gambit to "get Yamamoto." If this was how FDR would treat the Japanese code, what blunder might he commit that would jeopardize Enigma's secrets? Though finely barbed, Churchill's concerns were legitimate, and only time would tell.

The Americans waited with waning patience for the Japanese to announce Yamamoto's death, which they finally did more than a month after the plane had gone down. There was a minor scandal during the interim when everybody seemed to know that the intelligence came from radio decryption. High-ranking officers tamped down the rumors by spreading a cover story that coast watchers had seen Yamamoto get into a plane. Miraculously and despite widespread distribution, the true story remained a secret to the Japanese. Concealing ULTRA's secret was worth dying for, and the Navy had once again narrowly averted disastrous consequences. With the next gaffe they would not be so lucky.

In June 1943, Andrew J. May, the powerful chair of the House Committee on Military Affairs, returned from a fact-gathering tour of American military bases, including Pearl Harbor. May was an enthusiastic war supporter—the country was nearly unanimous in this conviction—but his blustery, rah-

rah bombast and the important committee soapbox he used to express it often rankled even the most ardent war supporters. In one typically unlikely fantasy, at the height of the war he called on the Navy to "steam into Tokyo harbor and blow the city to bits." For him, the Japanese were not a capable, tenacious, and formidable enemy, but racially inferior, stupid yellow "Jap" bastards. To illustrate how stupid they were, in a fit of braggadocio, he claimed to reporters that the Japanese couldn't touch U.S. subs because they didn't set the depth charges deep enough. The story hit the wires and received distribution far and wide, including the local Hawaiian newspapers.

The Japanese are by no means stupid; the effect of May's blunder was immediate. U.S. subs reported devastating depth charge attacks as the Japanese organized effective convoys and set their depth charges lower than 150 feet. Many subs' final reports came in the form of Japanese radio decrypts, when the waters of the Pacific closed in on them from all sides, a ghastly oil slick marking the location where all souls aboard had gone on eternal patrol. The entire Navy was outraged, none more so than Admiral Lockwood, who wrote, "Congressman May...would be pleased to know that the Japs set 'em deeper now." Although he would never atone for the many ships and hundreds of men his indiscretion may have lost, years later May was convicted of taking bribes in connection with his powerful post as chairman of the Military Affairs Committee.

In the small, tight-knit submarine community, the loss of each submarine came as a shock, and no one could grow accustomed to it. That the ships simply left without a trace only worsened the sense of dread, and the flurry of "overdue, presumed lost" notices coming to friends of many years lent a sense of panic. *Argonaut, Amberjack, Grampus, Triton, Pickerel, Grenadier, Runner, Grayling, Pompano, Cisco*, the *S-44, Dorado*...the seemingly unending list went on and on, each ship taking with it upward of seventy men, devastating wives and children, mothers and fathers, brothers, sisters, friends. Although the war was brutal in every branch of service, it was becoming apparent that the submarine service, the Silent Service, was the most likely to deal the card of death.

All across the nation, households with sons, fathers, or brothers in the service displayed a banner with a blue star in the front window to indicate they had a relative in the fight. If he died, the banner was replaced with a gold star, and many women became known as "gold star mothers." As the war gathered strength and shattered souls from house to house in communities great and small, the stars turned gold in the windows of houses like the turning of the autumn leaves. In neighborhoods and farms all across the country, some forlorn houses stood apart in that they had two, sometimes three gold stars in the window.

Jasper Holmes's wife, Izzy, made their house on Black Point Road almost a home away from home for many of the officers, especially on holidays. They frequently entertained Jasper's friends from Hypo and old submarine buddies. In keeping with the fatalistic times, some of the gatherings became wild. When Holmes related a story to his dinner guests about some friends at the University of Hawaii who were investigated for singing sentimental Christmas carols in German, a defiant Joe Finnegan assembled a choir of Japanese language students in a loud (and probably drunken) version of the Japanese navy's anthem, "Kai-gun Koshin Kyoku."

Though his duties as a division commander at the sub base probably precluded any exceptional wildness at the Holmeses', their friend John Cromwell dropped in more than most. Despite the risks involved, like the other division commanders, Cromwell wanted nothing more than to go out on patrol. Lockwood wanted his division commanders to get combat experience and sent ComSubPac staffer Frank Watkins out in the uss *Flying Fish*. Like the skippers he commanded, Watkins found that a submarine war patrol was not a piece of cake. Lockwood also wanted to experiment with the Germans' wolf pack concept of concentrating a number of subs on a convoy. Coordinating several submarines would throw the convoy off balance, and mutually supporting torpedo attacks from different locations would lead escorts on the wrong track. The Germans had used this to devastating effect in the North Atlantic, but it was all centrally coordinated by radio in the compromised Enigma code from Admiral Karl Dönitz's main headquarters. Dönitz micromanaged his skippers and was constantly giving away their locations by requesting frequent reports. The British and Americans were able to locate the ships using direction finding, DF, and in any event were able to read both Dönitz's orders and the U-boats' reports.

Since coordinating wolf packs from across the much larger Pacific was impractical, Lockwood and a brilliant submarine innovator under his command named Swede Momsen devised a plan to send a wolf pack commodore with three subs who would use one boat as his flagship. The skipper of the flagship would be in control of the ship, just as in a carrier task force. The ships would use a short-distance VHF radio signal called Talk Between Ships, or TBS, with a simple encoding system to communicate with one another so that long-range direction finders wouldn't be able to locate them. Two of the three ships would attack on the right and left flanks of the convoy in the hope that the first attack would drive the convoy into the path of the second submarine; the attacks would occur at different points along the base course of the convoy to reduce the chance of running into friendly torpedoes. The third ship would hang behind to pick off stragglers, make end-around runs, or look for other targets of opportunity.

Momsen's group of three subs, the *Grayback*, the *Plunger*, and the *Shad*, was able to sink some ships, but the TBS didn't work as well as they had hoped, and Momsen was unable to effectively coordinate attacks in the way they had planned. One of the skippers thought it a complete waste of time, but even if they hadn't been able to attack according to plan, their proximity to one another added eyes and ears to the area, giving better overall coverage. Lockwood was pleased with the results and gave Momsen a Navy Cross for his efforts. Moreover, he wanted to experiment with more wolf packs. It looked like John Cromwell might finally get his chance to make a war patrol.

In the summer of that year, Cromwell was able to visit his family in California. For his son, Jack, seeing him off to a seaplane at Treasure Island made an indelible impression. Like families anywhere who are seeing a relative off at an airport or train station, the Cromwells were understandably anxious, more so because John was going back to a war zone. His wife, Margaret, probably hoped that his promotion to captain would keep him away from the fighting, though she knew it was possible he might make a patrol—or even several—in a submarine. Given the prohibition against talking about operational details, especially in the Silent Service, he probably wouldn't have been able to tell her much, at least not in any detail. It would only have worried her anyway. Once he got to Pearl he could get around the censors through Izzy Holmes, who could send things along. Some officers went to great lengths to put their wives back home at ease, even writing weeks and weeks of letters in advance, and having a trusted friend post them during the weeks they were out on patrol.

As the Cromwell family waited on the ramp next to the seaplane, Admiral Nimitz strolled out to the terminal. He'd been in San Francisco on some business and said hello to Cromwell by name. For a Navy family, this was like being on a first-name basis with Clark Gable, a fact that the characteristically unpretentious John Cromwell would probably never have mentioned. His son was filled with pride for his dad, and for the opportunity to meet the famous Admiral Nimitz.

Eventually, the departure time came. Cromwell Sr. got on the plane with Nimitz and other officers bound for Pearl. His family waved good-bye to their father and husband. For the rest of his life, John Jr. would remember the roar of the plane's engines, how it taxied away from the pier, picked up speed, and lifted off, disappearing over the Golden Gate bridge.

# 10

# *Squalus*

*Sculpin*'s sixth patrol to the island fortress of Truk came without the benefit of Lockwood's improved torpedoes, but it mattered little. Although coral formations around the island created channels for incoming and outgoing ships, there were too many openings and the Japanese seemingly used them all. Chappell patrolled somewhat far from the island in the hope that he might be able to close on at least one of the ships or convoys, but he was unable to do so and had a disappointing patrol before taking the boat to Hawaii.

Before their final departure from Australia, the men took full advantage of everything Brisbane had to offer. Having gone on five patrols already, a certain fatalism set in among some of the sailors who had been in the war from the beginning. Judging by friends who had gone on patrol and never returned, they figured that you could probably rely on completing about five patrols, but beyond that your chances of surviving seemed to decline rapidly. Being young and mostly unmarried, they spent money and drank like, well, sailors on liberty.

First there was a question of booze. When the sailors finished drinking everything in Fremantle, Brisbane, and some of the smaller towns set up for R&R, some crews resorted to Prohibition-era solutions by making wine out of Welch's grape juice. When fermentation didn't finish before they went back on patrol, they sometimes brought the stuff onto the boat. Another solution was the ethanol alcohol fuel for the torpedoes, also known as torpedo juice or pink lady. It contained a noxious castor oil–like substance with powerful purgative effects. Naturally being tinkerers, some submariners set up stills in their hotel bathtubs to purify the alcohol, and on at least a couple of occasions the stills threatened to explode.

Since most of the men of fighting age had left Brisbane, there was no shortage of women. Love is unpredictable at any time, but in the context of war it often leads to wild, improbable romances. These were anything but "good old days," and caught up in the events so far beyond their control—a worldwide conflagration of such proportion it would make anyone feel small— the young men and women living through them sought comfort wherever they could despite, or perhaps because of, the mutability of their lives. Several men on the *Sculpin* made proposals to Australian women. As Mendenhall remarked, he thought some of the proposals might even be in earnest. Gunner's Mate Bob Wyatt, whom they nicknamed "Wyatt Earp," was a young rascal who upheld the finest traditions of the Navy. His first order of business in Brisbane was to go to the drugstore to buy several engagement rings. Since having multiple fiancées is not technically bigamy, he had little to fear but outraged fathers and a trail of broken hearts. Another *Sculpin* sailor learned a novel form of prophylaxis early on in his career. An avuncular older sailor counseled him to carry a bottle of whiskey around with him wherever he went. If he got lucky, he could pour the booze over his penis to ward away a dose of the clap (gonorrhea), herpes, or syphilis. If he didn't get lucky, he could ply a girl with the whiskey in the hope that he might.

Few are aware of it these days, but during World War II, prostitution practically had its own bureau within the War Department. Millions of men went through Hawaii on their way to the war, or on their way back home. Hotel Street in Honolulu had at least a dozen brothels where military men of all stripes literally lined up on the stairs, out the door, and into the street, where they were monitored by the shore patrol and military police. Some brothels even had their own peculiar architecture for the business: a bathroom with two doors leading to separate bedrooms. The price was three bucks for three minutes, after which was a quick cleanup in the bathroom, then out the other door to another customer.

Drinking and carousing was not for everybody, however. After being trained by his division commander John Cromwell, young quartermaster Bill Cooper came on the *Sculpin*. Tongue-in-cheek, Cooper would describe himself as a Tennessee hillbilly, but he was sharp as a tack and a keen observer of everything that happened on the *Sculpin*. Cooper had fatalistic thoughts similar to those of many of the other submariners about his chances for survival, but rather than living it up, he simply accepted the likelihood that he would die in a submarine and decided to become a Christian and leave it in God's hands. Though never tempted to emulate his crewmates' bawdyhouse antics, neither could he condemn them. They were all so young, so recently separated from their boyish world of comic book heroes and baseball icons. Separated from home and everything they knew, in private moments they suffered a desperate loneliness and the real possibility of dying under horrible circumstances, far away from everyone they loved. Some of them were beginning to realize that the modern submarine warfare they were conducting was far removed from the heroic, romanticized Hollywood images they'd grown up seeing and believing. When the water closed in around a submarine for the last time, it was just pure death. If their number came up, they wanted to have enjoyed as much of life with their allotment of time, whatever that may be.

For the officers there was the additional burden of command, writing reports, and wangling whatever they could for the benefit of the boat. In their off-hours they played cards at the Officers Club with their counterparts from other subs, commiserating about lousy torpedoes, grief from their superiors, and bad news from home. For the officers of the *Sculpin* these bull sessions often included the officers of her sister ship, the *Sailfish*. They were in the same division and had been chasing each other across the Pacific, often berthing on opposite sides of the same dock. In an entry in Mendenhall's war diary, he mentions one such meeting he had with a classmate, Benjamin Jarvis, the torpedo and gunnery officer on the *Sailfish*. Jarvis had recently graduated from the sub school in New London, and as Mendenhall put it, "I helped him with some of his questions and offered solutions we had reached in *Sculpin*." Just how that would play into a future tragedy remained to be seen; at that time either man would know only of the tragedy that had bound the two ships together years earlier. The curious story of how the ships' histories had begun to intertwine included the legendary Charles "Swede" Momsen.

Momsen's involvement with the submarine force began long before he solved Lockwood's torpedo problems and became the

Pacific Fleet's first wolf pack commodore. He was haunted by the deaths of submariners, and every technical innovation he ever devised was brought about by the horrors of dying in a submarine. Momsen was the skipper of the USS *S-1* when the USS *S-51* went down off the East Coast near Block Island in 1925, and was among the first on the scene. A liner, the *City of Rome*, had accidentally rammed the *S-51* in the fog after the submarine had surfaced. When Momsen arrived there was no sign of the sub except an oil slick and telltale bubbles. He tried to communicate with the boat, but received no reply, and at that time there were no means for him to rescue the men below, or for them to do anything for themselves. Momsen waited, horrified and helpless, as time crept long past when there was any possibility of survivors. A World War I–era lightship, the USS *Falcon*, took part in the salvaging operations, and after raising the *S-51* they discovered evidence that the men had made a frantic attempt to get out as the ship sank. One of Momsen's officer friends had nearly rubbed the skin off his hands trying to open one of the hatches in a desperate attempt to get out, but at the depth that the *S-51* had plunged, the pressure of the water pressed against the hatch so hard that he would never have been able to get it open. It distressed Momsen to think of his friend's last waking moments, and he racked his brains to devise a way to save the sailors of sunken submarines.

Momsen submitted an idea to use a diving bell as a rescue chamber to the Bureau of Construction and Repair. A diving bell is a vessel with an opening on the bottom that can be lowered into the sea. As the bell gets deeper, the water pressure pushes against the air inside the bell, decreasing the volume of air inside. Divers inside the bell could increase the amount

of air inside, thereby equalizing the pressure of the surrounding sea, and pushing it back out the bottom opening. To lower
the bell, the divers allowed water to come in. To raise it to the
surface, they pushed water out by bleeding air into the bell—
much like a submarine's ballast tank. Momsen's design called for
a rubber gasket along the bottom of the diving bell to create a
seal between the bell and a smooth collar around a submarine's
escape hatch. The young Momsen foolishly followed protocol
and submitted the design to the proper channels in the Navy's
constipated bureaucracy of the time, and predictably, the Navy
did absolutely nothing with it. Oddly, the Bureau of Personnel
then transferred Momsen to the very unit charged with inves-
tigating unsolicited technological suggestions such as his diving bell rescue chamber. After sifting through his predecessor's
paperwork, he found his submission at the bottom of the pile,
untouched. Despite fervent proselytizing about his idea, it hit the
intransigent, hidebound staffies with a resounding splat. Momsen decided to let it rest, and after doing so, another submarine,
the *S-4*, went down off Cape Cod.

This time the ships above were able to confirm that there were
six survivors, as they tapped out messages against the stricken
sub's hull. For the press, in an age where the nascent titan of
radio communications was revolutionizing journalism much like
the Internet did years later, the sinking offered the irresistible
story line of survival against the odds and possible rescue. But
the Navy knew the odds, and just as with the *S-51*, time ran out
for the six unfortunate souls sealed in the iron coffin of the USS
*S-4*. Their last testament before succumbing to carbon dioxide
poisoning was the words *Please hurry.*

The terrible spectacle caught the Navy off guard. Each

submarine sinking was becoming a national sensation that led to questions about the advisability of even having submarines in the U.S. Navy. Momsen went back to the drawing board, and once at his new billet, the Submarine Safety Test Unit, he conceived an ingenious device that the press would come to call the "Momsen lung." It would revolutionize submarine safety and become standard equipment not only in U.S. submarines but in submarine navies throughout the world.

The lung was a breathing apparatus with a mouthpiece leading to a tube with two valves. Exhaling opened one valve to admit the air into a rubber chamber that resembled a hot-water bottle. The chamber contained soda lime, a substance that scrubbed the exhaled air of $CO_2$. When the diver inhaled, another valve opened, admitting the scrubbed air back into the diver's lungs. Charged with an initial amount of oxygen, the device would keep a submariner breathing and alive long enough to ascend to the surface. But great depths had physiological effects that Momsen had to take into account in order for submariners to escape safely.

At greater depths, water pressure will push against a volume of air; conversely, when that same amount of air reaches shallower depths and correspondingly lower water pressure, the same amount of air expands. For example, if you take a deep breath of pressurized air at a depth of 200 feet, then move to the surface, that breath of air at the surface could expand to be two breathfuls, causing the lungs to become overextended. Men holding a single breath of pressurized air at a mere depth of eighteen feet have died on the surface. So Momsen introduced another valve in the Momsen lung that would let excess air pressure out of the lung as the diver ascended, thus avoiding the possibility of bursting lungs and pulmonary embolisms.

A similar principle was at work inside the divers' bodies in an excruciating phenomenon known as the bends. The lungs introduce tiny air molecules into the bloodstream by forcing them into solution, much like carbon dioxide bubbles under pressure in a bottle of soda pop. Oxygen and nitrogen molecules—the main components of ordinary air—are everywhere in the body's tissues, but when a diver's body is submerged in deep water, the gas molecules in the tissues are under pressure. If a diver surfaces too fast, the pressure keeping them that size suddenly leaves, and the molecules come out of solution. The effect is like taking the cap off the soda bottle, and the gas molecules in the body tissues now effervesce. Unable to absorb the volume of bubbles, the body fills with gas that can't escape, and in extreme cases turns into a horrible, bloated, fizzing balloon. Unless a diver can be quickly repressurized in a barometric pressure chamber, they suffer a sudden, painful death as blood vessels burst all over the body but especially in the brain, heart, and lungs. Momsen had heard of divers surfacing too quickly and bloating at the surface, and had previously chalked it up as an old sailors' tale, but on further reflection he incorporated this into his escape regime. As he tested his lung at greater depths, he rigged an escape line with markers at certain depths. The diver would have to stop at each marker for a certain amount of time to allow the body to adjust to the new depth, thus avoiding the bends.

Despite misgivings that he may have missed something crucial that could prove deadly while implementing his lung, Momsen successfully tested it on himself and others at the Sub

Safety Test Unit. And rather than going through regular channels, as he had with his rescue chamber, he decided to make an
attention-getting public test. The Navy brass was caught off
guard again, and before they could do anything about it the
press had dubbed his remarkable device the Momsen lung. The
invention did much to improve his credibility, allowing him to
finally start work on the rescue chamber, starting with experiments on the salvaged *S-4*, the same submarine that had killed
its previous crew. Momsen worked with Allan McCann on the
final design before being transferred yet again, and when the
Navy unveiled the finished project as the McCann rescue chamber, regular Navymen widely acknowledged that Momsen had
gotten the short end of the stick. It was a reprimand for embarrassing them with his innovative Momsen lung. Nevertheless, by
hook or by crook, Momsen had gotten the rescue chamber built,
and it would get its first tragic test a few years later when the
*Sculpin*'s sister ship, the uss *Squalus*, went down.


For the men of the Silent Service, the *Squalus* disaster was the
first glimpse of what it might be like to dive for the last time.
At half past eight on the morning of May 23, 1939, the *Squalus* began a normal test dive in preparation for formal trials and
induction into the fleet. The captain, Oliver Naquin, was trying
to shave fractions of a second off their crash dive so the boat
would qualify for service in the fleet. Before diving he called for
full speed so the boat would have momentum as it went down,
and no fewer than three people watched as every single red light
on the Christmas Tree indicator flashed to green: safe to dive.
They bled air into the boat to confirm its airtightness, flooded

the ballast and bow buoyancy tanks, and continued the dive. But as they passed fifty feet, the boat shuddered.

A shock wave of compressed air hit the men from the engine rooms forward as thousands of gallons of water flooded the engine and maneuvering rooms. The deafening cascades of water instantly flooded the after battery. The men on the control room battle phones heard frantic screams and cries through their headphones from men drowning in the near-freezing water, which was flooding the engine rooms. The watertight door to the forward engine room closed, and for one man transfixed by the sight, the glass porthole offered a vista of drowning men that would fill a lifetime of nightmares. Unable to look away, he watched as the inky water rose above the porthole until the engine room was as black and devoid of human life as the sea all around.

The after battery was also compromised, however, and he and the other men there had to retreat to the control room as the freezing water seemed to stab their skin as it rose alarmingly fast. Pipes burst throughout the boat, causing leaks that gushed like fire hoses that knocked the men down. As the men in the mess room strained against the rising water to get forward into the unflooded control room, the lights went out. They flopped around in the disorienting darkness, the water roaring in their ears, trying desperately to get to the watertight door before it closed. One, two, three came in. The boat was on an up angle, and the water accumulating in the after battery was like a lake as it started to slosh over the doorsill into the control room. Four, five men in. The man at the door started to close it when in the utter dark his eyes made out a ghostly glow straining in the water toward him. The water rose higher, spilling into the control room like water from a cup. If he waited any longer they might all die. The faint white apparition loomed closer, gasping and flailing in the water, appearing finally as the last man to escape the after battery. They could wait no longer for a man they'd left in the latrine, another sleeping on his bunk, and yet another down below in the battery compartment, to say nothing of the poor souls in the engine rooms. The man at the door strained to pull the heavy steel watertight door toward him to seal the after battery and all within, hoping against hope that he wouldn't see the face of a friend bobbing behind the glass porthole, his eyes filled with despair, accusation, eventually oblivion.

While the *Squalus* was filling with water and sinking, the diving party tried to blow the ballast and the bow buoyancy tanks, but it was no use. Saltwater came into the forward battery, shorting out circuits and beginning the process where the lead-acid batteries created chlorine gas, which would lead to an eventual explosion. One man had risked his life to throw open the old-fashioned blade-type switch as it glowed blue with an arc of dancing lightning sparks. The skipper went about the boat getting reports. Most of the men were whole, if shaken, and cold. So much air had been pushed forward by the surge of water that they were almost unable to open a tin of rockets. Naquin knew immediately that theirs now was a race against time; surely the sub base in Portsmouth would notice their absence and send someone to investigate, but if not, it would be a matter of how long their oxygen would last. He sent up the emergency telephone marker buoy, as well as a series of distress rockets in the hope that someone, perhaps a local fishing boat, might see them. He also gave orders for the men to rest, not speak, and conduct themselves with a minimum of effort, so that they could conserve the oxygen supply. They spread powdered $CO_2$ absorbent on the bunks to scrub the air, and distributed the boat's Momsen lungs. This was not only a pragmatic effort to have them ready in the event that they should have to quickly leave through the escape trunks, but also as a precaution against the possibility of chlorine gas poisoning from the batteries.

The men huddled in the dark for hours, sleeping where they could, eating canned fruit, and sending more rockets. Several hours later they heard propellers up above. They sent up another rocket to catch the boat's attention and waited by the buoy telephone. Then there was a voice on the other end—coming from their sister ship, the *Sculpin*. They were overjoyed, but the conversation was cut short, and with it their chances for survival. A seaman on the *Sculpin* had tied the rescue buoy's line to a cleat on the *Sculpin*'s teakwood deck. Since the line had no play, it snapped when the *Sculpin* rose on the swell of a wave. In light of this new development, a rescue diver wouldn't have a link leading him to the stricken *Squalus*, and would have to practically search by hand in the dark swirls of muck 250 feet below the surface.

The temperature in the *Squalus* plunged as the hull's steel rested in the icy waters. The roving columns of light emanating from their flashlights and head lanterns revealed shining brass valve fixtures, gray paint, pale wet faces, and the vapor coming from their mouths and nostrils in the chill air. Up above, the *Sculpin* had leaned a spare anchor from its chain locker to act as a grapnel. A tugboat dragged the anchor back and forth along the seafloor, trawling for the *Squalus*, hoping to make a connection for when the divers arrived. The Navy mobilized its rescue fleet, including a steamer from the sub school at New London, Connecticut, which had a McCann rescue chamber.

As more ships churned in the water overhead, the men in the *Squalus* tried to communicate with them via Morse code by banging on the hull. The ships above could hear them, but just barely, and responded by asking questions about the state of the ship. Since their hammer blows against the hull were so faint, the men had to tap out each word as hard as they could three times. In the damp chill, this was hard work, and as the air grew more toxic with $CO_2$ they started to succumb to hypoxia. Thinned of life-sustaining oxygen, the air was beginning to give them the symptoms of a hangover. First drowsiness, then nausea, splitting headaches, weakness, and lack of coordination. Worst perhaps in this situation was the sense of detachment, muddleheadedness, and fuzzy thoughts. The men beating out messages on the hull sweated with their exertions in the cold, thin air until exhausted, when they huddled into a cold corner of the boat, shaking with chills. Naquin spread out more $CO_2$ absorbent and bled oxygen into the compartment for the first time. He didn't know how long they would be down there and wanted to pay out as little oxygen as possible. In between messages the men listened for replies from the ships above, often hearing instead the slow dripping of water into the hull. Like any submarine submerged for too long, the *Squalus*'s many valves and hull openings would leak, and the hull would fill drop by drop until the air remaining at the top of the compartments was at the same pressure as the sea around the boat. But that would occur so slowly that they would be long dead before seeing it, unless they were able to get out somehow.

Despite their grim circumstances and the increasingly narcoleptic atmosphere, the men maintained good spirits and upheld the Navy's tradition of order and discipline. Perhaps with an appreciation of the finality of over a hundred pounds of pressure pressing in on them and limited air supplies, their thoughts turned inward like men awaiting the gallows, yet they also curiously clung to hope. They speculated about what they might like to have as their next—or perhaps final—meal, and a nice steak seemed to fit the bill. Despite all this, they were still humorous young submariners with a blue streak a mile wide. One of them cracked wise and told his crewmates that he'd rather have a blonde.

Finally, early the next morning they heard stomping noises on the deck above them, as though someone were walking back and forth. It was in fact a diver, trying to attach a line to the escape hatch above the forward torpedo room. A small cheer rose—they were going to get out of here after all. Without benefit of special diving gases, it was a remarkable feat for the diver, a young man named Martin "Skee" Sibitsky. Later in the morning, Swede Momsen gave orders to the two men in the rescue chamber as they lowered the bell down to the hatch, clamped the rubber gasket down onto the collar, and made the world's first submarine rescue. After charging up the forward torpedo room with some fresh air and delivering hot coffee and sandwiches, the rescue chamber left with a handful of survivors.

When they reached the unbearably bright light of the surface and stumbled onto the deck of the USS *Falcon*, the crew of the *Squalus* realized for the first time that the entire world was watching. A flotilla of ships of various sizes—some Navy, some chartered—bobbed around the *Falcon*. Press photographers snapped pictures and churned away at old-style moving picture cameras. In a foreshadowing of the ubiquitous news chopper phenomenon, planes buzzed and circled with more reporters and photographers. Radio journalists dashed off reports on live radio while wire reporters called in or telegraphed their stories to newspapers as near as the *Squalus*'s home port of Portsmouth and as far as cables could reach around the globe.

With the first handful of rescued sailors was the roster of *Squalus* crewmen both living and dead. When the rescue was announced over live radio, the news understandably caused powerful waves of sobbing—for some of joy, for others anguish and despair. Thirty-two men were on the list of survivors, though one man was mistakenly left off for several hours, causing his wife to collapse once when she thought he'd died, and another time when she learned he had survived. Despite hoping against hope that the remaining twenty-six men aft of the control room had survived but had been unable to communicate by tapping, a fifth and final dive to the aft torpedo room confirmed their deaths. Throughout the entire ordeal, the faithful sister ship, *Sculpin*, had stood by and gained a reputation as one of the "good" ships—a billet any submariner could take with confidence.

When Navy salvagers eventually raised the *Squalus*, photographers took spectacular pictures as its bow rocketed out of the water. President Roosevelt remarked that the scene reminded him of a sailfish crashing through the surface. After refitting, the Navy recommissioned the *Squalus* as the *Sailfish*. Investigators trying to determine what had caused the catastrophe eventually traced the problem to a link that closed the main induction valve: the huge hull opening that admitted air for the engines. A burr left from the metal-casting process to manufacture the link sometimes opened the valve, even after it had been closed. It was a dangerous glitch that appeared in several of the other boats of the class, including the *Sculpin*, which the Navy found and fixed.

Despite the change in name, the *Sailfish* remained an object of curiosity, scorn, even outright hostility. It was a cursed vessel that had killed half its crew, a hard-luck boat, an evil omen. Superstitious sailors wouldn't go on it. One wag at the Portsmouth Navy Yard called the resurrected boat the *Squailfish*, and the name stuck. When strict by-the-book man Mort Mumma became the skipper, he did everything in his power to strike the former ship's history from not only his memory, but everyone else's as well. One of his stranger standing orders was to forbid its former skipper, Oliver Naquin, from ever setting foot on the boat. One day before the war, while the *Sailfish* was berthed at Pearl Harbor, the order was actually carried out, leaving a nonplussed Naquin to simply walk away down the pier.

Try as he might to obliterate any mention of the *Squalus*, suppression has a curious way of forcing unexpected feelings out of the woodwork. In the case of Mort Mumma, the memory of the ship and the awesome responsibility of being its skipper finally caught up with him on the *Sailfish*'s first war patrol. It would be a grave error, however, to call his bravery into question. As a leader of PT boats later in the war, Mumma would fly into the maw of danger several times with distinction. Mumma's nervous collapse had less to do with the pressure of the situation and everything to do with the ghost of the submarine *Squalus*.

# 11

# Rest and Recuperation

The thing that we want most of all
Why it would be ecstasy,
Give us thirty days' leave with traveling time
In the Good Old U.S.A.
   —"Dear Mr. President"
      S-Periscope, uss Sculpin shipboard newsletter
      December 1942

When the Sculpin came back to Hawaii after its sixth patrol, the captain and crew got the news they'd all been waiting for since the beginning of the war: They would be going to San Francisco for a major refit that would take enough time to allow them to return to their hometowns and visit their families. Turnover in the crew had brought in new faces, but for more than forty sailors it had been nearly two years since they'd been stateside, let alone at home. Bethlehem Steel would conduct its first submarine refit of uss Sculpin at Hunter's Point, while the men fanned out across the country in search of family, friends, and lovers. Like nearly every other military unit at the time they were a mixed lot. They hailed from all across the United States, from the hill country of Tennessee and small towns in Texas, to New York City and the suburbs of Chicago. They were the sons of admirals and immigrants, members of the upper crust, and the recipients of Depression-era soup kitchen hospitality.

Corwin Mendenhall got married and honeymooned at this time, and Lu Chappell likely visited his wife, Marion; their son, Lucius Jr., and daughter, Mickey, were away at boarding school. For the skipper and his family the separation had gone on far too long, the duties of his command straining tenuous ties drawn tight by the dangerous nature of his duty. The wartime censorship of letters did nothing to help the situation in that he could write little more than that he was doing well. Marion did clerical work at local shipyards and continued to act as an organizing figure among the wives of the other officers, but under the pressure she became increasingly ill, overwrought, and morose.

The exec, Charlie Henderson, left the *Sculpin* for "new construction." He would go back east to commission the new submarine USS *Bluefish*, bring it back to the Pacific theater, and conduct war patrols. In his stead they got Al Bontier, a redheaded lieutenant from Missouri who was described as being quick-witted, and seemed to be on the short list for command of his own boat. Jack Turner, the engineering officer, also left to become the exec of the USS *Ray*, while George Brown took his place. Brown was a compact young man from New York who in the future would give Park Avenue as his address. He'd attended Yale University and loved to bet on just about anything with Mendy, particularly about who sighted more targets while on watch. Despite what appears to have been a rather privileged upbringing, he'd trained as a diesel specialist and on first sight of his new boat rolled up his sleeves and got down to business with the black gang as they cleaned oil filters, replaced cylinder liners, and performed other messy machine maintenance. Since everybody of that era had to have a nickname, he drew his—Sammy Glickstein—from the protagonist Samuel Glick of the popular novel *What Makes Sammy Run?*

As "George," or the most junior officer on board, they got the enthusiastic young Joe Defrees. His father was Admiral "Rollie" Defrees, a friend of Admiral Lockwood. Joe also had a special relationship with the boat in that his mother had christened the *Sculpin* when it was first launched in 1938.

George "Moon" Rocek, a tall young motor machinist's mate who had been on all six previous war patrols, took a train back to his hometown of Cicero, Illinois. He'd grown some since he'd joined the Navy three years ago, and like many submariners he now sported a beard. When he got into town, his first visit was his father's tailoring shop. He said merely, "Hi," but his appearance had changed so much from the boy he'd once been that his father didn't recognize him at first. "It's me, George!" he said. His father's eyes flashed with recognition, then with tears.

His brother had coincidentally come back from service in the Marines, and the local hometown paper made a big deal of their return with a prominent story and photographs of the young Roceks, who appeared awkward and unaccustomed to such attention. Walking up and down the streets of his hometown brought back memories, though the war years had changed the place substantially. There were U.S. War Bond advertisements and war propaganda posters everywhere. The economy had picked up because of war-related industries, but that didn't mean a new coat of paint on most people's houses. The government had rationed nearly everything for the war effort, so now in addition to money you needed coupons to buy staples like butter, milk, eggs, and flour.

Rocek likely walked past the lamppost where he'd gotten his nickname, "Moon." As a kid, he hung out with a crowd of neighborhood kids who resembled those in the popular Hollywood film shorts *Our Gang*. Rocek had gotten a particularly close summertime haircut, and under the light of the lamppost one summer night, one of the kids remarked that his head glowed like the moon. Rocek was able to shake the nickname when he got into the Navy, but after receiving another close haircut on the *Sculpin* during the "crossing the line" ceremonies, one of the shipmates made the same observation and the childhood nickname stuck for life.

Even though the *Sculpin*'s refit took much longer than expected, the leave time ended all too soon and the men found themselves in barracks near the dock. Some had detached for service in other subs or new construction, and new hands came in. The boat had quite a few alterations. They cut down the conning tower so that it would cast a smaller silhouette when running on the surface, moved the 3-inch deck gun forward of the conning tower, and added two machine gun supports onto the conning tower. They'd also added Kleinschmidt desalination stills, which would allow them to produce enough freshwater to have the occasional shower. The most important addition was something called SJ radar. Whereas the old SD-type radar could sense planes a few miles out it was neither directional nor terribly accurate. The new SJ radar could pinpoint ranges and bearings of ships, and most important it could "see" ships up to fifteen miles out in daylight and night, under any weather conditions.

It would allow them to accurately obtain and track targets long before a lookout could see them, and also find navigational fixes like mountains and islands to confirm the sub's position.

After reaching Hawaii, the *Sculpin* initiated new crewmembers with practice drills directed by their division commander, John Cromwell. They also got a final crewmember, Lieutenant I. J. "Pete" Galantin as a PCO, or prospective commanding officer.* The Navy sent out PCOs on active war patrols so they could gain experience from seasoned skippers, and though he would stand watch and perform other functions, Galantin was not in the line of command. After Cromwell was satisfied that the *Sculpin* was ready for duty, Admiral Lockwood sent orders for the *Sculpin* to patrol Area 3, the so-called Empire Waters directly off the coast of Japan. Area 3 bristled with mines, anti-submarine escorts of all descriptions, Q-ships to lure unwary sub skippers, and land-based air patrols. There were also rumors that the Japanese were now using radar as well.

Just a few days out from a refueling stop at Midway Island, Frank Alvis, the communications officer, was decoding radio messages from Pearl when he came across a message heading containing the word ULTRA. There was a certain protocol for such messages: They were to be decrypted on the top secret ECM, then further decoded only by the skipper, who used a onetime strip cipher to derive the ULTRA message. Lu Chappell went to his quarters with the message. By now the men on the boat had taken notice of these unusual events. Chief of the boat Weldon "Dinty" Moore, also known as "Magic Eyes" for

---

*Galantin later headed the Polaris missile program and rose to the rank of full admiral.

his sharp vision on deck watches, was usually first among the enlisted men to know if something was afoot. Although the chief was not an officer, as one of the most experienced submariners on the boat and ombudsman for the enlisted men, he wielded a great deal of influence. Some chiefs were more than qualified for command, and in a few instances became skippers. George Rocek would come to call Moore an "express man," because he often knew what was happening even before the officers—even back at Pearl.

Fifteen minutes after going into his quarters, Chappell showed the orders to the exec, Al Bontier, and burned the paper cipher strips. Stepping into the control room, he ordered a change of course and speed, and started to look at charts on the plotting table. They would be gunning at top speed to get into position somewhere, presumably for a rendezvous. All around the control room the men exchanged glances and wondered what could be so important. A few hours later, the radarman detected a ship at about 4,000 yards; one of the lookouts caught a glimpse of the ship at the same time, flashing a light in the gloom of the night. Uncharacteristically, Chappell continued, not even stopping to check to see whether the small ship might develop into a convoy. This happened again at half past six in the morning, but Chappell ran the *Sculpin* on the surface well past dawn. They spotted another ship at ten in the morning, but maintained their course. After tracking it for half an hour, they submerged and continued along the path to their rendezvous.

All seemed quiet the next day when they were apparently where they were supposed to be, about 300 miles southeast of Tokyo harbor. But Chappell raised the boat in broad daylight twice to get a fix on the sun for navigation, and surfaced for good at about half past eight in the evening. They patrolled back and forth along an eight-mile line in anticipation of their meeting, which came so quickly at midnight that they hardly had a chance to react. On first sight, Lieutenant Galantin's knees were knocking so hard he could hardly stand up.

In seas so calm that a pebble would make ripples for miles, what appeared to be three mountains glided silently along the horizon. They were two aircraft carriers—one of which was probably the *Hiyo*, as well as a cruiser. George Brown had the watch and immediately called the skipper to the deck. The radarman detected the ships at just about the same time and gave the range as 11,500 yards on a bearing of 190 degrees true. Chappell sounded general quarters while peering through his binoculars at the massive ships. Mendy was getting the bearings and ranges to put into the TDC so they could determine a course change. Chappell asked Mendy for the ships' speed and the approach bearing they should take to get as close as possible for a good shot.

"Twenty-two knots, sir, two-four-two degrees."

"Come to course two-four-two. All ahead flank."

"Coming to course two-four-two, sir. All ahead flank, sir."

"Make ready the tubes. We'll fire four from the bow and turn around for another four."

The carriers were clipping along so fast, and they were so far away, that within minutes the *Sculpin* was soon as close as it could come to them before the range would start to widen. They were 7,000 yards away, and if they fired torpedoes now, the torpedo track would be a full 7,850 yards. It was a long shot, but Chappell decided that even a long shot at targets this important was worth the effort.

"Set torpedo speed to slow."

"Torpedo speed set to slow, sir."

"Take a final bearing."

Mendy called over the battle phones: "Set!"

"Fire one!"

Quartermaster Billy Cooper clicked a stopwatch as the surge of air punched the torpedo out of the boat and started up its motor. Twelve seconds later, Chappell called out again, "Fire two!" then, "Fire three!"

No sooner were the words out of his mouth than there was a massive explosion nearby. One of the torpedoes—probably the first—had prematured. Everyone slumped. How could this be? Surely the lookouts on the carriers had heard and seen the massive explosion. Chappell fired the fourth and final torpedo, then changed course for a stern shot. The men on the deck watched impassively, muttering profane Rosaries of malediction to high heaven against the Bureau of Ordnance as they waited to see the inevitably poor results. After several minutes they heard explosions and watched as the carriers, untouched, flashed blinker signals back and forth as they pulled farther and farther away from the *Sculpin*. They were now so far away that Chappell decided not to try the stern shot, and he wheeled around once more to give chase. But they'd likely picked up speed and, within minutes, they slid away into the inky night. Soon the radar could no longer make them out.

Hoping that the distant explosions had been a torpedo hit, Chappell followed the carriers in case there was a cripple waiting to be sunk, but nothing developed, and he could only conclude that he may have hit one and caused some damage. They would learn later from ULTRA radio decrypts at Pearl Harbor that they had not even accomplished that. Chappell transmitted a message, while the carriers went along their path. One of the carriers was the *Hiyo*, and the next day it would meet the USS *Trigger*'s underwhelming torpedo attack, leading to Nimitz's order to deactivate the magnetic exploders.

Chappell sent out a disappointing contact report and chugged north to their original patrol area off the northeast coast of Japan's main island of Honshu. As they made their way north, the temperature gradually became cooler. The waters and weather in this area were peculiar, especially for a submarine. Warm water currents flowing up from the south mixed here with cold water currents coming down from the north. Rather than mixing into a happy median temperature, there were interlocking fingers of cold and warm water layers. The varying densities of the intermingling waters made for turbulence, and the *Sculpin*'s diving crew struggled to maintain control, especially at periscope depth. Another phenomenon was that the varying layers created a sort of underwater muffler; the sound waves bounced around and dissipated in the confused water. This would be useful when trying to evade a pinging escort, but a disadvantage to getting a sound bearing on ships up above. The weird water also created strange unsettling fog patterns, where visibility ranged from zero to 5,000 yards over the course of a few seconds. When they got to the patrol area, the temperature had plunged to the mid-40s and the air was moist. Running around on the surface was like traveling through clouds. Since it was so cold they couldn't run the air-conditioners, and the moist air created condensation on the electrical parts. Soon the radar set—their best hope of peering through the weird, cloudy gloom—began to short out. However, neither Chappell nor other skippers liked to use the radar too much when they were this close to enemy shores; the radarman could sense "radar interference" when the Japanese were using their own radar, which could give away the *Sculpin's* location.

They patrolled for a few days, occasionally sighting small fishing boats and sampans. They also frequently heard depth charges or other underwater explosions, but without seeing any ships. Chappell suspected that freighters and cargo ships were crawling up and down the coast near the shore, well beyond the hundred fathom line: 600 feet. Chappell couldn't cross that line; in the event that the sub sank in salvageable waters, the Japanese might discover codebooks and technology such as their ECM encryption/decryption machine.

One night at dusk about twelve miles northeast of Kinkasan Island, a promontory they'd been using for navigational fixes, Joe Defrees spotted a medium-size transport and four smaller ships: a tanker, two cargo ships, and an escort. They were crawling up the coast near the shoreline, and Chappell inched in as close as he dared while Galantin watched closely. Mendenhall was tracking the convoy at a speed of 10 knots and a range of 9,000 yards. Chappell had plenty of time to set up before they neared. "Battle stations, torpedo," he ordered. "Make ready tubes five through eight"—the stern tubes.

The men repeated his orders and brought the boat around as Chappell gave bearings and ranges from the periscope. Pete Galantin and Al Bontier took turns looking through the scope, wheeling around the conning tower like a cat swishing its tail as they looked for planes or other escorts, before focusing again on the transport, taking a reading, and dipping the attack scope down again. When the torpedomen in the after torpedo room had loaded the fish and Mendenhall had a solution, Chappell came back up with the periscope and started firing.

"Fire five!"

The fire controlman pushed the plunger; the ship shuddered, and the men's ears popped as a huge swoosh of high-pressure air entered the boat.

"Five's away, sir."

The quartermaster Bill Cooper clicked his stopwatch.

The soundman reported: "Torpedo running hot, straight, and—"

Once again, the first torpedo exploded after traveling only about one boat length. The boat shook violently, catching some men off guard as they struggled to stay upright. Dinner plates in the mess jolted free and fell onto the deck, breaking noisily.

"Goddamn it! Another premature!" said Chappell. The men were stunned. It was absolutely quiet throughout the entire boat. Though the skipper was still peering through the periscope, the crew didn't dare sneak glances at one another but stared solemnly at the switches and gauges at their stations. They'd never, ever heard the skipper like this. *"FIRE SIX! FIRE SEVEN! FIRE EIGHT!"* he yelled, watching as the torpedoes went along their way. "Full speed! Hard-a-port! Make ready tubes one through four!" Chappell was coming around for a bow shot.

The men on the transport had seen the torpedo explode and were running around on the deck. The ship started to turn toward the *Sculpin*—the officer in the wheelhouse was watching the torpedo wakes make their way toward his ship, and he was trying to run up between the torpedoes before they hit. The other ships in the convoy turned toward the shore as the escort made a beeline for the transport. Chappell saw one of the torpedoes explode slightly forward of the middle of the transport, but no one heard it due to the strange thermal layers.

Still monitoring the stopwatch, Bill Cooper reported, "They should have got there by now, Captain."

The escort—a little antisubmarine patrol craft—had changed course again, this time toward the *Sculpin*—and was only about 500 yards away.

"Take her down!" Chappell ordered. "Two-five-oh feet."

*Tiktik bang! Tiktik bang!*

"Two-five-oh feet, aye aye, sir."

*Tiktik BANG!*

"Passing one-oh-oh feet, sir."

*Tik BANG!*

"One-five-oh feet."

*Tiktik bang!*

They waited in the depths for more depth charges, but the first five turned out to be the last five, and though unnerving, after twenty-five minutes Chappell was back at periscope depth, making observations. Unfortunately, the convoy had been able to slip away while the *Sculpin* evaded the escort.

The faulty torpedoes nagged at Chappell. The torpedo shops had tried to finesse the magnetic warheads so that they were more sensitive; now they seemed to him too sensitive, exploding just after they armed. They were demoralizing, and he'd have liked nothing better than to deactivate the magnetic influence warheads. Some of the skippers were doing that already, but the staffies had grown wise and started painting over the screws to indicate whether the torpedomen were tampering with their beloved design. Not to be outdone, the devious skippers countered by sending out their torpedomen to shake down the torpedo shops for the different colors of paint so they could cover their tracks. All against orders of course.

The weather continued foggy with occasional patches of visibility out to 5,000 feet. The radarman got interference on his set from Honshu, indicating that the Japanese were also using radar; *Sculpin* would have to use their radar sparingly so close to the enemy lest they give their position away. The soundman also picked up the ghostly sounds of screws out in the distance, but since the water was troubled they were unable to get a good fix on what was out there in the billowing, cloudlike fog.

Chappell decided to take a few days to make an exhaustive review of their remaining torpedoes. During that time they ran into several fishing boats and picket vessels too small for their torpedoes, and Chappell chose to surface and attack one with a nighttime gun action. Joe Defrees went up with his gun crew and readied the 3-inch deck gun as well as the two machine guns. Crewmen passed shells from a watertight locker to the breech on the gun as it blasted away at the hapless vessel, the gunpowder's smoky vinegar smell lingering in their nostrils and at the backs of their throats. The gunnies got a solid hit on the fourth shell and continued the volley for half an hour, eventually shooting the machine guns at the burning wreck. Satisfied that at least their deck gun worked if their torpedoes didn't, they left the sinking sampan and submerged at daybreak.

Sinking the sampan up close and personal seemed to buck up the crew a bit. While submerged the next day, they saw another, smaller, wooden sampan that was bristling with radio antennae. Clearly this was a picket boat used to report on subs like the *Sculpin* rather than an innocuous fishing boat. Chappell decided to play the pirate once again, this time during broad daylight, and he called his men in again for deck gun action.

Chappell surfaced the *Sculpin* in the midst of a huge cloud of fog and closed on their target. The men on the rickety wooden sampan saw the terrible, silent apparition looming out of the fog bank, the deck gun leveled on them. Within minutes the ship was ablaze and sinking. The *Sculpin* drew up with a boarding party consisting of Lieutenants George Brown and Joe Defrees, and three enlisted men. As they drew near, they saw men bobbing in the water, hiding behind the boat, clutching the floating wood debris. George Brown boarded first, followed by the three enlisted men. Other enlisted men started shooting at the sailors in the water. Joe Defrees misstepped on his way over the gunwale of the sampan and landed in the water. The bullets were flying now and he bobbed up, yelling, "Don't shoot me! Don't shoot me!" Corwin Mendenhall ordered the men to stop shooting at the sailors, while Pete Galantin stared in horror at the mess of blood, mangled limbs, and sightless eyes of two Japanese sailors sprawled on the deck:

> How different, how personal was war when the target was flesh and blood instead of steel. The stained water sloshing over their firm flesh, tiny purple craters erupting where machine gun bullets had swiftly ended their involvement in a war not of their making. I recall thinking how firm and strong their bodies were, even though they ate mainly fish and rice.

Brown and the other men were able to get a few documents and charts of some possible intelligence value, as well as a dummy wooden machine gun and a samurai sword as loot for the captain. The *S-Periscope*, the *Sculpin's* unofficial newsletter, heralded Brown in a comic send-up of a citation for his action:

## UNIQUE ACTION AND DECORATION

For the second time in as many issues, the *S-Periscope* presents to its readers the account of singular action, which was rewarded by an original citation and decoration. A complete survey of Navy files indicates that this was the first award of its kind ever given. This unusual citation is listed below:

Special award of the Leather Heart to Lieutenant G. Estabrook Samuel Glickstein Brown, Jr., USNR: Wounded in Action.

On June 19, 1943, Lieutenant Brown was scratched behind the left ear when he gallantly attacked, single-handed, and captured one Japanese superfine Wooden machine Gun from the bow of the *Miyashio Maru*. Lieutenant Brown was conspicuous in his dauntless attack and easily overcame the resistance of no less than ten enemy fishing lines. During the fray he stumbled and fell. One of the bamboo poles, seeing the opening, treacherously attacked, wounding behind the left ear. He calmly continued his mission in spite of blinding pain and unceasing agony.

For such outstanding and courageous action Lieutenant Brown is awarded the Leather Heart. This medal is authorized to be worn while in the head, the ribbon of golden (baby) brown to be worn on sleeping attire.

Less amused was the captain. The carnage—and some of the men's reaction to it—distressed Chappell. At heart he was a bookworm, a Southern gentleman, and a gentle soul. He regretted the attack, and years later sought to return the sword to its owner's family. Although Chappell would never conduct gun action again, the men of the *Sculpin* would see carnage like that again under different circumstances.

They continued the patrol, popping in and out of the weird fog banks. Sometimes they could see their only navigational aid, the peak of Mt. Kinkasan, poking up through the dense fog layer. While submerged and tracking a destroyer that was appearing and disappearing in the fog one day, head navigator and exec Al Bontier asked the skipper to confirm their position by sighting Kinkasan. "Captain, we sure could use a fix. Could you give me a cut on Kinkasan or anything else? I think it will bear about three-zero-zero."

"Up periscope."

Chappell grabbed the periscope ears and swung the scope around and back again, peering through the fog. "Oh, yes; here it is. Stand by for a mark." He paused, his back clearly tensing as the knuckles on his hands clamped hard on the handles. "Mark the bearing! It's a ship—trying to ram us—take her deep! All ahead full! Flood negative!"

George Brown eased the *Sculpin's* nose down as fast as he could without dangling her rear end in the air. Pete Galantin stole a look through the periscope before they went under: The Japanese ship was so close, perhaps ten feet away, he could clearly read the Plimsoll line markers on its side. "Those rivets looked like dinner plates," Chappell told the crew. Neither the crew nor the soundman heard the ship coming because of the weird thermals masking its approach. When the soundman finally located the freighter, it was practically on top of them, then its sound strangely died out again at perhaps 200 yards. Fortunately they were able to get down fast enough to avoid being sliced in half by the ship.

When a few minutes had passed they came back up to periscope depth and played cat-and-mouse with two antisubmarine patrol boats that sporadically pinged them. The soundman reported that the ships up above were getting contacts, but the confused waters masked the *Sculpin's* location, and the Japanese were never able to locate them precisely. Chappell made two more attacks during the patrol, and even went against orders by deactivating the magnetic warheads, but was still unable to get hits with the remaining torpedoes. When he got back to Pearl, he was reminded that he had "greatly exceeded authority" in doing that, but his timing was fortunate. The day after he gave the order to use the contact detonators, Nimitz had given the same orders for the entire Pacific Fleet, and none of the commanding officers saw fit to chastise him in their endorsements.

After eluding the *Sculpin's* torpedoes on this war patrol, the Japanese aircraft carrier *Hiyo* also averted disastrous consequences when the skipper of the submarine USS *Trigger* fired a full salvo of torpedoes, resulting in four direct hits. When the code breakers confirmed that the Japanese acknowledged the hits in a radio broadcast—and the fact that only one torpedo detonated properly—Admiral Nimitz called a meeting with Admiral Lockwood to determine what to do. Despite the overwhelming evidence that the magnetic exploders were an abysmal failure, many in the submarine command stupidly refused to acknowledge the fact. Neither Admiral Withers nor Admiral Bob English, Lockwood's predecessors as ComSubPac, had seen fit to test the torpedoes for effectiveness. When division commander George "Turkey Neck" Crawford gave an order for the boats in his division to deactivate the magnetic exploders, Withers went so far as to berate Crawford, saying, "You tell those skippers to use the magnetic exploder. I *know* it works. I was at Newport when it was tested. I don't want to hear any more discussion about it. If I hear one more word from you on the subject, I'm going to send you to general service."

Many of the staffies under the Withers and English administrations—most of whom had never seen a shot fired in anger—were also peevish and often wrote excoriating endorsements on the skippers' war patrol reports. This did nothing to improve morale, and led one skipper to write a poem called "Squat Div One":

> They're on their duff from morn till nite;
> They're never wrong, they're always right;
> To hear them talk they're in the fight—
> Oh, yeah?
>
> A boat comes in off a patrol,
> The skipper tallies up his toll
> And writes it up for all concerned.
> He feels right proud of the job he's done,
> But the staffies say he shoulda used his gun!
> Three fish for a ship of two score ton?

Outrageous! He should have used but one!
A tanker sunk in smoke and flame—
But still he's open wide to blame.
His fish were set for twenty right—
That proves he didn't want to fight!
Oh, yeah?

The freighter he sunk settled by the stern—
With depth set right she'd split in two!
So tell me, what is the skipper to do?
He's on the spot and doing his best,
But that's not enough by the acid test.
The staff must analyze his case
And pick it apart to save their face.
Just because you sink some ships
Doesn't mean you win the chips—
You've got to do it according to Plan;
Otherwise you're on the pan!

So here's to the staff with work so tough
In writing their endorsement guff—
Whether the war is lost or won
Depends entirely on "Squat Div One."
Oh, yeah?

Bob English, the ComSubPac at the time, flew into a rage and went on a witch hunt for the scribe of this "subversive literature." When skipper Art "Otts" Taylor was confronted as the author, it took quite a bit of diplomacy on the part of his immediate superior to talk English away from serious disciplinary action.

It was a stroke of good fortune that the division commander, Captain Clifford Roper, was able to prevail upon Admiral English, because Taylor's next patrol was good enough to earn him a second Navy Cross.

Regrettably, none of this did anything to solve the torpedo problem. When Charlie Lockwood became ComSubPac, the entries in his wartime diaries about torpedo performance read like the doleful chronicle of a nagging, persistent toothache. At the conference, both Nimitz and Lockwood rued the potential sinking of the *Hiyo* and the risks skipper Roy Benson and the crew of the *Trigger* took in executing a near-perfect torpedo attack. Nimitz was originally a submariner himself, and had taken command at Pearl Harbor by hoisting his flag on the deck of submarine USS *Grayling* because most of the vessels suitable as flagships were lying on the bottom of the harbor. As a solution to their problems, Nimitz suggested that they deactivate the magnetic detonator. According to Layton, Lockwood said, "I can't order that, but I wish that you would."

"I can and will," said Nimitz.

The order was a slap in the face to the Navy bureaucracy that had championed the magnetic detonator ad absurdum. The initial results from the contact exploders seemed to confirm that Nimitz's order was the right decision. But less than a month later, there was another wrinkle.

Jasper Holmes continued to pass on hot tips to the submarine command through the secret telephone. By mid-1943, Hypo had become so adept at cracking the Japanese codes that the American submarines seemed to have them before their intended recipients. Since the port directors were broadcasting the convoys' precise scheduled noontime positions for each day's transit, it was a relatively simple matter to divert a submarine going to or from its patrol area to intercept a convoy. Some skippers became so dependent on these tip-offs that they actually complained when a convoy was a half hour late. Holmes generally contacted Dick Voge when he had hot dope, but when Voge wasn't in, Holmes's old friend of the family, John Cromwell, or "Uncle Jack" to Holmes's son, Eric, often answered on the other end of the line.

Holmes served up the massive, 19,000-ton cargo ship *Tonan Maru III* to the sub command, which in turn assigned Dan Daspit, commanding the uss *Tinosa*. On July 24, he spotted the heavily laden former whaling ship and was able to fire four torpedoes. He observed two hits, but they didn't seem to faze the *Tonan Maru* in the slightest. The big ship turned away while Daspit hastily fired another salvo, this time stopping the ship dead in the water. Since there were no escorts and the ship wasn't particularly well armed, over the next hour and a half he coolly and methodically circled around the dead duck and proceeded to fire one torpedo after another at close range, making observations of each hit on the stationary target.

Amazingly, none of the nine subsequent torpedoes succeeded in detonating when they hit the ship. One even glanced off the side, flew about a hundred feet in the air, and after splashing back down, went in a different direction. Having fired no fewer than fifteen torpedoes at this prize target to no effect, a destroyer came upon the scene, forcing Daspit to dive. He left for Pearl with the last torpedo secured for inspection. Lockwood was of course angry with the results, but also saddened. Not only had the torpedoes been running too deep, the magnetic exploders malfunctioned, and now Daspit's near-laboratory conditions demonstrated that even the contact exploder was incompetently designed, insufficiently tested, and irredeemably worthless.

Lockwood gathered a team of trusted friends, including Swede Momsen, to identify and solve this latest problem. Momsen suggested that they fire live torpedoes at a nearby cliff until they got a dud, then salvage the torpedo and study its defects. Lockwood was leery of such a dangerous enterprise, writing that, "I suspected we would find ourselves shaking hands with St. Peter when we tried to examine a dud warhead loaded with 685 pounds of TNT."* But both he and Admiral Nimitz assented to the test, which took place on August 31, 1943, and resulted in precisely what they had predicted: a dud. A boatswain's mate named John Kelly found the torpedo in fifty feet of water and attached a line to it. They carefully raised it up to the deck of a submarine rescue vessel, where Lockwood, Momsen, and others examined the warhead's detonator. The torpedo was supposed to explode when a firing pin at the tip of the nose struck an object and traveled along a guide to the detonator cap. What had happened was that during the collision with the cliff wall, the guide became deformed, and although the pin did strike the detonator cap, it didn't hit hard enough for the cap to explode and detonate the rest of the Torpex explosive. Hence, a dud. Subsequent tests with torpedoes (with the Torpex removed) dropped from a crane onto a steel plate showed that glancing blows—as opposed to perpendicular blows—had a failure rate of only 50 percent. Lockwood instructed all boats already on patrol to try for glancing blows,

---

*Actually, the explosive in the torpedoes of the day was Torpex, a combination of TNT and other additives to improve the explosive effect of the TNT.

and had technicians modify all detonators at Sub Base Pearl. Nearly two years into the war, Charlie Lockwood had finally solved the torpedo problem.


While Lockwood was fixing the torpedo problems, Chappell would conduct his eighth and final war patrol, along the China coast. The traffic they found there was mostly small sampans, fishing boats, picket boats, and escorts that didn't justify the use of torpedoes. In one surface attack on a freighter, the balky torpedoes failed yet again and the *Sculpin* had to beat a hasty retreat from the deck guns of a small escort vessel. Billy Cooper was on the deck with the skipper as the shells started to land quite close, and recalled how the unflappable skipper stood his ground, recounting a droll anecdote of the Philippines from before the war. No one remembered just what he said, because they were wiping water off their grim faces. The saltwater spray kicked up from the shells was splashing around them while Chappell spun the characteristically laconic story in his soft Georgia drawl. Chappell got a Purple Heart for taking a small bit of shrapnel in the back that day, to keep company with the two Navy Crosses he had earned on previous patrols. He left with the ship's bell, hand-sewn battle flag, and a warm send-off from a genuinely appreciative crew.

The executive officer, Al Bontier, also transferred off the *Sculpin* and like so many other submariners would eventually lose his life. As skipper of the USS *Seawolf* he was mistakenly caught by a U.S. Navy patrol plane, then depth-charged by a U.S. Navy destroyer. All hands died. Lieutenant John Allen replaced him as exec on *Sculpin*. Corwin Mendenhall also transferred off the boat for new construction as exec of the USS *Pintado*. That left George Brown as the engineering officer and Joe Defrees as torpedo and gunnery officer. The *Sculpin*'s new skipper was Lieutenant Commander Fred Connaway. As a tall, blond-haired, blue-eyed boy, he'd grown up on the banks of the Mississippi River in Helena, Arkansas, and lettered in track at the Naval Academy. After graduating in the class of 1932 he joined the surface fleet, then continued his education at the sub school at Groton and with postgraduate work back at the academy. Like Pete Galantin, he'd served aboard another submarine, the *Sunfish*, as a prospective commanding officer under skipper Dick Peterson, and the exec of the *Sunfish* would later write of his tenure there that:

> Our first patrol was unsuccessful, the second was successful; the third was unsuccessful; the fourth was successful. The one element which was notably present on the fourth patrol was Fred Connaway.... Both Peterson and Fred planned the next day's work in *Sunfish* with enthusiasm and obvious good results.

As division commander, John Cromwell trained this new group of officers and men in exercises off the waters of Hawaii, but this time with more emphasis because he would be leading a group of three ships on a wolf pack, and the *Sculpin* would be his flagship. In meetings with Admiral Lockwood, they probably agreed that, as a new skipper, Fred Connaway might benefit from Cromwell's experience. Cromwell would also have learned from Admiral Lockwood about an upcoming offensive, as well as the wolf pack's participation in it.

By late 1943, the Navy had finally built up enough ships to go on the first real offensive since Guadalcanal. The Japanese had consolidated their initial successes at the beginning of the war by building a series of island fortresses around the empire of Japan, offensive positions that would have to be neutralized before the Pacific Fleet would be able to concentrate on the ultimate goal of invading Japan's home islands. The Navy's first offensive in this new push would be called Operation Galvanic, a bid to invade the coral island atolls of Tarawa and Betio in the Gilbert Islands. Cromwell's wolf pack would be stationed farther west at the Japanese stronghold of Truk in the nearby Caroline Islands chain, where the Japanese Combined Fleet often assembled large task forces. If the Japanese staged a counterattack from Truk, Cromwell's wolf pack would be in place to attack the carriers, battleships, and cruisers as they came out of the northern channels, as well as give advance warning of their approach.  ·

As a major participant in the Combat Intelligence Center, Jasper Holmes was busy preparing reconnaissance, weather, and other intelligence reports for Galvanic. Though neither he nor Cromwell would have confided to Izzy Holmes that Cromwell was going on a war patrol, she was an extraordinarily canny woman with many years' experience as a Navy wife. Jasper couldn't dissuade Izzy from keeping a running tab on all their friends in the sub force who went on patrol; she'd often ask him, "Isn't so-and-so due back soon?" As an old family friend, she must have known what was happening when she helped John Cromwell shop for Christmas presents in downtown Honolulu for his family. Since Cromwell was likely pressed for time, Izzy also offered to wrap the presents and send them home to his family in Palo Alto in time for Christmas. With any luck he'd be back too soon for them to find out—or worry—about his impending war patrol.

Cromwell also likely received a separate, classified briefing, probably from Jasper Holmes himself, since Holmes was the Intelligence Center's liaison to the sub force at Pearl. Even though Holmes's old boss, Joe Rochefort, was stuck commanding a dry dock stateside because he had directed Hypo's decryption activities, Cromwell was embarking on an endeavor that could conceivably make him a prisoner of the Japanese and leak the same information, if in lesser detail. Holmes had briefed Cromwell countless times with hot tips for the sub force while standing watch at the sub base, hot tips with such exact details that Cromwell doubtless knew they came from decryption of Japanese codes. It's entirely likely that as a division commander he'd been officially read into the program. As such, he simply could not be taken alive; if captured they would inevitably torture him. Holmes was only too aware of the fate that befell American POWs. For many years after the war he kept in his attic a photostat of captured documents. One of them detailed surgical experiments conducted on American POWs. The polite term for the operations, if such could be applied to it, was "vivisection": The Japanese surgeons had cut out the POWs' livers to see how long it took the men to die.

# 12

## The Day of My Calamity

On the night of November 18, 1943, the *Sculpin* cruised north of the string of tiny Pacific islands consisting of Truk Atoll, looking for the reinforcements that naval intelligence had predicted would stream into the area. They'd received an ULTRA two days before, directing them to this location. The *Sculpin* had surfaced on the warm tropic waters shortly after dusk, and had charged her batteries on the surface for about five hours, when at half past midnight the radar operator acquired a target. It seemed like a convoy.

Captain Fred Connaway, Commodore John Philip Cromwell, and three lookouts were on the bridge at the time. Lieutenant Defrees clambered quickly up to the bridge. Mindful of his role as commodore, Cromwell went below so as not to fetter Connaway's command of the ship. Joe Defrees was practically unable to contain himself; all his hours of training on the Torpedo Data Computer and endless studies of the *Sculpin*'s past attacks had brought him to this point, in what would become an all-too-real battle between ships.

News about the radar contact rippled through the boat like a shiver. Bits of tantalizing information drifted in from the bridge

and the control room like windblown leaves, drifting and fluttering from man to man on whispers before a hushed gust of
excitement moved them ever deeper along the length of the boat.
Throughout the night-long chase and the ordeal that would end
it, a talker in each compartment would get play-by-play updates
on the battle phones and would relay these to the men in their
compartments when circumstances permitted. As the skipper
gave orders, as new information about the contact came in—
whether from the periscope, radar, or sonar—and as the men in
other compartments gave reports, everyone on the boat would
piece together a sense of the situation.

The lookouts scanned the horizon in the direction of the
radar contact, practically scouring the binoculars with their eyes,
looking for a mast, a smudge of coal smoke, an incongruous
motion or flash against the horizon—any sign, however subtle.
About four minutes after the radar contact, the moon loomed
at the edge of the sea to coast slowly in its course. It was a gib-
bous moon on the wane; a little more than half full, but light
enough to make darkness visible and to draw the inklings of
form between the sea and the heavens. According to Lieutenant George Brown, news drifted in from the bridge confirming
the contact: a freighter, a light cruiser, and what looked to be no
fewer than five destroyers.

Connaway gave chase, leaning on all four diesels. Defrees
went back down to update the TDC to plot the zigzag course
of the convoy with the latest bearings as they came in from the
bridge. Minutes ticked by as the plot emerged from the sum of
zigzags northwest, then northeast: a speed of 14 knots, the course
due north. Since Cromwell was coordinating the wolf pack, he
doubtless conferred with Connaway. With so many escorts,

the freighter or transport seemed to be crucial to an upcoming engagement; if not troops, it was probably carrying important cargo. According to some sources, Connaway speculated that the freighter might be a troop transport, but from Japanese documents we now know that it was a capital ship: the 5,160-ton submarine tender *Chogei*. The light cruiser was the 6,300-ton *Kashima*, and two of the escorts were the destroyers *Wakatsuki* and *Yamagumo*.

If the *Sculpin* made haste, it would be able to make a classic end-around at the periphery of the convoy for a submerged attack just as dawn broke. Cromwell evidently chose to maintain the radio silence that had begun on November 7 between the *Sculpin* and the other boats in the wolf pack until after an initial attack. He must have surmised that it would be best to maintain the element of surprise—the submarine's greatest asset—and to transmit the information about the convoy after the *Sculpin*'s presence had been revealed in the form of torpedoes and sinking Japanese ships.

The engines of the *Sculpin* hummed through the night as the ship sliced through the warm water and the main induction drew the damp tropical air through the compartments from bow to stern. Close and dank as it was, it would be some of the last fresh air the crew would breathe in the many long, desperate hours ahead. The lookouts and radar operator gave updated course and bearing information as the ship made its way past the convoy during the night-long maneuver. Shortly before 6:00 A.M., the contrast between the stars and dark night sky shifted almost imperceptibly as twilight began to illuminate the *Sculpin*'s last day on the surface. Even with her low-slung profile, the *Sculpin* would be easier to detect with each degree of the sun's rise.

The ship took its final position, in the twilight at about half past six, fifteen minutes before daybreak. The gray trumpet-shaped horns signaled the command to dive with the shrill bark of *oo-OO-gah, oo-OO-gah* as the crew cleared the bridge and sealed the hatch. The diesels shut off, the electric motors took over, and the main and exhaust induction sealed. The diving crew watched the Christmas Tree as the board lights flickered from red to green, then Lieutenant Brown, the diving officer, ordered high-pressure air into the hull to test the seals; everyone's ears popped as the pressure rose. When the boat held water he called out, "Green board! Pressure in the boat!" Connaway ordered a dive to sixty-five feet under the keel—periscope depth.

After going full-bore all night, the four massive, noisy diesel engines had now gone silent. The only sounds were the gentle hum of the electric motors, the hydraulic pumps making subtle adjustments to the planes and rudder, and the occasional release of air or water into the tanks as the diving crew adjusted the trim. With the ship now sealed off from the ocean, the tempera-ture climbed as the engines' heat radiated in waves throughout the boat, borne aloft by the air along with the odors of diesel fuel and cigarette smoke, the smell of the submariners' bodies and of fresh coffee in the galley. The humid air and cigarette smoke hung like a warm, wet film in the dim incandescence of the bare lightbulbs hanging from electrical cords. A glance in any direc-tion revealed a stark apparition of the taut, pale faces and ghostly bare bodies against a dark backdrop of the gray-painted surfaces of machines, wires, and tubes. As with cold-water pipes in the basement of a house at the height of summer, the hot air inside the submarine condensed on any portion of the boat that was cooled by the seawater and not insulated with cork—parts of the hull, the miles of pressurized tubes, the hatches. First the exposed metal hazed, then beads formed, becoming rivulets that dripped into tiny pools throughout the boat.

The skipper ordered "Up periscope" from the conning tower. The massive tube glided up from the well leading all the way down to the keel with the muffled whine of the hydraulic pump. Connaway seized on it immediately; he had only a few moments to make his observations before a sharp-eyed lookout on one of the Japanese ships might detect the periscope's telltale "feather." He took the freighter in his sights and sang out the readings for Defrees to compute on the TDC.

"Bearing...Mark! Angle on the bow...Range...Down periscope!"

Defrees plotted the bearing, speed, and range on the TDC. The attack setup was ideal. In a few minutes the skipper would raise the periscope and take the final bearings for the attack. The men in each compartment hung on every word. In the forward torpedo room, the torpedomen made ready for action.

"Up periscope," the skipper ordered.

"Up periscope, aye aye, sir," came the reply.

Connaway shifted left and right until the freighter was in the crosshairs. Inexplicably, he started shifting the periscope as he tracked the image.

"Down periscope!"

"Down periscope, aye—"

"—TAKE HER DOWN!—"

"—aye aye, sir!"

Something had gone terribly wrong; a command to take her deep at the penultimate stage of an attack could mean only one thing. The men cast furtive glances back and forth as the skipper calmly slid down the ladder to the control room. What had he seen? As diving officer, Lieutenant Brown ordered the negative tank to be flooded. The valve opened, air hissed and sizzled noisily out of the tank, too noisily for Brown's comfort. But the boat took on a steep down angle and dove quickly below the surface. Connaway said that just as he was preparing the final bearings, the convoy suddenly swung on a direct course toward the *Sculpin*, as if to ram.

By way of confirmation, the sonarman noted that the scream created by the cavitation of collapsing bubbles in the convoy's wake had increased in pitch; the convoy was picking up speed. Tense minutes went by as the convoy approached, the sound of their screws becoming ever louder throughout the boat. The men went about their business, listening intently, waiting for orders. The seasoned veterans listened for the telltale sound that depth charges make when they splash on the surface of the ocean. As the *Sculpin* went ever deeper, the bathythermograph—a device to locate cooler, denser layers of water that could mask the sub's noises and reflect sonar pinging—indicated no thermals. Under these conditions, the sonic quality of the water was as good as a telegraph indicating the precise position of the submarine. The glass-smooth sea was no comfort either; with no waves to whip up confusing background noise, the calm conditions were ideal for a destroyer looking for a submarine.

But the sounds of the screws came and went. The men heard no splash of depth charges, no pinging, and eventually, no screws. Given the extraordinary measures the Japanese were taking with this convoy, Connaway and Cromwell agreed that they should surface and try another laborious end-around, this time with the possibility of engaging under the more favorable condition of night. For the men, it was slightly disconcerting to have two men in command, like having two skippers, neither of whom they knew well.

The ship came to periscope depth and Connaway made a sweep of the area. There was by this time heavy fog on the sea that probably drifted in thick clots, but he could discern the vague outline of the convoy as it steamed away to the north. Curiously, the sound operator didn't report anything unusual.

"Down periscope," Connaway called.

"Down periscope, aye aye, sir."

"Prepare to surface." The horns rang through the boat three times. "Two engines."

"Two engines, aye aye, sir," came the word from the maneuvering room.

As quartermaster, Bill Cooper was on the ladder to the bridge, waiting for the boat to surface so he could open the hatch. Lieutenant John Allen was behind him. As the water crashed off the deck of the *Sculpin*, Cooper spun the wheel; the pressurized air rushed past him. The water ran down through the port as he flung the hatch open. He and Allen ran onto the bridge with their binoculars to scan the horizon. The fog hung all about the boat. According to Cooper, who was looking aft, "I said to Allen, 'I don't see a thing.' And he says, 'Look at this. What is that? Is it a crow's nest I'm looking at?'"

Cooper spun around to fix his binoculars on the crow's nest of the *Yamagumo*. The *Sculpin* went into an immediate emergency dive. Allen dove down the hatch, followed by Cooper, who closed it and hung on to the lanyard while Allen spun the wheel to dog the hatch. Connaway looked through the periscope as the ship dove. The destroyer had by now turned and was approaching rapidly with a bone in its teeth at a range of about 6,000 yards.

The crew assumed that the convoy had left behind a sleeper. George Brown thought that the noise from flooding the negative tank about an hour ago had given up their position. But if the *Yamagumo* had been traveling at an estimated 14 knots, it is unlikely that the *Yamagumo*'s passive sonar could detect anything through the rush of water. Connaway had surmised that the Japanese had sighted their periscope. But recent translations from the destroyer's logs tell us that the *Yamagumo*'s first indication of the *Sculpin* came at this time, when a bridge watch saw her surface on the port beam at 8,000 meters—about 8,700 yards. The logs gave no explanation as to why the *Yamagumo* was so far behind the rest of the convoy; it seems that its position was just dumb luck. But luck comes to those who are prepared for it, and the attack that the *Yamagumo* would wreak on the *Sculpin* would prove to be a textbook example of excellent seamanship on the part of Commander Ono Shirou, the captain.

The *Sculpin* took on a tremendous down angle as the ship rigged for depth charges. The sonar operator reported that the sound of the screws was making a straight line for the *Sculpin*, and fast. But his report became redundant as everyone on the boat heard and felt the loud, insistent, rhythmic *shh-shh-SHH-SHH-SHH-SHH* of the destroyer's approach. Sounds carry through the water at five times the speed of sound through the air, and though the relative loudness told the men when the destroyer came closer or went farther away, the sound hit all sides of the boat and vibrated through the hull at roughly the same time, so no one but the sonar operator with his directional baffles could tell whether the destroyer was to port or starboard, fore or aft.

The temperature in the boat began to rise. Pinpricks of sweat opened on the men's skins as their clothes became damp with perspiration. The sound of the destroyer's screws became unbelievably loud as it passed overhead; according to Edwin Keller, a signalman on his first submarine war patrol, "The screws sounded like a freight train coming through a tunnel. You could hear them coming from a long ways off. I looked around and saw [signalman] Tom Brown on his knees, blessing himself. Brown had made one patrol before, so he knew what to expect." Now the seasoned sailors like Brown heard the sound they all dreaded: depth charges splashing on the surface at thirty-second intervals.

Three splashes followed three more. They waited for the charges to drift inexorably down, listening yet to the sound of the destroyer charge away on the surface. Suddenly, the shock waves ripped up and down the length of the boat in a series of short, sharp, loud cracks that broke the glass on instruments and literally turned the cork insulation into powdery chunks that fell to the floor. With each explosion the damage became worse— the massive force of the water damaged the sea valves around the diving station.

Shortly after the last depth charge, the *Yamagumo* slowed and commenced pinging in a methodical and unnerving sonar search that would last over a half hour. The minutes ticked by as the sonar operator reported the position of the destroyer on the points of the compass. A damage report came from one of the engine rooms: An exhaust valve had developed a crack; water was gushing into the compartment. The starboard propeller shaft packing had also come loose. It was a precision-ground part with close tolerances, but now it was out of true and whined with each turn. Worse yet, water started to gush in from the damaged packing, adding to the flooding from the exhaust valve. The *Sculpin* was rapidly taking on water.

Forty minutes after laying the last depth charge, the *Yamagumo*'s sonar operator heard an echo and evidently shifted to short scale. Over the next nine minutes the *Yamagumo* turned toward the *Sculpin* to lay down another string of depth charges.

Keller recalled what he heard over the battle phone: "On the telephone, I can hear the soundman and tracking team. They would say, 'He's at 145...150...160...170...he has turned towards us...he's coming in.'

"At that point I got scared."

The crew heard the splashes of ten depth charges. The men waited in dread as the rear of the boat continued to fill with water, slowly taking her out of trim with an up angle that was at first barely noticeable, then increasingly alarming. The string of depth charges started to explode all around them at thirty-second intervals, each closer than the last: *bang, bang, BANG, BANG.* Each concussion peeled up the length of the steel hull and rocked the boat so hard the men practically expected the metal around them to splinter into thousands of shards. The ship's plates and thousands of welds groaned as they adjusted to the powerful compression and rarefaction of the water. The explosions shook the men inside like rag dolls.

Each explosion added more and more damage to the boat. *BANG*—the pipe flanges chuffed a fine mist, then started to spray high-pressure water into the boat like a water fountain. Men worked desperately to tighten the already wrench-tightened nuts and bolts keeping thousands of gallons of water out of the hull. *BANG*—the pressure gauges in the control room dipped, then popped with the tens of thousands of pounds per square inch of additional pressure. They, too, now filled with water and started to spray everywhere. *BANG*—at the diving station, Lieutenant Brown watched as "the hands of the depth gauge fell off in front of my face." Unbeknownst to the men of the *Sculpin*, the broken depth gauge would later create the most catastrophic incident to come. *BANG*—leaks sprang up forward on the starboard side as the battered engine coolers started to give, then flood. *BANG*—now the electrical system shorted, plunging the boat into the utter, terrifying darkness of the bottom of the sea. The light now absent, the other senses assaulted the men's overloaded minds: the sound of men breathing, of water dripping, of the destroyer's propellers cutting neatly through the water with maddening rhythmic insistence—*SH SH SH SH SH*. Orders from the skipper. The smell of fresh seawater and now the taste of it, dripping down their faces and onto their lips. *BANG*—the temperature rose throughout the boat to 90 degrees, then 100. The air was stale and it became difficult to breathe. Each explosion left their ears ringing. The beams of flashlights roved in jagged arcs as the electricians worked to locate the short and restore the lights. *BANG*—the hull imparted a tingling sensation to any body part that rested against it, like the "bee stings" in your hands when you hit a baseball on the odd part of a baseball bat, and the vibrations seem to travel up to your elbows. *BANG*—the split in the exhaust valve became wider, the shaft packing looser, admitting even more water into the flooding engine rooms. Now that the boat had taken a drastic up angle, the skipper had to rev the motors just to maintain depth, and the shaft leading to the propeller now howled in protest, telegraphing their position to the destroyer above.

To their credit, the men never faltered, never gave each other a sense of panic. With everything going on around them, they could not lash out at their attackers, and should the depth charges pull their minds from their moorings, what could they do? With their hearts in their throats, if the waves of panic rose and let fly the screams and curses on the tip of their tongues, the Japanese sonar operator might easily hear them. They could only sit there in mute horror and allow the situation to play out. Some men closed their eyes and said their Rosaries. Some sat in twitchy anticipation. Perhaps most deeply affected, some stared to a point far off in the distance and glazed over.

The hundreds of gallons of water aft were by now so heavy that the ship's up angle was over 13 degrees. Though the crew raced the engines to maintain depth, the *Sculpin* went to 300 feet below the surface, then continued to dive. She was barely under control. Working against the odds, the electricians were able to restore the lights. But when the crew turned on the bilge pumps and trim pumps to equalize the weight distribution, the pumps refused to take up suction and quit entirely. Connaway sent Lieutenant Brown aft to check on the situation. Before leaving the dive station, he warned Ensign Max Fielder to be careful about the depth gauge. His warning would prove prophetic.

For all the damage the boat had taken, some men were surprisingly oblivious to their precarious existence. Keller, who was sitting in the galley with the cook, saw Brown on his way aft to the engine rooms. He asked the lieutenant when they would shake the Japanese.

"We're not going to lose them," Brown said. "They have us."

This was devastating news to Keller. Perhaps all the radio serials and comic books of his youth had led him to believe that no matter what the odds, the good guys always win. And he was one of the good guys, after all. Until that moment he was doubtless too young to seriously contemplate the possibility of his imminent mortality, leastwise today, now, or in the next few minutes. He was left with the horrifying implication that today might be his day to die. But could it really be possible? As he would discover, not only was it possible, it was inevitable. If not him that day, too many of the familiar faces around him would soon be extinguished.

What Lieutenant Brown discovered aft was an absolute mess. It appeared that the bilge pumps and trim pumps had burned up. They could raise the stern of the boat by putting a bubble in the fourth main ballast tank, but Brown thought that the water sloshing around might short the main electrical leads to the motor. The only thing to do to get the water forward was to arrange the sailors into a bucket brigade. The temperature in the boat was by now 115 degrees. The men fell in line and started passing the hundreds of gallons of water down the line, one bucket at a time. The brigade started in the aft torpedo room, gingerly passed the maneuvering room with the exposed "cage" where the ominous black electrical cables conducted hundreds of amps, past the forward engine room, the galley, the after battery, the control room, all the way to the forward torpedo room. It was exhausting, backbreaking work in the hot, stale air.

Making a sweep with the sound booms, the sound operator found the unmistakable swish of rain hitting the surface of the ocean. Connaway steered the ship toward the rain in the hope that the sound, however faint, might mask their escape. The boat crept toward a depth of 400 feet—well beyond test depth and approaching crush depth, where the boat would buckle, then implode. The men in the control room played cat-and-mouse with the destroyer above, which had fallen silent. Other men bailed water forward, which improved the trim. By degrees, the boat came back under their control. There were no depth charges and since the danger seemed past, the cook started to make a meal. After about two hours, Connaway surmised that enough time had elapsed for them to come up for a look. The diving officer, Max Fielder, planed the boat up and blew air into the tanks.

Much of what happened next comes from accounts conflicted by terror, anguish, and the outrageous reversals of fortune. Keller was on the battle phones again when a panicked voice in the forward torpedo room came through the line.

"WHAT ARE WE DOING ON THE SURFACE? THE BOW IS OUT OF THE WATER!"

The damaged depth gauge that Brown had warned about had stuck somewhere along the way up. Accounts vary about what depth it indicated—some say at 125 feet, another at 170 feet—but no one looking at the broken depth gauge when the boat broached survived that day.

*"Emergency dive! All ahead full!"* Connaway ordered. If he looked for the destroyer before the *Sculpin* made its next-to-last dive, the image would have filled the scope. According to the *Yamagumo*'s logs, the sub surfaced at approximately 900 yards. Since neither the *Sculpin*'s sound operator nor anyone else in the boat heard the *Yamagumo*'s screws, the destroyer may well have been dead in the water, a most peculiar decision on the part of its captain.

Sixteen minutes later, perhaps after getting a full head of steam, the *Yamagumo* had swung around to a position over the *Sculpin* and dropped four depth charges. Six minutes after that they dropped another three on the same spot. Then they resumed pinging.

As the *Sculpin* plummeted toward the ocean floor, the depth charges exploded all around with such force that several lightbulbs simply popped to splinters. The radio transmitter ripped from the bulkhead, and the receiver was smashed beyond all repair. Worse yet, the jarring concussions severely damaged the outboard vents in both torpedo rooms, likely making the torpedo tubes inoperable. The pinging continued unabated and a few minutes later became insistent as the *Yamagumo* acquired the *Sculpin* and rushed to drop ten more depth charges. The steering mechanism now broke, and the men strained with the work of moving the rudder. The descent was so rapid that they were in danger of losing control of the boat. After going back to the diving station, Brown put a bubble in the bow buoyancy in a desperate effort to stop the free fall.

Keller sweated in the 115 degree heat as he listened, unbelieving, on the battle phones: "I remember hearing reports from the forward torpedo room that we were at test depth, and then a steady count in tens as the sub sank. And then a report we were below crush depth."

Beyond 400 feet, they had passed any reasonable expectation to survive; the ship simply was not built for these depths. Taking a fleetboat below 500 feet was madness; it was playing chicken with a brick wall at a thousand miles an hour. With a boat as damaged as the *Sculpin* it was certain, unalloyed death. Bill Cooper heard a report from one compartment that a pressure gauge was reading 350 pounds per square inch; for a rough estimate of depth, he doubled the pressure reading. At this depth the pressure was like an infinite number of hypodermic needles ground to the sharpness of a single water molecule running over the body of the boat, tirelessly trying every hairline fissure and mediocre weld, insidiously probing the threads of every valve. Nature abhors a vacuum, and if the tiniest fissure occurred *anywhere* between the hull and the water, the boat's relative vacuum could suck thousands of gallons of water through the fissure as it equalized the pressure inside. It would shove everything— dinner plates, bedsprings, torpedoes—through the path of least resistance. The force could shoot a man through a keyhole.

The air in the bow buoyancy tank took effect, the boat at first leveled off, but then took another alarming up angle as the ship rocketed toward the surface with the speed of an air bubble. They were now in danger of whipsawing back up through the surface again.

"Vent bow buoyancy!" Connaway ordered. The crew's ears popped as the air from that tank went into the hull; according to Brown the pressure in the boat was becoming dangerously high. The crew discovered that the hydraulics on the planes were also not working and rushed to start cranking them so as to level the boat. The crippled ship's ascent stuttered, then stopped, by some accounts at approximately 100 feet. To maintain that depth, the motors ran at 170 turns. The *Sculpin's* screaming screws were straining the batteries to their limits. Connaway asked the maneuvering room how much juice they had. The answer: only enough for a few minutes.

Although their logs make no mention of it, the *Yamagumo's* sound operator likely detected the *Sculpin* at this time because the destroyer dropped another ten devastating depth charges. The shock waves rang the *Sculpin* like a giant bell, creating ever more damage—the hydrophone's sound heads were driven up into the hull; as a result they could no longer hear the destroyer's movements beyond what rattled through the battered hull. The concussions shook the boat so hard that even now both torpedo rooms reported cracks where the torpedo tubes met the hull. Although they did not know it at the time, the periscope shears were also bent, and the metal around the conning tower was crumpled.

It was six hours to sundown. The stricken ship could not maintain this depth without batteries. There would be no chance to recharge them on the surface. Connaway announced that they would battle-surface. The gun crew would engage the destroyer while the rest of the crew abandoned ship. Then he or one of the other officers would scuttle the *Sculpin*.

Now Cromwell came out of the darkness of the control room: The destroyer *must* be nearly out of depth charges. They should wait it out. Connaway and Cromwell went back and forth in impassioned whispers. The men heard Cromwell next:

*"Keep her down! Keep her down!"*

# 13

## Acknowledge Receipt

Jasper Holmes read through the decrypts of Japanese radio messages as they came in. Lockwood's torpedo fixes and deployment of U.S. submarines using ULTRA had become so effective that the Japanese became alarmed by the loss of tankers and freighters. So many ships were going down now that the shipyards in Japan were staggering under the demands for replacement merchant ships. Compounding the problem of lost ships was the loss of raw materials they carried. The Combined Fleet had created a new unit specifically designed to train and deploy escorts in convoy tactics, and the radio traffic reflected the Japanese navy's panic. There were radio direction finding bearings, reports of torpedo attacks and sinkings, even reports about periscope sightings.

Going through the decrypts, Jasper Holmes came across an informational message from the Truk port director that seemed to suck all the air out of the room. He put it down, then reread it, and turned it over in his mind. The communication would occupy his thoughts for the rest of his life, but now more than ever. He picked up the receiver on his desk and called Dick Voge, former *Sailfish* skipper and now Admiral Lockwood's chief of staff. While waiting for Voge to answer, he might have hoped to hear the voice of his old friend John Cromwell, and realized that it would probably never happen again.

Thanksgiving fell on November 25 that year. Once again the Holmeses had their annual feast for all the lost lambs whose sweethearts were stateside, and although they had twice as many guests as the previous year, the news about Operation Galvanic dampened their spirits. Aerial assaults and a heavy bombardment from battlewagons had turned the coral atoll of Tarawa and Betio into moonscapes, but the Japanese had so entrenched themselves into every nook and cranny, the marines had no choice but to fight inch by bloody inch for control. By the time it was all done, nearly 5,000 Japanese and 1,000 marines had died. The result was a hell on earth. It was impossible to bury the dead fast enough, who bloated and split in the sweltering equatorial heat. The roaring stench was indescribable.

For Holmes, the new invasion yielded more documents. Among them were several diaries; the Japanese soldiers and marines seemed to have a diary mania. Some yielded useful information, and others, as Holmes put it, had real literary merit. The intelligence center was also gathering more evidence about prisoner abuse and war crimes. The Japanese ascribed to the tenets of Bushido, which as a cultural concept could be roughly translated as chivalry. Part of Bushido was to die an honorable death as a warrior, even going so far as to perform seppuku, or ritualized suicide. But to be taken prisoner was a form of moral disgrace, and commanders in the field received little in the way of direction as to how to treat American prisoners. Many were humane and went to great lengths to conform to the Geneva Conventions as they understood them, wherever possible. But many Japanese treated POWs with unspeakable brutality. Among the documents that Holmes came across was an interrogation manual documenting techniques for interrogation: "Methods in which pain is inflicted may be used...in applying the third degree, it is preferable to use a method in which the interrogator does not feel himself as being cruel and which the prisoner is not injured so as to leave a permanent scar." There was another clue to the dubious interrogation tactics: "If the prisoner complains repeatedly that he is thirsty and asks for water, this is a sign that he is in agony such as one experiences just before confessing matters of a vital nature."

Despite these tactics, and much worse, the Japanese interrogators seldom gained intelligence of any practical use.

In light of what was happening to American servicemen, the case of the *Sculpin* could not be less galling. According to Holmes, "On 29 November Lockwood ordered Cromwell to form his wolf pack. Still, nothing was heard from the *Sculpin*. Lockwood canceled that order and directed the submarine to reconnoiter Eniwetok and report." The *Sculpin* didn't respond.

At home, Holmes watched with peculiar dread as Izzy wrapped the presents for the Cromwell family. Izzy was unaware of what had probably already happened, while her husband tried his best for a poker face. Later, when she cheerily announced to Jasper and their son, Eric, that she'd been to the post office to send the parcel along, she asked, "Isn't John due back soon?"

Holmes sat down in the living room and looked away. To Eric, he was visibly anxious, uncomfortable.

He turned the ULTRA decrypt over in his head:

*November 20, 1820 hours. From: CinC 4th Fleet. To: _____.*
*Forty-one prisoners (among them three officers) from the submarine*
*sunk by the YAMAGUMO have been turned over to _____.*

Izzy cocked her head. Had he heard her?

"Jasper—?"

Holmes shook his head, frowning.

No more questions.

End of story.

"—oh. Oh. *Oh.*"

It must have been apparent to Holmes that if Cromwell were captured he had not yet divulged the secrets of ULTRA, because the code breakers at Hypo continued uninterrupted. There were of course other alternatives.

In late November, Lieutenant David A. Ward came across a message garbled with gobbledygook, but also mentioned three ships: the heavy carrier *Zuiho*, and the smaller escort carriers *Chuyo* and *Unyo*. Most of the rest was unreadable, but did specify times and coordinates. Looking at the charts, Ward saw that if his guesses were correct, ComSubPac probably had several boats that might be able to intercept what appeared to be the battle group, so he rushed the information along, hoping he might be able to get more precise information later.

At Holmes's daily coordination meeting for the submarine command, Dick Voge became more and more excited as he looked at the plot, speculated about the positions of three of their subs, then went back to the plot again. As Holmes recalled, Voge said, "This is where we get a carrier."

Though impressed as always by Hypo's code breaking, Holmes was doubtful about the possibility of actually sinking an aircraft carrier. He'd seen all this before—the decryption of a carrier's itinerary and plot, followed by hasty ULTRAs posted to multiple submarines along its path. Then inevitable failure because bad weather had hampered exact navigational fixes for both target and submarine, or the torpedoes failed, or the convoy was heavily defended. Even the legendary Voge himself had been incorrectly credited for sinking a carrier that had actually turned out to be a seaplane tender. But Voge insisted on success this time; they'd fixed the torpedo problems, and the poor bastards had to get lucky sometime. To settle the matter, Holmes and Voge made a wager of one dollar, with both men hoping Holmes would lose.

Patrolling off Truk, though not part of Cromwell's wolf pack, was the USS *Skate* under Gene McKinney. Lockwood sent him an ULTRA about the carriers coming out of Truk, and McKinney spotted them on the morning of November 30. The *Skate* submerged on the convoy's track as the huge carriers zigzagged; McKinney set up a bow shot on the *Zuiho* when the carrier made a radical turn. He fired three torpedoes, one of which seemed to hit the *Zuiho*, but it had no effect. The carriers put on steam and eluded him.

The next skipper to receive one of Lockwood's ULTRAs was John "Junior" McCain* on the USS *Gunnel*. Like McKinney before him, McCain was able to spot the fast-moving convoy in time to submerge on its track, but another radical zig by the

---

*McCain was the father of presidential candidate John McCain.

*Zuiho* threatened to ram the *Gunnel*, and McCain had to evade. He did manage to fire four torpedoes and heard four explosions, but neither he nor Hypo could confirm any hits, and the convoy got away.

The carriers *Zuiho*, *Chuyo*, and *Unyo* seemed to enjoy charmed lives, untouched by American torpedoes despite the submariners' best efforts. Despite his own wishes to the contrary, it was looking like Jasper Holmes's prediction was going to come true. Their one last hope was Dick Voge's old boat, the *Sailfish*. Although all the plankowners who had survived the sinking of the *Squalus* had since gone to other ships, the hard luck seemed to follow the ship and its crew. Yet another skipper was relieved after a bad patrol, and the new skipper, Bob Ward, was untested. The barometer was also dropping in Ward's area, signaling bad weather and poor navigation for both parties, making an interception unlikely. If he did manage to intercept the Japanese ships—and actually get a hit—the carriers had formidable hull plating that would be difficult for the torpedoes to penetrate. Even if everything did go their way, Holmes had precedent on his side: No American submarine had ever sunk a Japanese aircraft carrier.

# 14

## Rocks and Shoals

"Keep the ship down!" Cromwell yelled at Connaway.

The *Sculpin* was rising to the surface. Although the sound-man on the *Yamagumo* already had a good idea of the *Sculpin's* exact location from the whining of her screw bearings, once they made the surface the destroyer could ram the submarine or blast it out of the water with its superior guns.

"They might be out of depth charges—the men counted fifty-seven!" continued Cromwell. "Even if they do send more down, it would only be a few."

"We have no batteries left."

"But we still have air in the tanks. If we can stay down a few hours..."

"It's *six hours* to sunset. We have *no batteries*. We are flooding and we have *no pumps*. We have to surface while we can *still bring her up.*"

*"Keep the boat down! That's an order!"*

"I am the captain of this ship. I am responsible for this ship and its crew. And I give the orders, Captain Cromwell."

For the second time that morning, the ocean parted over the *Sculpin* as it broached the surface of the water. Cromwell and

Connaway were yelling at each other at the top of their lungs. Aghast at the argument raging between the skipper and Captain Cromwell, Chief Weldon Moore asked, "Make ready the tubes, Captain? Captain? Should we make ready the tubes?"

"No, just battle surface," Connaway replied.

The order stabbed Bill Cooper in the gut—what the hell were they going to do? He wished that the experienced Chief Moore were the skipper. Cromwell was still arguing with Connaway.

"Captain, permission to open the hatch?" Bill Cooper asked.

"If we ever get back to Pearl I'm going to court-martial your ass!" Cromwell shouted at Connaway.

"Lieutenant Allen! Lieutenant Brown!" Connaway shouted, "make damn sure this ship is scuttled!"

"Yes, sir! Captain! Permission to open the hatch?" the exec, John Allen, asked. While Connaway and Cromwell were still arguing, *Sculpin* was a sitting duck. "Oh for Chrissakes give us a fucking chance!" someone muttered.

Exasperated, Allen nodded to Cooper, who turned the wheel on the hatch. The hatch practically blew off its hinge as the pressure in the boat blasted it outward. Cooper jumped out onto the deck, followed by the gunnery crew. What they saw took their breath away: On a sea undulating with gentle whitecaps rolled a destroyer the size of a light cruiser not more than 1,000 yards away. It had three mounts, each with two 5-inch guns, and elsewhere was bristling with machine guns. It simply stood there, the cruelly sharp bow followed by clean lines, the smoke rising from its stacks, impassive and majestic as death itself.

"Boys," Cooper said, "it's right over here on the port side, about half a mile."

The exec stayed in the conning tower with the radar operator. Joe Defrees—the gunnery and torpedo officer—was neither in the control room, nor the conning tower, nor on the bridge. There was in fact no officer on the deck. Defrees may have been trying to fix the outboard vents on the torpedo tubes so that Allen, in the conning tower, could draw a bead on the destroyer: If they were able to get off some fish, they might be able to get the destroyer before it got them—it was *that close*. In the control room, George Brown sent two men to the torpedo rooms to ready the tubes; he intended to shoot torpedoes from the control room. For their part, the men on the *Yamagumo* recorded that the *Sculpin* was severely damaged, its periscope shears bent and broken.

Despite the lopsided fight, and the sheer enormity of their orders to attack the leviathan Japanese man-of-war, the gunnery crew ran to their little 3-inch gun. Chief Moore, Herbert Thomas, Warren Berry, Bob Wyatt, Joe Baker, Ed Ricketts, and Harry Milbourne prepared the deck gun for action. One man pulled the watertight plug out of the muzzle while another prepared the breech. A third opened the watertight locker on the doghouse and broke open the shells for the gun. Two others got the horizontal and vertical spotting gear ready. Eldon Wright and others passed shells, singing "Praise the Lord and Pass the Ammunition." Ed Ricketts loaded a shell into the gun.

Bill Cooper helped gunner Jim Harper mount a 20mm machine gun he'd dragged up from the control room, but the sight of the huge *Yamagumo* looming over them was inescapable. Neither he nor Cooper could get it to fire, and Harper's helper didn't arrive.

The gun crew got the first round off, which went over the *Yamagumo*'s bow and splashed behind.

The crew listened to the deck gun's report as the gunner's mates fired and reloaded, fired and reloaded, *bang…bang…*the second shell fell short as the destroyer put on steam and started to make way.

A salvo from the *Yamagumo's* 5-inch guns straddled the *Sculpin* as huge geysers of water erupted on either side of the submarine. It seemed to take forever for the water to stop splashing. The *Yamagumo* was going around the *Sculpin* to gain a position so that the deck gun would be masked by the conning tower.

"Let's go down to the deck and help them bring up the ammo," said Cooper. Harper nodded and went along one side of the conning tower while Cooper ran along the other. The *Yamagumo* fired another salvo from behind the *Sculpin*, and this time a shell found its target. The raking shot hit the air induction pipe behind the conning tower with a deafening explosion, sending a torrent of hot scrap metal flying forward. Bill Cooper was thrown down onto the deck, stunned. His ears were ringing—both eardrums had split—and his back was filled with incredible pain. Lifting his head, he saw Jim Harper, who had been on the other side of the conning tower as they'd raced forward. One of his arms was missing. Crimson blood stained his white T-shirt from what was left.

The *Yamagumo* now opened fire with its machine guns and several men not yet hit by the shell that had destroyed the main induction fell as the bullets splashed all around them and ripped up the teakwood slats of the deck. Fireman Alex Guilot passed ammunition despite deep chunks missing from his chest.

Another volley of 5-inch shells penetrated the conning tower and exploded inside. George Brown confirmed that the exec, John Allen, and the radarman, George Embury, were killed.

We do not know where Lieutenant Commander Connaway or Lieutenant Defrees were at this point, only that they did not die in the conning tower. Lieutenant George Brown succeeded to command.

Another shell hit, this time above the forward torpedo room, injuring several men. As the new skipper, Brown knew that he had to scuttle the ship—it was too far gone and they'd never outrun the destroyer, and he said as much to Cromwell. "Go ahead," he replied. "It's the right thing to do."

Cromwell sat down on an ammo box in the control room and pulled out a photo of his family.

Brown gave the order: "Emergency speed! Abandon ship! You have one minute! Abandon ship!" In case the battle phones had been damaged, he sent two runners to either end of the boat, who yelled the orders at the tops of their lungs.

Waiting in the engine room, George Rocek was tending to the engines when the order to abandon ship came. The crewmen were absolutely stunned. This couldn't be happening to them. They were going to die out there, all alone. Some remained at their stations. Others sat down to contemplate their fate. Still others made their way up the ladders and opened the hatches. The battle topside was raging, and the men heard the guns roaring, the Japanese bullets riddling the sides of the submarine and tearing through the wooden deck. One man panicked uncontrollably because he couldn't swim and he didn't have a Mae West life jacket.

In the after battery, Ed Keller watched in horror as Bob Carter went up the ladder into the withering machine gun fire, only to come back down again, decapitated. Duane White put Carter's body on the green linoleum and backed away.

George Goorabian was next to go up the ladder, followed by Keller, who told White to hurry up.

Dripping with sangfroid, White simply said, "Them sons a bitches have got me this far. They can take me the rest of the way." White shook out a cigarette from a pack in his pocket and lit up.

As he came up the hatch, a shell hit Goorabian squarely, slicing him in half in a sudden puff of pink mist. Another shell hit so soon afterward that Keller was blown up and out the hatch, seriously wounded. The *Yamagumo* recorded that "black smoke started to rise from the submarine's rear hull area." This may have been a shell hit or exhaust from the *Sculpin*'s engines as they sputtered and started.

George Rocek got out through a hatch and ran toward the conning tower. He saw the bloody mess of what had been a crewmate on the deck. He'd gone into a door on the conning tower called the doghouse when a shell hit, sending hundreds of pieces of shrapnel like fine, curled iron shavings through his legs. The concussion momentarily stunned him and he stood there blinking, seeing, but curiously unfeeling and unaware. When he gathered his senses and realized he was still alive, he jumped into the water. Bill Cooper had been thrown into the water, unconscious.

Other men were jumping in as fast as they could while the *Sculpin* pulled away. George Brown's two runners returned to the control room. Everyone had received the orders to abandon ship, but some decided to stay. Ensign Fielder, who had accidentally broached the boat due to the faulty depth gauge, played solitaire in the wardroom as he waited to die. Sitting next to him was one of the cooks, Eugenio Apostol, who preferred death to capture. Brown tried to get Captain Cromwell to go topside, but he explained that he knew too much, and that he couldn't afford to divulge his secrets in the event of torture. Also apparently choosing death were Lieutenant Defrees, as well as skipper Fred Connaway, if they were not already dead.

Chief Machinist Phil Gabrunas stood by, waiting for Brown to give the order to scuttle. Brown nodded. It was time to scuttle the *Sculpin*. They opened valves to flood the submarine and scrambled up to the conning tower. Brown got through the hatch to the conning tower as the water reached it. Gabrunas was right behind him, but the water was spilling in through the hatch already. Brown never saw Gabrunas again.

Inside, the cataracts of water quickly poured thousands of gallons into the compartments. Books, papers, and those left behind rose with the water, more quickly than they could have imagined, as the men pressed up toward the remaining air overhead, then took that first gulp of saltwater. Those still alive to see the *Sculpin*'s last dive described it as seeming ordinary, as though it were merely slipping down the ways like the day she was launched by Mrs. Joe Defrees. The waters churned and bubbled around the *Sculpin* as the periscope—the very last thing they ever saw of the ship—grew smaller and eventually disappeared with a momentary flash of white water, then vanished as though the uss *Sculpin* had never existed at all.

There was a massive underwater explosion, followed by another—possibly the engine blocks cracking and the batteries exploding.

For the men still on the surface, grievously wounded and exhausted from their efforts, the ordeal had only just begun. George Brown and Weldon Moore gathered the men together as best they could. Bill Cooper became conscious again; he didn't know how long he'd been in the water. Ed Keller didn't have a life preserver and swam over to Jules Peterson and Del Schroeder, who did. John Rourke had also been unconscious and was in very bad shape. A shipmate helped keep him afloat, but his head dunked under the water several times, and he took several choking gulps of water. The *Yamagumo* went back and forth as sailors on the fantail shot at the men in the water with machine guns. Del Schroeder took two bullets in the chest and died; Dowdey Shirley was either shot in the water or died from shrapnel wounds he had received on the deck. Other men were losing blood and near death. Henry Elliott had a bullet hole in his hand, Charlie Pitser had one in his arm. Bill Welsh also had wounds to his arm, above his eye, and torso, and was fading in and out.

The *Yamagumo* slowed and threw over lifelines to the men in the water; according to one account, some of the men swam away, and Eldon Wright initially thought he'd do that. But he changed his mind and swam toward the destroyer with the others. They pulled themselves out of the water onto the deck of the *Yamagumo*, where the excited Japanese sailors gestured and yelled to them in Japanese. They motioned the men forward to the forecastle of the ship, where other sailors bound their hands and feet. While Bill Cooper was helping a fellow *Sculpin* crewman forward, a Japanese sailor stopped Cooper and made him drop the man. While incapacitated, the man was still conscious. The Japanese sailor then rolled him over the deck and into the water. Cooper remembered this man as Claiborne Weade, but other sailors claimed it was Bill Welsh.

The Japanese destroyermen likewise stopped two men helping John Rourke, who had swallowed a great deal of seawater and was barely conscious. But Rourke may have seen what had befallen the other sailor, and in a final, desperate burst he scrambled away on the deck toward the forecastle, thereby saving his life. On their way up the rope and while on the deck, the men's hearts sank when they saw that the *Yamagumo* had only three depth charges left; maybe they really could have held out and survived. But in truth, any one of the explosives could have been the one to split the *Sculpin* in half with all men aboard. Their fates were sealed and there was no going back to what might have been.

The men of the *Sculpin* sat on the forecastle, bound hand and foot, shivering with exhaustion and nerves. Most of them were wounded, some seriously, and the blood from their wounds pooled around them like the floor of a charnelhouse. As the *Yamagumo* headed back toward Truk, they made a head count: Forty-one men had survived the sinking of the *Sculpin*. Lieutenant George Brown and Ensigns Worth Gamel and Charles Smith were the only officers left. The seas kicked up that afternoon, and the destroyer started to roll and heave while storm clouds gathered. It started to rain on the men, and the Japanese sailors gave them a tarp, as well as hardtack biscuits and a little water. Even now the interrogations started. Torpedoman Herbert Thomas was among the first to undergo the process, and they asked him detailed questions about the Pacific Fleet's composition and placement: How many battleships? How many submarines? Where were the carriers? Were any of the battleships raised on Pearl Harbor? They became frustrated with Thomas's noncommittal answers and started beating him. Where were the U.S. Navy's secret island bases? Where did they refuel? All the while, the beating continued. Under duress, Thomas resorted to the classic tortured man's confession, and revealed a secret refueling depot between the Marshall and Gilbert islands. The interrogators looked for maps of the area in question and showed him a map dated 1820, where he indicated the general location of the secret island. But he failed to mention the unicorns and leprechauns that lived on the Big Rock Candy Mountain there, and when he got back to his shipmates, he spread the word for them to repeat the lie.

The next day the *Yamagumo* reached Truk lagoon. To conceal the Japanese navy's strength there, the submariners were forced to wear blindfolds, but occasional peeks revealed an awesome sight: battleships, cruisers, destroyers as far as the eye could see. Their guards took note of this and cuffed the curious men. After a trip in a launch to the dock, the men got into trucks for a ride to a barracks away from the harbor. Their blindfolds and clothes were taken off and they found themselves in a compound with three cells that were about seven feet by eight feet, with a hole in the corner for the latrine. So many men—about fourteen—were packed into each cell that none of them could lie down, so they simply stood there naked, sometimes crouching. The guards came by to beat them with clubs through the single window. If they spoke, they would reach through the window with a long club and beat them about their heads and shoulders. If they tried to lie down, the guards would beat them. One of the guards, whom they called "Tulagi," was particularly vicious and beat them just for the hell of it.

They sweated in the oppressive tropical heat, but received no food and no water. The interrogators brought them out one by one for questioning, where they were asked about their duties, how the submarine operated, what kind of equipment they used, and the equipment's specifications. The interrogators creepily referred to them by their first names. If they didn't answer questions quickly, the guards beat them. If they were caught out in a lie, the guards beat them. When they asked for water, the guards beat them.

By the second day the men were out of their minds with thirst and pain. They hadn't gotten any food or water, and no medical attention for their wounds. George Rocek's legs were peppered with shrapnel-like shavings from a metal lathe, and the sores and wounds had begun to fester. Other men had gashes or were riddled with bullet holes and were missing chunks of flesh. Joe Baker, who was missing part of one of his calves, cried piteously through the night for water. The guards became upset, and beat him and the men around him. Having no other alternative, his mates had to muzzle him to prevent further harm to himself or them.

On the third day, Bill Cooper was at his wit's end. Though he had no open wounds, his back was severely injured. While doubling over in pain, the real agony was the fact that they had had no water for three days, and he and the rest of the men came to the conclusion that the Japanese intended to kill them from exposure. "I was so thirsty I prayed to God to take my life," Cooper later said. Baker recalled that ants, maggots, flies, and mosquitoes were "pestering the wounded and getting into their wounds." Despite their dehydration, exposure to high temperatures, and beatings, the interrogators gained only one thing: the identity of the radarman, whom they beat mercilessly for technical details of the sub fleet's radar program. The interrogators were especially brutal with the officers, who endured the longest and worst treatment. As ranking officer, George Brown asked over and over again for food, water, and medical treatment for his men. The guards responded by beating him.

But that day they got food, a rice ball cooked in seawater, which made them even thirstier. For their thirst they also each got a single teacup of water. It was the same on the fourth day. On the fifth day, a group of officers in snappy-looking uniforms came and asked in English for the ranking officer. George Brown identified himself. The officers were sniffing the horrible smell coming off the men as the translator asked questions—had they received medical care? No, Brown answered, and hoping they might be delivered he detailed their treatment thus far.

One of the officers was visibly outraged and punched another officer in the face. This was probably Admiral Mineichi Koga, successor to Admiral Yamamoto after the Combined Fleet commander's death. Koga had previously commanded the General Staff's intelligence division, and although there was little love lost between him and Americans in general, he doubtless valued the possible intelligence they might glean from the submariners. His outrage may have stemmed from humanitarian motives, or the possibility that the submariners might render up their souls before their secrets, or that the POW camp commander had disobeyed direct orders.

Whatever the source of the officer's rage, the POW camp commander followed the letter of the command if perhaps not the spirit. The men received water and used Japanese navy uniforms to cover themselves. They could also avail themselves of the tender mercies of the camp's medical care. Charlie Pitser's arm was seriously wounded, and he left the cell for dressings. The pharmacist's mate, Paul Todd, was astounded to see Pitser come back again with his arm completely amputated. The surgeon had taken a scalpel and sliced the flesh of his arm to the bone, then taken a hacksaw and sawed his humerus below the shoulder. The surgeon administered no anesthesia, not even aspirin, and an interrogator questioned him throughout the procedure. Henry Elliott, who had been shot in the hand, also had his hand amputated under similar circumstances.

After ten days at Truk, on November 30, an interrogator told them that they would become guests of the emperor in Japan. That afternoon, the guards put blindfolds on them, and the submariners got into trucks that brought them back down to the harbor, where they boarded the small carrier *Unyo*. Their captors then divided them into two groups, and unbeknownst to them at that time, in doing so they were separating the quick from the dead. Half the men remained on the *Unyo* while the other half went to her sister ship, the carrier *Chuyo*.

On board the *Unyo* the men were taken to a barren but clean brig. They received food and water regularly, and the Japanese sailors taught them stock phrases to stand at attention, ask to use the bathroom, and say good morning. Aboard the *Chuyo*, however, the men had filthy, cramped quarters. There was no ventilation and the Americans wilted in the oppressive heat. The guards lowered food through a door in the ceiling, but the men still lacked sufficient water.

Both ships were large compared to the submarine they were accustomed to, but as a storm began to break, even these large ships started to buck and roll. As the storm reached typhoon proportions, the ships seemed to slow down on the enormous waves, and although the severe weather shifted them this way and that, the men sensed that the ships had stopped zigzagging.

# 15

## On *Sailfish* Account

Bob Ward, the new skipper aboard USS *Sailfish*, was en route to a patrol area in Empire Waters when he received an urgent ULTRA from Dick Voge. It directed him to take a precise position 300 miles southeast of Tokyo Bay by December 3 to attack the carrier convoy that McKinney and McCain had missed, but as they approached, the barometer fell, the clouds gathered, and it started to rain. The wind kicked up to a speed of 50 knots, and soon the men on the bridge of the *Sailfish* were riding waves the height of a two-story building. At the crest of a wave, the bow came out of the water; and since the bow was no longer supported by water underneath it, the lookouts watched as the bow visibly drooped before crashing into the base of the next wave. The waves crashed all along the boat with the force of thousands of tons of water—enough to rip radio aerials off the superstructure and the teakwood slats off the deck. The bow planes were taking a severe beating, as were the men, who had to lower their binoculars before the next wave crashed into them. There was also the very real danger of getting "pooped," or having hundreds of gallons of water come down the open bridge hatch and into the control room. The conditions made precise navigation next to impossible; no celestial objects were visible, and even if they had been, the severe wave action made accurate sextant readings extremely difficult. Ward tried to con the ship into position using dead reckoning—a calculation of compass bearings and speed from the last known position. Their location became less and less accurate as they got farther from the known point, and the navigation was exacerbated by the unpredictable wave action.

But at ten to midnight the radarman miraculously picked up a contact looming in and out of the mountainous waves at a range of about 9,500 yards, and a few minutes later he was able to determine a course of 320 degrees and a speed of 18 knots; the bearing was constant and they were not zigzagging, probably due to the weather. In the succeeding minutes he started picking up contacts everywhere—ahead, behind, some small, some large. For the radarman to have picked up anything in the huge waves portended very large ships, but on the bridge, neither Ward nor any of the lookouts could see anything; the waves now loomed over and enveloped them with a sight not unlike driving a car into the side of a hill. After the approach officer calculated the track of the targets on the TDC, Ward changed course to intercept them and gave the order to load torpedoes forward and aft. In the rough seas the *Sailfish* could manage only 12 knots at top speed.

At midnight, one of the target ships turned on a searchlight that glowed an unearthly green across the storm ravaged sea. The light started blinking, but Ward doubted they'd seen the *Sailfish*. He dove to a depth of forty feet because he was also concerned that if he fired torpedoes on the surface, they'd broach in the valleys of the waves and come off course, or would slow down on their way to the target and miss altogether. Even submerged near the surface, depth control was tricky as the sub bobbed up and down on the waves, threatening to broach as they approached their target. Ward knew the attack was damn near impossible—he couldn't even see the target and didn't know what kind of ship it was, only that it was huge. Nevertheless, he had to try.

When he and the lookouts had gone down below and sealed the hatch, he called for the periscope. They were very close now to the targets, but Ward could hardly see anything; the waves towered over the periscope shears and crashed over the lens, giving the skipper only momentary glimpses from time to time. However, Ward was able to make out vague shapes: "The picture looks as though we are on the left flank of a fast group of men-of-war, consisting of a destroyer, then possibly a cruiser, then a carrier or battleship, then another carrier or battleship with possibly something beyond that."

Ten minutes later he fired the bow tubes at the first of the two largest pips on the radar screen. While they were coming hard aport to bring the stern torpedo tubes to bear, they heard deep explosions in the water corresponding to the first and fourth fish. Ward was at the scope, but he hadn't been able to see anything because a wave had churned up in front of the lens. A cheer went up throughout the boat—in spite of everything, maybe they did get the bastard after all. Their cheer was short-lived, however, as two depth charges rocked the boat.

"Take her down!"

The *Sailfish* dipped gently down as the planesmen carefully turned their wheels to make the ship go deeper. As they took on more depth, the sea suddenly became calm and the boat stopped rocking back and forth; for the first time since the beginning of the storm they were now gratefully under the waves.

*Tiktik Bang. Tiktik Bang.*

The depth charges were nowhere near. They listened to the roiling sea above, but the water was so troubled the soundman was unable to make out anything above them, or the splashes of the depth charges as they hit the water. Luckily, the conditions were advantageous since the destroyers wouldn't be able to detect the *Sailfish*. They evaded as seventeen more depth charges rained down, thankfully far away from them, and when they surfaced two hours later, they couldn't make a contact save for the radarman, who picked up a pip again northwest of them at 8,400 yards. Ward leaned on the engines, hoping it was the large, crippled ship they'd hit, but the waves were if anything even higher, and he could barely stand on the bridge let alone make way. As they approached slowly throughout the early morning hours, the pip on the radar screen turned into two, one going slowly at a few knots while the other circled around.

The men of the *Sculpin* heard the two explosions at around midnight; the deep, sharp *thrum* of the concussions blasted them off the tatami mats on the floor of the brig. Alarm bells and sirens went off throughout the ship. Their very first thought was that a U.S. submarine had gotten a couple of torpedoes off, though for the first time in their lives they had mixed feelings about sinking Japanese carriers.

Throughout the sleepless night the men heard Japanese seamen running up and down the corridors, the ringing thuds of wooden beams thudding along the stairs and banging against the steel walls. Finally, they heard hammers and mallets hitting wedges. Dinty Moore speculated that they were shoring up bulkheads. If he was correct, the *Chuyo* had serious structural damage. Shortly afterward they smelled the first whiff of something burning, then the eerie sight of smoke curling through the hatch of their cell like a snake making its way into the room. They listened as the storm tossed the boat up, held it there, then crashed it down again with the sound of fine sea spray like waves crashing on a beach. Underneath this sound was a curious sloshing, dripping sound coming from below, separate from the storm outside. As the sloshing grew louder, the boat's violent turns up and down the sea swells become less pronounced; they were taking on water, maybe counterflooding to keep the carrier on an even keel. Finally, the Japanese seamen's banging stopped. They heard voices in the corridor, shouting. Men ran up and down the corridor, their footsteps making splashing sounds as they ran. The smoke was getting thicker now, pooling upside down along the ceiling as the smoke gathered and sought admittance to the level above. They experienced relative quiet—no more voices, no more footsteps, just the creaking of the ship as it rode the sea swells, the crashing of the waves along the side of the ship, and the gathering water pooling and sloshing up and down the corridor outside the hatch.

Water started to come in through the sill at the bottom of the hatch.

They banged impotently on the hatch with their soft, fleshy fists, yelling for someone to let them out of the brig. But no one came—only the sounds of the storm and sloshing water, up and down, up and down. The water had pooled up on the floor of their cell and was running up and down the room with the pitch and roll of the boat, soaking their feet and trousers. They tried the wheel on the hatch, which was dogged shut. As they turned the wheel completely open, they discovered that the hatch was locked from outside.

The ship was sinking and they'd been left belowdecks.

One of the men started bashing the latrine and succeeded in wrenching the long, thin steel pump handle from its flushing mechanism. The other men leaned into the door, trying to force the lock outside the cell. They pushed and pushed as far as the hatch would go, and shoved the pump handle into the gap between the hatch and the sill. With one last bash from their shoulders and the leverage provided by the pump handle, the door came off its hinges and splashed in the flooded water of the darkened corridor. The men cheered.

Aboard the *Sailfish*, Bob Ward cautiously approached the great hulk struggling in the distance, which was underway but very slow—he still hadn't actually seen the target well enough to identify it. As morning approached, the rain stopped but the huge wave swells continued to crash over them and into the bridge. Shortly before six in the morning, Ward knew that in order to finish off the big ship—whatever it may be—he would have to do it quickly before the sun rose. Even though the radarman told him they were over 3,000 yards away, he decided to fire another salvo from the bow tubes.

The approach officer on the TDC had been tracking the slow-moving target and already had a solution.

"Fire one! Fire two! Fire three!" Ward ordered.

"All fish running hot, straight, and normal," the soundman reported. The quartermaster kept his eyes on his stopwatch. At this range it would take over two and half minutes to find out what would happen. The night sky was lightening into an over-cast morning, the clouds dark and swirling.

In the distance, Ward saw one of their torpedoes explode like a giant, fiery muzzle flash, then they heard the torpedo's report muffled through the clouds and fog. When another torpedo hit, there was a massive, ominous sound—Ward described it as "like a battleship firing a broadside—even with the locomotive rumble so characteristic of sixteen-inch shells."

Through the night, the men of the *Sculpin* had tried to get top-side before the ship sank. The corridors outside their cell were pitch black and filled with smoke. Chief Weldon Moore suggested that sailors who had served aboard big surface vessels lead the search for a way out, while the others trailed behind, holding hands. Amputee Charles Pitser led the rear.

Blindly groping along the walls, they felt their way down the corridor like rats in a maze, grasping at hatch handles leading to more darkness, dead ends, despair. Doubling back they finally opened a hatch into another corridor, which seemed to be promising, and soon they were in a food storage area with crates of soda pop. Having had very little water in the days since they left Truk, they chugged the soda quickly and kept on going until they reached a level where they encountered Japanese seamen, who rushed past them without any concern whatsoever. The Americans figured that things must be pretty bad if no one took any notice of twenty-one prisoners wandering around. Slowly making their way up through the ship they found life preservers and put them on, and, finally, the men made their way to the flight deck.

The sun hadn't risen yet but the skies were continuing to lighten.

Pandemonium reigned as the Japanese sailors ran this way and that among the smoke and flight equipment. The submariners were astounded to see officers in life preservers barking orders to ordinary seamen, who had no time to put on their own life preservers. Elsewhere, the sailors were lashing timbers together to make life rafts. One officer finally took note of the submariners and stripped them of their life preservers, then got some rope and started tying them together until the rope ran out. They were in the process of untying themselves when the second volley of torpedoes hit with two massive explosions. Sailors fell to the deck and shook their heads from the shock, then slowly got up.

The men on the bridge of the *Sailfish* saw star shells and antiaircraft fire come from the target. They were firing everywhere and nowhere, reflexively lashing out at their unseen tormentor for several minutes until the tracers started coming exclusively at the *Sailfish*. Ward pushed the button on the klaxon twice to dive. The lookouts came down from the periscope shears amid the *oo-OO-gah* of the klaxon. As they settled into the calmer waters of the depths they heard four depth charges, but none of them was close.

Ward circled warily around the stricken ship for an hour and a half, making occasional periscope observations in the huge waves. In a sudden clearing, he finally got a good view of the target, and realized that he and his crew were probably making history. "Boys, it's a carrier," he said. The crewmen gushed—none more so than the veterans who'd started the war thinking they'd sink the entire Japanese fleet single-handed. Certainly everybody was happy for the bragging rights, and for their skipper, who would surely get the Navy Cross.

As the *Sailfish* approached the helpless carrier, Ward saw a destroyer. The sea was as high as it had ever been, and with the sun overhead, they were in danger of being spotted. Still, he had to get up far enough to be able to see the carrier. "When we are at sixty feet there is nothing but green waves with the scope looking into or under a wave most of the time," wrote Ward. "At fifty-five feet we damn near broach and still can only see about twenty percent of the time."

By 9:30 A.M., Ward was within 3,000 feet of the target. He watched through the periscope, fascinated. He could not fathom why the rest of the convoy, save a single destroyer, had abandoned the carrier to this fate. There were airplanes on the forward part of the flight deck, and hundreds of Japanese sailors dressed in navy blue on the aft part of the flight deck, "enough to populate a fair sized village." They looked to be preparing to abandon ship. Ward turned the boat around for a stern shot. Three minutes later *Saifish* fired from tubes five, six, and seven. The crew heard two torpedoes hit, followed by the unearthly sounds of the ship breaking up, like sticks cracking underwater, and a sound like a whale crying. Then the muffled *Ka-thunk* of two distant depth charges. Ward was frustrated because he couldn't see the torpedoes hit, and gave the order to come around again for another salvo from the bow tubes. When he brought up the periscope at 9:51 A.M., the carrier was gone, and with it, half the survivors from her sister ship, the USS *Sculpin*.

The *Chuyo* shuddered. The carrier's bow quickly tipped down and the list became more pronounced. The structure of the ship's plates and bulkheads couldn't handle the torque as it tipped forward, and as the deck shifted underneath them, the *Sculpin* survivors heard sounds that made their hearts leap into their throats: It was as though a 600-foot tree made of steel was bending in the howling wind, groaning and whimpering like an earthquake underneath their feet as the inch-thick plates buckled and screamed, tearing apart in broad gashes like a tin can. They trembled at the sound of inch-thick rivets popping.

Rocek looked at Chief Moore, whose eyes bulged, his mouth agape. "Let's go!" Rocek called out. The list became more vertical as the deck quickly lowered to meet the sea, the thirty-foot swells crashing onto the deck and receding with foamy turquoise tendrils. "Let's go!" Rocek repeated, but Moore sat there aghast and overwhelmed. It would be the last time Rocek would ever see his chief. He started to slide on his backside down the rough wooden deck, leaving Moore behind, and he fell into the shockingly cold water as the ship quickly sank behind him. Among the jetsam of logs and papers and oil of the sinking ship, he started to swim away as fast as he could.

When forty million pounds of steel disappears on the surface of the ocean, a ship of that size doesn't simply slip under the water like a bathtub toy. As the *Chuyo* descended, the water around it surged to fill up the space where the ship had been, causing a sucking action in the middle of the ocean. As Rocek and the other survivors tried to swim away, they were caught in the current leading straight down to the sinking ship, sucking them below the surface of the ice-cold water, then into the inky depths.

Wild thoughts flashed through Rocek's mind's eye—the escape from belowdecks, the interrogators beating him on Truk, the sight of the dead sailor on the deck of the *Sculpin* as he abandoned ship—the flickering images of memory gathered in speed and intensity more vivid than life itself: the smell of a woman and the ocean on a starlit Brisbane beach, a sailor shaving his head after crossing the line, another sailor he knew at sub school, the smell of burning wood and singing songs around a campfire at a hometown pig roast, his first love, his boyhood friends under the glow of the street lamp outside the house, his father's voice saying grace before Christmas dinner, his mother holding him in her arms, until finally a sense of himself long before he was aware of his name, like a glinting shard of diamond, glowing dimmer like the sun above him as he sank deeper toward the bottom of the ocean, until like some preconscious dream he felt his leg kick, and then the other kick, and his hand paddled, and then the *Chuyo* hundreds of feet below him turned sideways and rendered up its soul in the form of a gigantic bubble that had been trapped above the flight deck, approaching Rocek, overtaking him, raising his body to the surface, where he gasped as though for the first time, like a full-grown newborn man, looking with crazed eyes at the overwhelming splendor and the horror of his world.

Jasper Holmes and Dick Voge got their first confirmation that *Sailfish* had made contact with the convoy in the form of a Japanese "submarine attack" message. Later, Bob Ward sent his first radio serial confirming the victory.

Holmes and the sub command were jubilant, and he made out a large ceremonial check drawn "on *Sailfish* account" to settle his bet with Dick Voge, who framed the check and kept it over his desk.

Only later would they realize what had happened on the *Chuyo*, that their ability to decrypt the message, indeed the ability to even make the attack on the *Chuyo*, was predicated on the fact that John Philip Cromwell had kept ULTRA's secrets with him aboard the USS *Sculpin*, now under 5,000 fathoms of water.

# 16

## The Torture Farm

When the *Sculpin* survivors on the *Unyo* arrived at the Japanese naval port of Yokohama, their captors tied their hands and made them wear blindfolds. The weather at this time of the year—early December—was quite cold as compared to the tropical climate at Truk, and though there was frost on the ground the men received no shoes. After walking down the gangplank, they marched barefoot on frosty cobblestone streets until they reached a railroad station, where they took a train about thirty miles south to a place they learned was Ofuna, or "the torture farm."

Ofuna was a little larger than a football field and had three prisoners' barracks arranged around the perimeter of the field. The men learned that the Japanese navy ran the camp to interrogate special prisoners, mostly submariners. They also discovered that through a cute interpretation of international law, the Japanese had classified them not as prisoners of war but "unarmed combatants." As such they would be afforded no protections under the Geneva Conventions, including provisions governing contact with the outside world, how the guards would regard their dignity as human beings, and whether they would be tortured.

Lieutenant Commander John Fitzgerald, former skipper of the USS *Grenadier*, had been captured several months previous, and had undergone several forms of torture. While interrogating him, his captors had run a penknife under his fingernails and had pried them off. They had stabbed his hands, and even more painful, they had driven pencils up between his fingers. One man was hanged from his thumbs for ten days, another lost a tooth during a beating.

Fitzgerald had also undergone what he called "the water treatment." The guards strapped him to a table, elevated his feet by about 30 degrees, covered his mouth with their hands, and poured water into his nostrils, asking questions all the while. After a few minutes he passed out, and when he came to, the process started all over again. For hours. He was barely able to muster any sort of answer, let alone tell them what they wanted to know, and when he was lucid he told them only lies and misleading half-truths. This was waterboarding. After the war the Allied war crimes tribunals classified the practice as a form of torture, a war crime, and handed down prison sentences spanning decades to its practitioners.

After receiving canvas shoes, the men retired to the barracks. Each man occupied his own room of four feet by eight feet. The next day, they got a new prisoner, as Joe Baker recalled: "Just before lunch, George Rocek came into camp all black and burned as though he'd been in a fire. His clothes were all ripped and his eyes were sticking out of his head as though he had seen a ghost."

Rocek's survival was nothing short of miraculous. Nearly everyone on the ill-fated *Chuyo* had died, including all of Rocek's shipmates. After he rose to the surface, he spotted a raft with a

Japanese officer on it. Several men were floating in the water and holding on for dear life as the mountainous sea swells rose up and down. Rocek tried to hold on to the makeshift raft along with the cook, Maxiso Barerra, and Ensign Charles Smith. Sometimes they'd lose their grip and have to swim in the cold water to get back to the raft. For hours they watched a Japanese destroyer going around in circles, charging up and down the waves at high speed. They hoped to God it wouldn't leave them here, and eventually it slowed down to pick up survivors. Rocek grabbed on to a rope, but the Japanese officer on the raft stepped on his face and he was cast free until he got an elbow onto a Jacob's ladder—a web made of rope slung over the side of the ship. He was by now so exhausted that he couldn't get his feet into the web rungs, and held on for dear life as they pulled the Jacob's ladder up onto the deck with him still attached like a crab. He flopped over the side facedown, where he panted stock-still until they turned him over and realized that he wasn't a Japanese sailor. Yelling in Japanese, the sailors around him gave him some kicks and pulled him up to toss him overboard again, but someone intervened and he was spared. He watched as other sailors leaning over the rail on the fantail poked long sticks into the water—were they hitting Barrera and Smith, or trying to save them? Rocek never found out. He was the only American survivor of the catastrophe.

Rocek was led to a door off the deck and stuck in a room, where one kindly machinist gave him biscuits, while another sailor came in drunk to beat him. Eventually he began to shiver uncontrollably, and sometime during the night he found a large vat of water. It felt so warm he took off his clothes and simply sat down in it, soaking up the warmth until the next morning. Eventually he was brought to Ofuna, where he took a hot bath with a couple of his shipmates, though none of them could talk about what had happened because of the guards.

At Ofuna, the rules were simple: No talking among prisoners, ever. The punishment was a swift and savage beating with clubs—as Fitzgerald described it, like "the old circus tent stake driver pounding the peg into the ground." The guards also meted out this punishment for a variety of other perceived infractions, including spilling food, going to the benjo (latrine) without asking permission, failing to salute in a manner to their liking, and just because they felt like it. Despite the dangers of punishment, the Ofuna prisoners carefully instructed the *Sculpin* survivors what they'd already revealed during interrogation, including the many lies they'd told, so that the new prisoners would perpetuate the misinformation. Another purpose was to avoid punishment; the interrogators compared answers from different sailors for contradictions and follow-up questions. Interrogations began the next day with particular emphasis on George Brown, whom they viewed as a particularly valuable source of information, and who suffered the most at their hands.

During interrogation, the prisoner was literally under a gun. If he didn't reply quickly enough he received a strike from a club. The interrogators, nicknamed the "Quiz Kids" or "QKs," wore business suits and often identified themselves as graduates of American colleges. They usually spoke fair English, sometimes even pitch-perfect, but their knowledge of the language didn't extend to American slang or common idioms, and the men frequently found themselves trying to formulate bum dope answers to avoid being a stool pigeon, if you catch the drift.

During the sessions, the interrogators revealed the state of Japan and the war through their line of questioning: Were there sub bases in Fremantle and Brisbane? A secret fueling depot at the Australian port of Darwin? How did the sub command decide to recognize and reward whether a skipper damaged or sank a Japanese ship? When would the skipper send radio messages, and how would he code them? Where would the Allies strike next—the Marshalls, the Philippines, Formosa? Over time, the men could appreciate that the noose was slowly drawing closer around Japan, and that it was rapidly losing supplies. Most revealingly, the interrogators also fielded questions about the prospects for peace. Would the United States initiate negotiations? What terms would they seek? Could the Soviet Union—which at this time in the Pacific war was neutral—broker a peace agreement? Who would negotiate for the Allies? How should they interpret "unconditional"?

When the men weren't being interrogated, their days were fairly quiet and they sat on benches around the field. The guards sometimes held their bayonets to a dozing man's eye, hoping to skewer it if he happened to startle awake. The prisoners developed a means of communicating with each other by exerting subtle leg pressure to the man next to them. When a guard withdrew, they'd cough to let the man know the coast was clear. They were fed three times a day, but throughout the winter the men rapidly lost weight. The daily allotted meal ration was precise to within a few grains of rice—213 grams—as well as 500 grams of vegetables, though they usually received only about 200 grams of vegetables, supplemented sometimes by soups made from bones and intestines from a local slaughterhouse.

By late January, the interrogators had gleaned about as much as they thought they could from most of the *Sculpin* crew, and although the crew didn't have a choice they were "offered" a transfer to a work prison, where they would be allowed to register with the International Red Cross as prisoners of war and write letters to their loved ones. This came as a great relief because they thought that nothing could be worse than Ofuna, and they seized on the opportunity to let their families and sweethearts know that they were alive.

Eleven of the *Sculpin* men left Ofuna for the train station, bound for an old mining town in the mountains north of Tokyo called Ashio. They would be followed by their other shipmates in June and July of that year. As an officer with potentially relevant information, George Brown stayed at Ofuna. When the men arrived, they soon discovered that the conditions at Ashio were even worse than Ofuna.

Since it was in the mountains, Ashio was colder. The men received thin blankets made from wood pulp and went to their barracks, a drafty, low-slung building with four ineffectual potbellied stoves. There they found some Javanese and Dutch prisoners captured earlier in the war. Their meals consisted of a gruel essentially made from chicken feed: a wormy mixture of corn, barley, and rice. Sometimes they received fish guts, shark heads, and small sand sharks. The tatami mats on their pallets were crawling with lice and fleas that infested their clothing and feasted on them all night long. Rats crawled all over the barracks at night, and the latrine was overflowing. The bath was frozen, so there was no opportunity for them to clean themselves or wash their clothes. With the unsanitary conditions and starvation diet, the men quickly succumbed to diarrhea and dysentery, and they started to lose weight even faster than at Ofuna. If they became too sick to work, they were put on a strict water diet, "for their health."

After their arrival they were marched through the little town of Ashio to their work duties. Curiously, the authorities decided to observe the Geneva Convention rule prohibiting the parading of prisoners as objects of curiosity and derision, and the people of Ashio were hustled inside their houses or along side alleys until the prisoners had gone past. Ungovernable as they are, preschool children sometimes raced out and made faces at them.

Ashio was a 400-year-old copper mine that had ceased operations several years earlier. Safety issues and environmental degradation at the mine led to an unusual riot earlier in the century, and as the mine's copper ran out the company owning the mine shuttered it. Since America's submarines were by now strangling Japan's access to raw materials, the need for electrical wiring and brass shell casings became acute, and the Japanese government decided to reopen the mine. The men divided into three groups: miners, loaders, and smelters. George Rocek and Bill Cooper went deep into the mine to drill holes for dynamite blasting. Others became muckers, and used shovels to fill a dozen or more mine trams—per man—with tons of raw ore during their ten- to fourteen-hour shifts. Others worked by transferring the ore into hopper cars, and yet others like Herbert Thomas worked in the smelter to boil the ore down into copper. It was heavy, dangerous, and toxic work that took its toll on all the prisoners.

The men working in the mines started out by attaching a carbide helmet torch to their heads and stripping down; it was hot in the mine and they didn't want to soak their uniforms. There were earthquakes and collapses while they worked; sometimes large boulders fell from the mine ceiling and crushed men. The work was also exhausting for men who were not sufficiently fed. When they left the mine, they were covered with sweat that saturated their clothes and made the trip back to the camp as cold as could be imagined. Some caught colds that developed into pneumonia. The Javanese prisoners were especially vulnerable, since they were unaccustomed to such cold, and several died.

By the summertime, the men of the *Sculpin* resembled cavemen. They had not shaved or had haircuts for several months. The overflowing latrines attracted swarms of flies and maggots, and the exhausted men's bodies gradually broke down. They contracted pellagra, a disease that covers the skin in lesions; it is caused by nutritional deficiencies in people who eat grains almost exclusively. Malnutrition also caused beriberi, with symptoms including an alarming swelling of limbs, numbness, joint pain, eventual incapacitation, and heart failure. Although the camp director had received boxes of goods from the Red Cross, he failed to distribute them, leading many of the men to suspect that the guards were simply stealing the foodstuffs and letting them starve. On the day one of the townswomen just outside the gate accused the prisoners of stealing one of her daikon radishes, the guards rounded up a suspect and nearly beat him to death.

Despite the risk of being caught stealing, some prisoners did so anyway. When one Javanese man found three other Javanese stirring his pet dog in a cooking pot, he rounded up a posse of other Javanese and they killed the three offenders. During air raids, Herb Wyatt ("Earp") would often raid a Korean workers' commissary and hide the food. He was even so bold as to steal a Red Cross box from the camp commandant's office. It was too big to conceal, so he tied it up with string and hung it from a nail on the underside of a plank of wood that served as a latrine seat.

Every time they went to the benjo they reeled it back up, ate a can of Spam or a Hershey's bar, then put it back down again.

The number of air raids increased, and one day they even saw a B-29 Superfortress dumping metal chaff to confuse Japanese antiaircraft radar. They received little news of the war, and missed the American offensives on Peleliu, Iwo Jima, the Philippines, and Okinawa. They sensed the war was going badly for Germany, and eventually got news that FDR had died. It seemed the war was coming to a close; if the Americans were near enough to launch air raids on the mainland, they must have taken some islands nearby, or perhaps they were using bases in China.

On August 14, 1945, Bill Cooper nearly died when a massive boulder fell near him, severing the pneumatic hose he used for his power drill. The honcho sent him back to the barracks, and the next day they were told that there would be no work; it was a holiday. The camp commandant and guards listened intently to the radio at noon that day as the emperor addressed the Japanese nation. It was the first time they had ever heard his voice, and his message was that Japan would surrender.

The *Sculpin* survivors were jubilant, their captors dumbstruck at having the tables turned. Through their dark ordeal for survival, the POWs had banded together and been as close to one another as brothers, and by looking out for each other they all survived. They'd each lost forty, fifty, even sixty pounds, and most of these once strong young men now weighed somewhere between ninety and 110 pounds. Though several were tempted to lash out at the camp guards who had made their lives so miserable, they preferred to raid the Red Cross boxes. Inside they found shoes, clothing, and food. They put on whatever they could and gave the rest to the townspeople who had shown them kindness by sometimes feeding them. They even gave candy to the children of the woman who had accused them of stealing the radish.

The camp guards left, and others took their place to paint "PW" on the barracks roof. Soon, American planes began parachuting food and other supplies to the camp. Eventually they got authorization to leave Ashio, and took the train back to Yokohama. Traveling through the Japanese countryside, they cheered at the sight of the first razed town they saw, and every razed town after that until the realization sank in that Japan was absolutely devastated, its people starving.

At the train station in Yokohama, they were reunited with George Brown, who was carrying forty-three small wooden boxes. He had been transferred out of Ofuna to another work camp where they were working on a dam under similarly hellish conditions. The boxes contained the cremated remains of the men who had died while working at the camp. The released prisoners were escorted to hospital ships in the harbor, and left Japan for Guam, where they received their final debriefing, this time by the submarine command. Though some were able to get a plane back to the States, most went in hospital ships or troop transports, and for them it was like their slow boat to China. There were standing orders to feed them anytime, day or night, as much as they pleased, and they took full advantage of the opportunity to eat everything in sight.

Once they got stateside, they were transferred to Navy hospitals, and after recuperating they traveled home to see their parents and sweethearts. Unfortunately, Bill Cooper's girlfriend had gotten married in the intervening time. George Rocek's family was overjoyed to see him—all their families were.

For the men of the uss *Sculpin* the war was over, but in a sense it never ended for them in their hearts. The intensity of their experiences would haunt them all their days, and it would chase them into their dreams; they had sacrificed the very essence of their youth when they were at their prime, and they had come within an ace of making the ultimate sacrifice many of their buddies had made.

# Epilogue

With its torpedo problems solved and dozens of new submarines coming down the ways, the U.S. submarine force eventually overwhelmed the Japanese empire, and sank over half the total merchant tonnage during the war. A large measure of their success was due to Hypo's ULTRA intercepts. Despite these victories, submarines worked most often behind enemy lines, and about one fifth of the sub force never came back. As a result, it was statistically the most dangerous service in the armed forces.

Despite the USS *Sailfish*'s reputation as a hard-luck ship, the crew continued to make successful patrols through the end of the war. Though the peculiarity of the *Chuyo* sinking escaped no one, less well known was the fact that by sacrificing himself to keep ULTRA's secrets safe, John Cromwell may have made the *Sailfish*'s successful attack possible.

For his extraordinary heroism in sacrificing his life to keep ULTRA secret, John Philip Cromwell posthumously received the Medal of Honor. His son, John Jr., stood in for him at the decoration ceremony. After graduation from the Naval Academy, John Jr. served his country with pride and distinction in the Navy. Margaret Cromwell worked at the registrar's office at Stanford University, where she steered young Eric Holmes toward the university's best classes and professors.

Lucius Chappell received two Navy Crosses for his grueling eight war patrols. His wife, Marian, contracted a fatal disease, and in May 1944, she shot herself in a San Francisco hotel room after he was reassigned to the Portsmouth Navy Yard. Chappell married a woman he'd met through George Brown, and they had a boy, Randy, and daughter, Conny. Chappell's children from the previous marriage—son Lou and daughter Mickey, who were teenagers by now—frequently clashed with their step-mother, and the children left. Chappell continued his career in the postwar Navy, but on several occasions his career suffered; although he kept quiet and followed orders, he refused to pol-ish anyone's shoes. After retirement from the Navy, Chappell served as a technical advisor to two Hollywood films, *Operation Petticoat* and *The Wackiest Ship in the Army*. In the latter movie he made a cameo appearance as an admiral. Later, he taught schoolchildren math and science, and eventually retired for good so that he could read his beloved Sherlock Holmes and classical literature. He died in 1980.

Jasper Holmes was very successful as an intelligence officer dur-ing the war, and organized thousands of pieces of intelligence from various sources into valuable reports used to plan the major offensives in the Pacific. After the war, he wrote or co-wrote sev-eral books about the submarine force and Hypo, including *U.S. Submarine Losses: World War II*, *Underseas Victory*, and *Double-Edged Secrets*. With Dick Voge he co-wrote the submarine com-mand's administrative history. After his final retirement from the U.S. Navy as a captain, he went back to teach at the University of Hawaii, where Holmes Hall is named in his honor. Although there was no circumstance where he could legitimately tell John Cromwell's wife what they knew about the sinking of the *Sculpin*, his conscience troubled him for years. His son, Eric, became a neurologist and wrote several science fiction works.

George Brown worked for Procter & Gamble after the war, and retired in 1976. He attended many submarine conventions and corresponded with many submarine veterans. A lecture series of the Cincinnati Navy League is named in his honor.

George Rocek continued with his career in the Navy as a diesel machinist well into the advent of the nuclear submarine fleet. He married and was widowed twice, and had several children and grandchildren. Despite the many times he nearly died and the many privations of his captivity, George proved to be among the longest-living veterans of both the *Sailfish* and the *Sculpin*. He died in August 2007.

Bill Cooper married his sweetheart and had two daughters after the war. He became an insurance salesman with the American Farm Bureau and sold real estate in Florida, where he is retired.

# Acknowledgments
# and a Note on the Text

No book comes together without great effort from many quarters, and in the case of this book, the list of those who have helped me is considerable. First and foremost I have to thank my wife, Kathryn, whose support was comprehensive, unwavering, and long-standing. It was she who allowed me to do what I needed to do and without whom the thing never would have been written. Her mother, Jane, was also a major factor by helping to watch our children while I was doing research far from home.

After several years in the book publishing business, I came across many very good literary agents, and there are a great many I have not yet met. But in my experience, Sorche Fairbank outshone them all for her patience, professionalism, sense of humor, and tenacity. I am truly lucky to be her client and to know her partner, Matt Frederick, who has always been very helpful. Sorche introduced me to the next person I have to thank, my editor at Grand Central, Rick Wolff, who believed in the project from the beginning and whose persuasive guidance and many detailed and incisive observations honed the book into what it is. Rick also came up with the title.

A great deal of research went into the book, and along the way I had a great deal of help from friends old and new. Tom Allen and his wife, Scotty, graciously took me in as a houseguest and showed me the ropes while I was conducting research at the National Archives and the Navy Yard around Washington. They are wonderful, warm hosts, great conversationalists, and fantastic friends. I only hope I will be able to repay them in kind. Tom's longtime friend and author of *The Death of the USS* Thresher, Norman Polmar, was also extremely helpful by taking time in his busy schedule to rid the manuscript of the many niggling, yet acutely embarrassing, errors I and I alone had managed to introduce, multiply, and magnify. Wendy Gulley, the archivist at the Submarine Force Museum Library in Groton, Connecticut, patiently and kindly supplied me with the ships' books and other materials. The National Archives in College Park, Maryland, is a national treasure that every American should visit, use, admire, and support. Without its fantastic people—the real vitality of any institution—its mysteries would be inaccessible. I had great allies in archivists Barry Zerby, Nathaniel Patch, Deborah Edge, Lawrence McDonald, Lynn Goodsell, Andrew Knight, Kevin Bradley, James Konicek, and that inimitable institution John Taylor. At the Operational Archives Branch of the Naval Historical Center, Dr. Akers and Tim Petit were extremely accommodating and knowledgeable resources. Jack Gustafson and William Lockert at the Wenger Command Display in Pensacola, Florida, make the best damn coffee in the Navy.

The research for the book was not, however, confined to archives. Many people gave quite a bit of their time to talk to me about their experiences during the war—most notably USS *Sculpin* survivors George Rocek and Bill Cooper, possibly the most notable and, thankfully for me, the longest living from either boat. Regrettably, George passed away shortly after our interview, but luckily his son, also George, was very helpful afterward. *Sculpin* crewmen Jack Connors and Herbert Thomas were also very helpful and informative. John Philip Cromwell's son was very generous with his time, experiences, and practical pointers about the U.S. Navy. Jasper Holmes's son, Eric, was likewise a terrific resource and eyewitness who gave freely of his time. Randy Chappell and Lou Chappell kindly shared photos and clippings as well as reminiscences of their father, skipper Lu Chappell. Anne Pope, daughter of Lieutenant Commander Fred Connaway, also kindly told me everything she knew about her father. I thank them all. Anthony and Patterson Taylor kindly gave permission for me to use their father's now-infamous poem "Squat Div One." Not every quote in the book came from research or my own personal interviews. I owe thanks to Carl LaVO for permission to use quotes from his book *Back from the Deep,* an excellent resource that comes with my recommendation.

Putting a book together—really putting a book together—is a laborious, handcrafted process requiring years of experience, good judgment, and conscientious hard work. That you are reading this now is the result of the work of Tracy Martin, Jim Spivey, Rick Scruggs, Fred Chase, Tricia Tamburr, Shauna Toh, Stratford Publishing Services, Ellen Rosenblatt, and Mari Okuda, and likely many others at Hachette Book Group whose names I do not know. Mari corrected the manuscript not only in English but the parts in Japanese as well, and asked a very good question about the many quotes used throughout the book: "How do we know that's what they said?"

Some submarines of the day did use rudimentary tape recorders that utilized wire instead of magnetic tape to capture what was going on, and some of these exist, but not for the USS *Sculpin* or the USS *Sailfish.*

In the case of the basic mechanics of commanding the submarines and following the captains' orders, I reconstructed the sequence of events from the skippers' patrol reports. During attacks on enemy ships and subsequent evasion, some of the accounts are given on a minute-by-minute basis. The command-and-response language was exceedingly specific and uniform throughout the submarine force; the skipper and crew conducted practice drills not only to run the sub but also to ensure that the skipper's commands were understood and that the crew complied in every respect. Because their lives depended on adherence to even the smallest details, submariners even had instructions on how to pronounce numbers—"four," for instance, was to be pronounced "FO-wer." If the skipper wrote in the patrol report that the submarine came to a depth of 200 feet, barring other circumstances such as loss of the control of the boat, that was always a result of his direct command, and Navy regulations stipulated that he give that command in the form of "come to two-oh-oh feet," and that the response would be "two-oh-oh feet, aye aye, sir." It is possible, though extremely unlikely, that the officers or crewmen would deviate from their training.

I've also included other sorts of dialogue outside the command-and-response structure, and in these cases I've relied on the written recollections of several eyewitnesses. You'll notice that there's no idle chitchat in the control room or elsewhere; unless it was remarkable in some way, no one thought to record it, and as such it is lost. But aside from the skippers' patrol reports, many participants wrote memoirs with direct quotes from the people around them. Corwin Mendenhall kept a secret diary—strictly against Navy regulations—and expanded on it after the war to write his book *Submarine Diary*. Pete Galantin also wrote about his experiences during the war, including his stint as PCO aboard the *Sculpin*, in his book *Take Her Deep*. Edwin Layton gives an excellent account of his time as intelligence chief for Admirals Kimmel and Nimitz in his book *And I Was There*. Jasper Holmes recounted his experiences in *Double-Edged Secrets* and his son, Eric, was able to corroborate the events and utterances of the Holmes household. John Cromwell's son likewise provided information about the experiences he had with his father. Holmes, Mendenhall, Thomas Dyer, and Joseph Rochefort also gave oral histories about their experiences during the war. After repatriation, the survivors of the *Sculpin* gave interviews to Navy personnel about the circumstances surrounding the sinking of the ship and their treatment at the hands of their captors. Interviews with two surviving *Sculpin* crewmen, George Rocek and Bill Cooper, gave me new material or confirmed what I'd already researched, as did the material from author Carl LaVO's interviews. In instances where eyewitness accounts were specific enough to be put in direct quotes in the references, I included them. If not, I simply paraphrased the conversation or the outcome of the conversation. It is possible that the eyewitnesses misremembered a specific event or misquoted a particular utterance. But after reconstructing the events dozens and, in some cases, hundreds of times, using all resources to cross-check and confirm what happened, in my experience their accounts have remained consistent. In the end, whether it is a patrol report written the day after an event, a book composed from diaries by an eyewitness, or an interview conducted sixty years later, these are the materials of history.

# Index